PRAISE FOR

The Child Is the Teacher

"Readers of feminist history will savor this evenhanded profile of a groundbreaking educator and businesswoman." —*Publishers Weekly*

"A balanced, well-written, and clear-eyed portrait of a complex, trail-blazing woman." —*Library Journal*

"An intimate, comprehensive biography...[an] absorbing narrative... that rewards both intellect and emotion."
—*Foreword Reviews* (starred review)

"[*The Child Is the Teacher*] goes beyond the typical accounts written by disciples...It is remarkable how much of Montessori's radical critique still rings true today." —*Reason*

"In over fifty years of reading and writing about Maria Montessori, I have never found a book, except those written by Dr. Montessori herself, that I could read from cover to cover. *The Child Is the Teacher* is essential for anyone interested in education, in Montessori schools for children, and in Montessori teacher training for adults."
—Susan Mayclin Stephenson, author of *The Joyful Child: Montessori, Global Wisdom for Birth to Three*

"Weaving history and narrative, Cristina De Stefano takes us on the journey of feminist radical and progressive educator Maria Montessori, from her early days in the anatomy room to the hollowed-out buildings of San Lorenzo, where she envisioned a new pedagogy that placed autonomy at the center of a child's social and intellectual development. A fascinating portrait of the controversial woman behind 'The Children's School,' *The Child Is the Teacher* shows how the revolutionary idea about children's rights depended on a new, peaceful philosophy of humanity."

—Jaipreet Virdi, author of *Hearing Happiness: Deafness Cures in History*

"Cristina De Stefano brings Maria Montessori to life in her important new biography, *The Child Is the Teacher*. With a fresh, objective perspective as a thoughtful Italian journalist, she gained access to many new original sources that offer a unique window into the life and thoughts of one of the twentieth century's leading agents of social change and the founder of a global movement to transform education that also led to contemporary brain research. Montessori's life is a fascinating story in itself. This book will be a must-read work."

—Tim Seldin, President of The Montessori Foundation and Chair of The International Montessori Council

"De Stefano's lively new biography of Montessori is a feast—a sympathetic yet clear-eyed view of a complex, revolutionary genius whose mission was to shed new light on children, revealing conditions wherein they become the hope for all humanity. The book is extensively researched and filled with novel insights and information."

—Angeline S. Lillard, Professor of Psychology, University of Virginia

"With extensive access to Montessori's unpublished diaries and letters, journalist Cristina De Stefano has written a compellingly readable account of the personal life of the famous educator."

—Dr. Mira Debs, author of *Diverse Families, Desirable Schools: Public Montessori in the Era of School Choice*

"When discussing a revered icon, approaching the myth without preconceptions or a sense of awe is a slippery endeavor. Cristina De Stefano succeeds in it, skillfully leading us in a narrative that perfectly incorporates her intense research." —*Robinson, La Repubblica*

"Maria Montessori's life is a complex tapestry, which Cristina De Stefano has rendered with fluid precision and documentary faithfulness."
—*La Lettura, Corriere della Sera*

The Child

Is

the Teacher

A Life of Maria Montessori

Cristina De Stefano

Translated from the Italian by Gregory Conti

OTHER PRESS NEW YORK

First softcover edition 2023
ISBN 978-1-63542-413-3

Originally published in Italian as *Il bambino è il maestro:
Vita di Maria Montessori* in 2020 by Rizzoli, Milan.
Copyright © 2020 Cristina De Stefano
English translation copyright © 2022 Gregory Conti
Published by special arrangement with Alferj e Prestia di
Valentina Alferj e Carmen Prestia in conjunction with 2 Seas Literary Agency

Production editor: Yvonne E. Cárdenas
Text designer: Jennifer Daddio
This book was set in Goudy Old Style and Wade Sans
by Alpha Design & Composition of Pittsfield, NH

1 3 5 7 9 10 8 6 4 2

Library of Congress Cataloging-in-Publication Data
Names: De Stefano, Cristina, 1967- author.
Title: The child is the teacher : a life of Maria Montessori / Cristina De Stefano ;
translated from the Italian by Gregory Conti.
Other titles: Bambino è il maestro. English
Description: New York : Other Press, 2022. | "Originally published in Italian as
Il bambino è il maestro: Vita di Maria Montessori in 2020 by Rizzoli, Milan"—
Title page verso. | Includes bibliographical references.
Identifiers: LCCN 2021033929 (print) | LCCN 2021033930 (ebook) |
ISBN 9781635420845 (hardcover) | ISBN 9781635420852 (ebook)
Subjects: LCSH: Montessori, Maria, 1870-1952. | Educators—Italy—Biography. |
Women educators—Italy—Biography. | Montessori method of education.
Classification: LCC LB775.M8 D4713 2022 (print) | LCC LB775.M8 (ebook) |
DDC 371.39/2092—dc23
LC record available at https://lccn.loc.gov/2021033929
LC ebook record available at https://lccn.loc.gov/2021033930

Cosette placed the doll on a chair,
then sat on the floor in front of it, motionless,
in an attitude of contemplation. "Play, Cosette,"
said the stranger. "Oh, I am playing!"
the child replied.

—Victor Hugo, *Les Misérables*

Contents

Part One: Constructing the Self (1870-1900)

Part Two: Discovering Her Mission (1901-1907)

Part Three: The First Disciples (1908-1913)

Part Four: Managing Success (1914-1934)

Part Five: Cosmic Education (1934-1952)

PART ONE

Constructing the Self

(1870-1900)

The adult must respect the child, his ego,

and the rhythm with which he

is constructing himself.[1]

A Little Girl

It starts with a little girl. She is sitting in a big classroom with a ceiling that's way too high. It is 1876 and the public primary school in via San Nicola da Tolentino, in Rome, is like all the others in the Kingdom of Italy: a prison for children. You sit still at your desk, you listen to the teacher for hours, you repeat the lessons in chorus. If you behave badly, you are punished. The little girl is six years old and she has hated it all since the very first day. In silence, she begins her personal rebellion against the institution. Her attention goes out on strike, and, in just a few months, she's the last in her class. "At school, I didn't study at all," she'll say as an adult. "I paid very little attention to the teachers, using the lesson time to organize games, plays."[2] And again: "I didn't understand the arithmetic exercises, and for the longest time I wrote down the answers using made-up figures, the first ones that came to mind."

Better at writing, with a passion for books, she's a born actress. When it's her turn to read out loud in class some touching tale, she makes everybody cry. She has an outgoing nature and, despite her young age, a powerful charisma. When it's time to play in the courtyard during recess, she's the boss, no doubt about it. If a class-mate protests, she shuts her up with a cutting remark: "You! Why, you are not even born yet!"[3] She's got the gift of gab and the security that comes from being a little girl whose family dotes on her. Since the day she was born, her parents have jotted down in a notebook every detail of her life as though she were a prodigy: her first words, her first steps, her chatty cheerfulness, and above all, her "vivacious and independent character."[4]

Her teachers are not enamored of her strong personality, her way of looking adults in the face without a trace of subjection. One day, one of them makes a sarcastic remark about the expression in "those eyes."[5] Offended, the little girl swears to herself that she'll never raise her eyes again in her presence. During the lessons she can't manage to get anything into her head. Learning poems and passages by heart is a torment. "One of the teachers was fixated on the idea of having us learn by heart the lives of great women, to inspire us to imitate them. The exhortation that accompanied these stories was always the same: 'You, too, can be famous. Wouldn't you like to be famous?' One day, I responded coldly: 'Oh, no, I shall never be that. I care too much for the children of the future to add yet another biography to the list.'"[6]

She has no appetite for competition. Faced with a classmate who is crying because she has been failed and cannot be promoted to the next year's class, she shakes her little curly head: "I couldn't under-stand her, because—as I told her—to me it seemed that one class was the same as another."[7] For her part, she gets failed three times, in the first, third, and fourth grades. You've got to apply yourself to achieve such a result, and she does. She takes long absences from school, complaining of all kinds of illnesses, doesn't listen to explanations in class, makes no effort to prepare for and pass tests. At home, when she has assignments to do, she comes down with serious migraine headaches and takes to her bed. No improvement, little improve-ment, her parents write in their notebook, resigned. They know their daughter's strong-willed character. They offer her private French and piano lessons, but it's not long before they have to give up on those, too. When she passes the primary school graduation exam, the girl is thirteen and looks like the older sister of her ten-year-old classmates.

Until her catastrophic collision with school, she had had a happy childhood, the adored only child of two already elderly parents. Her father, Alessandro Montessori, from Ferrara, a hero of the war against the Austrians, is a government employee. Her mother, Renilde Stoppani, from the Marches, is a schoolteacher who loved her work but had to leave it when she married. The little girl grew up between Chiaravalle di Ancona, where she was born on August 31, 1870, and Florence, before moving to Rome, following her father's work. The new capital of Italy, just captured by the Savoy monarchy, is still a small and sleepy city, all enclosed within a bend in the Tiber, from the Pincian Hill to Porta Portese, and quickly fades into a countryside of patrician villas and vineyards, where, when the nice weather comes, people go on outings or to gather chicory. Farther out, immense and infested with malaria, are the great fields and empty spaces of the Ager Romanus.

Her father works at the Ministry of Finance, while her mother devotes herself to raising her daughter. She teaches her the values of solidarity. She has her do knitting to make warm clothes to donate to charity. She encourages her to think about the poor and to befriend a neighbor girl who is hunchbacked. Maybe that's how she first gets the idea of becoming a doctor. "If I saw a poor child on the street I found him pale and thought he was sickly. Instead of thinking to give him my school snack, I thought about what medicine, what tisane could have cured him."[8] Her baby dolls are not for trying on clothes or bonnets but for acting as patients, lined up on the bed, while she goes around with a spoon to give each of them a dose of cough syrup.

Her upbringing at home is spartan. "We're not born to enjoy life,"[9] she'll say as an adult. And she'll gladly recount an anecdote from her childhood. She must have been very young. She has just come back to the city after a long stay in the country. She's tired, hungry, whining that she wants something to eat. Her mother, busy with their luggage, asks her to wait. Finally, her patience at an end, she hands her a piece of stale bread that's still in the house from when they left: "If you can't wait, take this."[10]

The Seduction of Theater

M y game was theater. If I happened to see someone acting, I imitated them with great vivacity: I got into the part to the point of going pale or hiccupping and crying and reciting fantastic things. I invented little dramas, improvised speeches, concocted costumes and sets."[11] While she is fighting her battle against primary school, she obtains permission to attend an acting course. Her father is against it but ends up, as he always does, by giving in to her insistence. He struggles to oppose his adored only daughter, who has an imperious character. That's how it is when she's a little girl and it will go on being that way all her life. "When she was there, nothing else in the room existed anymore,"[12] one observer will comment years later.

Her teachers at the acting school are enthusiastic. They say the girl has a great talent. They convince her parents to let her debut in theater, in her first official role. "I could feel it, too," she will write, recalling that period, "I was born for that and that was my passion."[13] At the last minute, however, she decides to give it up. It is a sudden choice, without explanations. "It was just one moment and I saw that

I was really headed for glory, on condition that I could get away from the seduction of theater." Throughout her life, she will often make these sudden decisions, based on instinct, in obedience to her inner soul. She believes in listening to her own calling, and in signs. She has a strongly mystic personality. One episode, recalled repeatedly by her biographers, is a prime example: "At age ten, she suddenly changed. She developed a remarkable interest in religion, and at the same time a sense of 'vocation.' Her parents realized it when she became seriously ill with influenza and the doctor told them to prepare for the worst. But Maria reassured her mother: 'Don't worry, mama, I'm not going to die. I have too much to do!'"[14]

In 1883, exactly when Maria, after being held back so many times, gets her elementary school diploma, the law in Italy opens the door to secondary school for girls. She declares that she wants to continue her studies, a choice enthusiastically supported by her mother. Her grades are not good enough for her to aspire to classical high school, so she settles for the Royal Technical School of Rome, which has just opened a section for girls. There are ten of them, a little group of pioneers, who soon become a team. Maria starts to see school with new eyes. The challenge of being part of the first group of girls to be allowed into the male world of higher instruction is finally something important, worthy of her attention. She quickly becomes a model student. Her father writes in the family notebook that his daughter now thinks of nothing else. Her migraines have disappeared. Every afternoon is devoted to study.

She attends the three years of technical school with excellent grades, and in 1886 she passes her final exam with an honorable mention. Her father would like her to enroll in Normal School, at the time the female school par excellence, which trains future teachers. But she doesn't want to hear it. Becoming a teacher does not interest her. When her application is rejected because her technical school diploma is not deemed sufficient, she does not hide her relief.

She insists on enrolling in the Royal Technical Institute of Rome. It is a very unusual choice. The few girls who go on in school do so to improve their culture before marrying, or at most to become a teacher. Not her; she says she wants to become an engineer. In the entire institute, there is only one other girl, by the name of Matilde Marchesini. During recess, their teachers lock them in the classroom so the boys won't bother them.

In the meantime, she has become a lovely young woman. She is short but shapely. She has curly hair and vivid black eyes, a way all her own of looking her classmates straight in the eye, with no timidity, and a beguiling laugh. An older boy, Giovanni Janora, starts courting her, "following her at a distance."[15] Confronted by Renilde, worried for her daughter's reputation, he explains that his intentions are serious. When he has finished school and done his military service, he says, he's going to ask for her hand. Reassured, Renilde gives him permission to come to the house on Sundays.

When they are informed about what is going on, the boy's family voices opposition, stating that he is too young to commit himself. Renilde, who has come to like him, is disappointed. Alessandro Montessori, on the other hand, is relieved. He likes the boy but finds him too gloomy, not cut out for his vivacious and expansive daughter. If it had worked out, the proposed engagement would have meant an early marriage and a completely different life. Maria would have been shut up inside of a middle-class living room, with children to take care of and evenings spent with her husband. Instead, the whole thing was called off. Her life story can go on.

Excellency, I Will Study Medicine

The next year, Maria is preparing for her final exams. She has decided to do something with her life, even if she doesn't know what yet. "Clambering my way along uncertain roads," she will recall years later, "I began my studies in mathematics, with the inchoate intention of becoming an engineer, then a naturalist, and finally I set my sights on the study of medicine."[16] Nothing can distract her from her studies. She's not even interested in the novelty of the year, Buffalo Bill's Wild West Show, which has pitched its tents in Prati, a vast open area on the other side of the Tiber used for military exercises. On show days, long lines form along the Ripetta port and the Sant'Angelo bridge. Maria looks on at all the hubbub with indifference on her way home from school.

In June 1890, now twenty, she passes her exams and takes her diploma from the technical school. Her mother encourages her to go on to university, her father hopes she wants to stop. He is proud of his brilliant daughter but he's afraid of ending up with one of those women in the house who are described by the prejudices of the time as mannish, all involved with their studies and incapable of being wives and mothers. When Maria declares she wants to be a doctor, he's against it but he knows there's no way he can stop her. If mother and daughter are allied, the battle is lost before it starts. He is meek, not given to conflict. In his daughter's memories, he is the one who put her to bed as a little girl, holding her in his arms and singing her a lullaby, a surprising image for a man of his time.

What truly worries him is the scandal. At the time, an upper-class girl was guarded like a precious object, waiting for a husband to come along. Imagining her sitting in a classroom full of male students is something unheard of. In recent years, the legal barriers to women's access to the university have fallen, but the cultural ones are still strong. "To come out a doctor, and in a certain way to cease to be a woman, a young girl would end up becoming chlorotic, perhaps consumptive, or mad, certainly neurotic,"[17] writes one professor, commenting on the arrival in Italy of the new fashion of women doctors.

Maria Montessori manages to obtain an interview with Guido Baccelli, the dean of the medical school. She finds herself before an elderly man, who listens to her with attention but in the end gently rejects her. Personally, he has nothing against the idea, even if he's already had female students in the department and he knows full well the agitation they provoke in a classroom full of young men. The problem, he points out, is that Maria does not have the required qualifications. Only those who have a diploma from the classical high school and have studied Latin and Greek can enroll in medicine. She does not get discouraged and leaves his office, declaring, "Excellency, I will study medicine."[18]

In the Montessori hagiography, this episode is used to develop the story of the enormous difficulties she encountered in her studies. She herself will say more than once that she was the first woman doctor in Italy, which is not true. She will talk of the opposition of the pope, of the masonry, of the strong opposition of academia; all things that on close examination turn out to be invented. Her professors show themselves to be understanding. Her problems in the classroom are caused more by her delicate sense of modesty than by the attitudes of the men around her. None of this takes anything away from the exceptional nature of her choice to pursue her studies at the university. Maria Montessori is a member of a group of pioneers: 132 out of a total of 21,813 enrolled students, if we consider the year of her graduation.[19] Before her, only two other women took their degree in medicine from the university in Rome.

To get around the problem of her inadequate secondary school diploma, she takes advantage of an article of the university bylaws. She enrolls in Science with the intention of transferring to Medicine, once she has passed the second-year exams. In the meantime, she has to make up for her lack of preparation in the classical languages. She knows that money is a problem and that her father disapproves, so she makes use of some connections among the Roman clergy. One newspaper story provides this account: "She turns for help to a friar and makes such an impression on him that the good religious man, seeing in her the will of God, promises to let her enter the seminary and attend the lessons in Latin and Greek, hidden, however, behind a wooden plank, so that her presence would not perturb the young seminarians."[20] When the poor cleric dies, she convinces her father to pay a teacher who comes to give her lessons at home. When she wants something, she is practically irresistible. One day they will say of her: "She sailed into situations like a battleship."[21]

The Anatomy Museum

Her days as a student are extremely long. Classes begin early in the morning and last until evening. After dinner, she has her private lessons in Greek and Latin. Maria Montessori takes her studies very seriously. That so many among the friends of her family and her fellow students smile at her desire to become a doctor only hardens her commitment. There doesn't seem to be anything else in her life. No more afternoons on the Pincian Hill, admiring the city from the big panoramic terrace. No more walks down the via del Corso, observing the high-society ladies passing by in their open carriages, their dresses fanning out around them like flowery corollas and their wide-brimmed hats flopping up and down to the rhythm of the horses' hooves. Every morning she goes to the university, her head full of projects. She thinks about her goal of finishing the first two years, after which her long-awaited studies will begin. "When I hear talk of medicine, it seems like I'm dreaming."[22]

Sometimes she carries with her a small bouquet of flowers, which her mother has prepared for her on the kitchen table together with her breakfast, as a feminine sign of encouragement. Things at medical school are not always easy. She has to win the acceptance of her classmates, hiding herself behind an air of ferocity. "She enjoyed telling the story of a boy sitting in the row behind her," another female student recalled. "This guy's foot kept making her desk shake. She didn't like the shaking at all, so she turned her head around and launched him an angry look. He then said to the guy sitting next to him, 'Another look like that and I'm dead!'"[23]

She is chosen to be the first to enter the classroom, so her contact with the other students is reduced to a minimum. She sits in the first row, by herself. She is always the last to leave. Her first trauma is anatomy class, obligatory even in the School of Science. In a world where it is considered indecent for a woman to show her ankle, she has to listen to explanations of the functioning of the human body and study detailed illustrations of every bodily organ. She gets upset from the very first day. Determined as she is, she is still a young woman of her time. When the professor talks about reproduction and the genital organs, the situation precipitates. Maria turns purple, feels faint. "That's the way my mother raised me. My ignorance made me so delicate and pure."[24]

The anatomy museum, with its dimly lit rooms full of skeletons and organs in glass cases, strikes her immediately as a spooky place. All she has to do is take a look out the window to understand just how much her choice is against the grain. While she's shut inside those dark rooms, the other girls are someplace else: "There was light out there, people walking, women dressed in bright colors. It all seemed so beautiful to me. A young milliner was standing in the doorway of a shop across the street. I felt a strong sense of envy towards her. She was outside, she was free, everything around her was alive. Her thoughts went no further than her hats."[25]

At home she tries to put a good face on things, but her parents notice right away that something is not right and they force her to open up. Her father takes advantage of the situation to ask her to interrupt her studies, which he considers scandalous. Her mother, though encouraging, is upset. Maria tries to play things down. She repeats that it was just the trauma of the first classes, that she is glad she didn't faint. Actually, she's worried, she knows that the lessons where she'll be asked to dissect cadavers will be starting soon. If she quits now, she keeps telling herself, she'll never be a doctor and all those people who thought her dream was absurd will be proved right. "All the admonitions I had been given when I decided to study anatomy came back into my mind: women doctors can't find work, nobody calls them, the only thing they earn is a general contempt."[26]

Lessons on the Cadaver

The first lesson in dissection is dramatic. The professor lifts the sheet, uncovering a female cadaver: "'It's a young lass!' the doctor said. The other young lass in there was me. Everybody looked at me."[27] When one of the male students reaches out a hand and starts feeling one of the breasts, Maria can't take any more and rushes out of the room. She walks quickly across the park on the Pincian Hill, her hat hurriedly plopped on her head and her books held against her chest. She sees a beggar sitting under a tree with her son. The sight makes her slow down, for no reason. It's the child that catches her attention. Like his mother, he's clothed in rags, but he seems to be somewhere else, immersed in observation of a strip of red paper he holds in his hands, passing it slowly through his fingers.

Recounting this episode, that detail will be what Maria Montessori will remember best. What she sees speaks to her, without her knowing exactly why. She doesn't imagine that years afterward, studying the striking attentive capacity of children, her way of understanding pedagogy will change forever. All she knows is that the sight of that little beggar intent on studying a strip of red paper in the midst of all that dirt and grime, isolated from everything around him, like a king in his realm, convinces her to return to the university. To focus on the detail, not on the whole. Recalling that moment, she will speak of a complete and utter illumination: "I don't know how to explain it. It simply happened that way."[28]

She asks to talk to the anatomy professor to explain her difficulties to him. He is very understanding and proposes to help her get over it immediately. He has them bring in the cadaver he was working on when Maria ran out of the classroom. His assistants come in, handling the cadaver clumsily. The arms and legs dangle in the air, sticking out from under the sheet. When the professor uncovers the body, she is again paralyzed from embarrassment: "My sense of modesty was too strong for me, I was about to faint at the sight of that naked woman."[29] The professor takes a hand, to force her to touch the cadaver. Maria pulls pack, upset by that gesture. We are in an age when no young woman would entrust herself to a man who is not part of her family, especially with no other people present. But he doesn't stop, he lifts the hand of the dead girl and rubs it on hers.

Being alone with her professor in an empty classroom makes Maria very uncomfortable. She knows too well that tomorrow that's all everyone in the department will be talking about. She would like to open the door but doesn't know how to go about it. She grabs on to a pretext when he, in order to cover up the smell of the putrefying body, lights up a cigar. She says to him, "Why is the door closed? May I open it?" And then, to keep from raising any suspicion, she adds, "Otherwise, we'll smother to death." With a calm, kind smile the professor points to the open window: "Don't be afraid," he says calmly between two puffs of smoke, "there's no danger."[30] The professor goes on with the lesson. When he has finished his explanations he accompanies her out into the courtyard so she can wash her hands in the fountain. As they are walking he slips an arm around her waist. Again, a less than totally appropriate gesture. Maria pulls away brusquely.

This episode, recounted by Maria in a very detailed way in one of her notebooks, enacts a curious ballet of gender conventions, fears, and relationships. One can almost see her as she blushes red every time the professor gets too intimate, torn between her disgust for the cadaver and her embarrassment for the situation she finds herself in, shut inside a classroom alone with a man. Everything about this passage speaks of her condition as a female student in a male environment, of a young woman venturing into unknown territory, where her presence is not contemplated. That she manages to overcome the obstacle anyway demonstrates the strength of her determination.

When the professor tells one of the orderlies to go buy some pastries, she looks at him incredulously. The last thing she wants in that moment is a pastry. But the professor insists. If you don't eat something right away, later it's even harder. "The pastry arrived. I grabbed it with that hand that moments ago he rubbed against the putrefying flesh of that young girl. Right there in front of him, but on the threshold of the exit leading to the hallway, I started to cry. The first bite just wouldn't go down. The orderly laughed. The professor encouraged me."[31] In the end she manages to swallow a few bites. The next day she goes to class and listens to the explanations of the cadaver with her classmates. When she gets back home, she writes in her diary: "It's raining—my spirit is calm. I intend to spend the day studying."

In the beginning, she pays an orderly to smoke next to her in the dissection room, to cover up the smell of the cadavers. Then she starts smoking herself. It's a habit that stays with her all her life, although she will rarely smoke in public. She passes the anatomy exam and goes on with her other exams. She also participates in the political life of the university. She joins with other students in the strike on May 1, a gesture that at the time amounts to a very explicit declaration of militancy, because May Day has just been introduced in Italy by the Socialist Party. Her professors convince her, however, not to participate in the workers' demonstration at Santa Croce, because there is concern about possible disorder.

Walks on the Pincian Hill

S he passes all her exams at the end of her first year. In a letter to a friend she describes herself during the Physics test, standing at the blackboard, a piece of chalk in one hand and a fan in the other. This detail is one of Maria's rare concessions to light-heartedness. She is so taken by the dream of becoming a doctor that she does not seem at all interested in what generally fills the lives of young women her age. Only in the summertime does she concede herself a few hours on the walking paths of the Pincian Hill. With her is Matilde Marchesini, her classmate at the technical school, and some other girls about whom all we know is their names: Clara, Dina. There is a high-society matron who has taken her under her protection and acts as her sponsor, promising her help for her future career.

Maria confides to her diary that she is attracted to a classmate, Riccardo Salvadori, who, like her, is enrolled in the School of Science with the intention of transferring to Medicine. When she meets him she feels suddenly weak under his gaze: "On my walks in the Pincian it seems to me that Salvadori considers me a woman."[32] Then she remembers that she is different from the other girls who play the flirt in the park under their bright parasols, looking for a husband. "Yes, I am a woman, and practical, because I have an ideal." The other girls her age are married or engaged, but she has no intention of being a wife. She has decided to become a doctor and she takes it terribly seriously: "I really must say it: on turning twenty, an ideal surged up within me; either that ideal or die."

After every encounter with Riccardo, she goes home agitated, and she has to shut herself in her room to calm down and try to think clearly: "What do I want? Oh beautiful, nothing. Marry him? Never."[33] Her classmate courts her, with elegance. One day when she doesn't go to the park because she doesn't feel well, someone knocks on the front door of the house. It's a waiter in livery from a café in the city, who has been asked to bring her a cup of hot chocolate. When she hears that at the end of the summer the young man will be moving to Milan, Maria thinks about writing him a letter to confess her feelings for him, but then she decides against it. She has chosen her road and she knows that it means not getting married: "Who knows how many new affections he will have in his heart. And I will always be alone! Alone!"[34]

At the end of August, she jots down a dream in her diary which seems to close that long summer, where love had put to the test her dream of becoming a doctor. It is a precious glimpse into her subconscious, and it contains all the ingredients of her life in that period: the lessons on the cadavers, the family's limited finances, her commitment to the poor, her attachment to her parents, her love for Riccardo Salvadori, all mixed together in a mysterious way, as always happens in dreams. It is long, but worth reporting in its entirety.

I left the house with my parents and, walking along, I came to an ugly place, full of poor people, but they weren't the usual beggars. No one was asking for donations, on the contrary, they all looked like distinguished people, but dressed in rags, and with haggard, frightened faces. My father said to me that the house we had just left was no longer ours, all the furnishings had been sold and we would be going to live with those wretched people that we were looking at. Let me go then, I said, I have to take some things from the house so I can have some memories. And I went back. There were already new people there, in the middle of our furniture, the house was beautiful, full of light, flowers. The people were so cheerful. I said: Let me at least take my memories! Here are your memories, they said. And they gave me a little case. Inside there was a skull of a dead person. The eyes were still in the sockets, but coming apart. I was about to take it, but I couldn't, it started to break, only some pieces of paper were left in my hands, and I pinned them to my chest. Then I went to school. It was a big conglomeration of stairs and hallways, all dark. Suddenly, I realized I had lost the pieces of paper. I ran into Salvadori and I told him. He ran to look for them, getting lost among the corridors. I went back to the lurid place where I now had to live. I saw a lot of people and with clothes that must have been elegant once but were now all filthy and torn. Everyone was looking at a place with painful curiosity. I looked at it too, and saw my father with a long faded overcoat in shreds. His face was green, all contorted, and he was hunchbacked. My mother wasn't there. I looked all around but I didn't see her. Then I grabbed the arm of a girl I didn't know, and while we were going along together I started to feel sick. Then, moving my tongue, I felt one of my front teeth move, and I spit blood. We went into a shop, dirty and ugly. They gave me a plate and I spit blood into it, and pulled out my tooth. Then, after that one another one, and then another one. I couldn't see them because they were covered with blood. Then the shopkeeper said to me, "Your mother is dead."[35]

Reaching Out to the People

In the summer of 1892 Maria Montessori finishes her first two years in Natural Sciences and applies for admission to Medicine. In February she is finally a student in the department of her dreams, enrollment number 1664, the only woman enrolled in that year. Her presence does not go unremarked. In the hallways her classmates often whistle when she walks by. She responds in a loud voice that everyone can hear: "The more you blow the higher I go."[36]

In those years, the School of Medicine in Rome is a center of progressive thought. The faculty includes professors like Jacob Moleschott, theorist of social medicine, Angelo Celli, a pioneer in the battle against malaria, Clodomiro Bonfigli, father of the university's psychiatric clinic. They are all very strong personalities with a profound influence on their students. It is a small school. The professors know all their students personally, take an interest in their personal lives, and often think of them as young friends. Maria is welcomed warmly by her professors and invited to join in their volunteer activities.

She participates in their expeditions into the Agro Romano, the poor rural area outside of Rome, organized by Angelo Celli and his German wife and nurse, Anna Fraentzel. It is her personal "reaching out to the people," and it is very traumatic. Having grown up in a protected, middle-class environment, she is not prepared for what she has to face there. "On a hilltop there rose up, similar to an encampment of Negroes, a lot of shacks with a small chapel in the middle, without a garden, without even one flower," Anna Fraentzel writes. "The shacks were one right next to the other and were made out of straw, canes, corn stalks, and dried leaves, with no windows and with a door, or rather an entry hole, so small that to enter you had to stoop down."[37] Getting those rustic people to accept the installation of mosquito nets is not easy. The women slit them so they can throw buckets of dirty water out the doorway and use them to make sieves for grain. Getting them to take quinine is an enterprise.

Maria also volunteers in the Soccorso e Lavoro (Mutual Aid and Labor) pediatric clinic established in the city to treat the children of the poor. Every day she sees dozens of pale, scrawny children with swollen bellies and hacking coughs. They have big, accusing eyes but not a single lament comes out of their mouths. Maria sees cases of malnutrition, rickets, tuberculosis, and other horrible things that can't be put into words. Every so often baby girls less than two years old arrive in the clinic with strange sores on their genitals. The doctor explains that there is a dreadful superstition in the back streets of Rome that syphilis can be cured by contact with baby girls. Men lure them into darkened entryways, attracting them with offers of candy.

Notwithstanding all the time she devotes to volunteering, she gets excellent marks. She wins a scholarship with a prize of one thousand lire, a considerable sum for the time, when university tuition was one hundred lire per year. The award comes at just the right time because her father has asked for early retirement for health reasons and the family income has been reduced. The news is reported in a Rome paper under the headline "Young ladies do themselves honor." It is not the first time that the local press talks about her. Some years before, she was mentioned for her participation in a festival at Villa Borghese, where she had the honor of offering flowers to the queen. During her fifth year, she wins the competition to become an assistant in Medicine—coming in ahead of students in their sixth year and new graduates, as her father records with pride in the family notebook—and starts doing clinical work in the hospital.

She is very impressed by Clodomiro Bonfigli, who teaches a course on the relationship between child rearing and mental illness. She decides to do her degree thesis with him in psychiatry, another pioneering choice for a young woman of her time. Her mother, as always, encourages her and helps her in every way she can. For every new course, she splits the binding of the heavy tomes, dividing them into smaller volumes, so they won't weigh too much in Maria's bag. In the evenings, she listens to accounts of the day's classes and reviews Maria's notes with her. When she was young, she wasn't able to enroll in the university, then prohibited to women, and her daughter's studies are her vindication. The light in Maria's room stays on late into the night. She herself will say, recalling those years, "I felt like I was able to do anything."[38]

In the final year of Medicine every student has to give a lecture to the class. Maria's lecture is awaited with particular interest. She enters the classroom feeling like a lion tamer who has to go into the cage with the lions. Her father had refused to accompany her, not wanting to give his approval to this crazy idea of public speaking. In the end, however, he lets himself be convinced by a friend and takes a seat in the back of the room. The lecture is a success. The audience responds with a long applause. When they realize that he is the orator's father, they all crowd around him to offer their compliments. Despite his worst fears, Alessandro Montessori is very proud of his daughter, who appears to be afraid of nothing. He describes her in a letter with these words: "The once young girl has become a woman, and an uncommon woman."[39]

Her final year at university is very intense, between classes, her internship at the hospital, and her study of the patients at the psychiatric clinic in preparation of her thesis. Maria graduates in July 1896. The city papers report the news, recounting that after the ceremony friends and professors got together at the Montessori home for refreshments. A chapter of her life comes to an end. "Now it's all over. All my emotions have reached conclusion. At this last public examination, a Senator of the Realm expressed to me his warm congratulations and stood up to offer me his hand,"[40] Maria recounts in a letter to a friend. "I must admit, however, that it all strikes me as rather silly. Everyone looks at me and follows me around as though I were a celebrity." Friends and family are amazed at this young woman who handles cadavers and examines nude patients without showing the least discomfort. "Nothing shakes me, nothing," Maria admits. "I talk out loud about difficult things with such indifference and cold blood that even my professors are left disconcerted, and I have the moral force that one would expect of an older woman steeled by experience."

When the celebrations are over, she goes back to work. Her degree thesis is presented to the Conference of the Phreniatric Society, not by herself directly, she being a woman, but by one of her professors. An article of hers is published in an important scientific journal. Since she is so skilled in the work of observation, some of her professors advise her to take an advanced course in Berlin with the greatest laboratory clinician of the time, Robert Koch. Her father doesn't have the money to finance her stay abroad; she applies for a scholarship but without success. Nevertheless, Maria will go to Berlin, and very soon, not as a physician, but as a feminist activist.

Up with Women's Unrest

T
hrough her volunteer work, she has come into contact with the feminists, who are very socially committed in Rome. She takes part in their political battles, from the protest against the Italian invasion of Ethiopia to the gathering of signatures in support of the struggle for liberation in Cuba. She becomes the secretary of the Association for Women, created by a group of activists to put forward a very radical program: community education, female suffrage, a law for the determination of paternity, equal pay for men and women.

This is the association that chooses her as the Italian delegate to the 1896 Berlin International Women's Congress. Everything about her makes her the ideal candidate: she's young, she's one of the first women doctors in Italy, she has demonstrated her ability to speak in public. The news makes it all the way to Chiaravalle, where a local feminist committee raises money to send to their illustrious sister citizen as a contribution toward the expenses of the trip. The Rome correspondent of a French newspaper interviews her before her departure. The journalist is expecting to meet an angry, mannish militant and is surprised to be greeted by a young woman in a "simple summer dress, with black hair, well combed, a thin, graceful waist, appetizing figure and complexion, seductive and healthy."[41]

In the interview, Maria talks about the internship she's doing at the hospital: "They have assigned me to the women's section, and I can assure you that the patients ask for me, they want me. You know, the patients are like children, they know intuitively when someone cares about them."[42] She recalls her university years with pleasure: "I must say, in tribute to my fellow students in Rome, that they always respected me; never was a word too gallant or too harsh directed at me." Impressed, the journalist comments: "Well chosen. The delicacy of a young woman of talent combined with the strength of a man, an ideal one doesn't meet every day."

The congress opens in Berlin on September 20, in the presence of five hundred delegates from around the world. The inauguration is disturbed by a demonstration of socialist women protesting outside the building against a congress they accuse of being bourgeois. Maria goes out and confronts the demonstrators, improvising a speech in the square. She climbs up on a wagon to be above the crowd. She is wearing an elegant dress, which highlights her thin waist. She speaks briefly, but with a sincerity that wins over her audience. She says she understands their anger. For women who live in poverty—she enunciates in Italian with its beautiful melodious cadence, while a feminist comrade translates every word into German—it can seem that the reforms are taking too long. But she asks, clasping her gloved hands together in a graceful gesture, that class differences not be allowed to divide women, sisters in struggle. At the end of her speech, she raises her hat, waving it like a flag, and shouts in a ringing voice: "*Viva l'agitazione feminile*" (Up With Women's Unrest).[43] The demonstrators, persuaded, applaud and wave their hats, imitating her.

During the congress she gives two speeches, one on women's associations in Italy and the other on women's work. In both cases she advocates for very polemical positions. Speaking of feminism in Rome, she criticizes the philanthropy of Catholic women whose aid

goes exclusively to Catholics, leaving others in need, but also the lay-
women's committee that supports the Mutual Aid and Work clinic,
because it helps very few people. In her address on women's work,
she recounts the difficult conditions of women of the popular classes,
things that she has been seeing for years volunteering: women who
work the same hours as men and then have to go on working at home,
with the smallest child sucking at their breast and the others grabbing
onto their skirt, often subject to beating, when their husband comes
home from the tavern. She urges politicians to bow to reality, and
cites as an example the new law that in Italy allows women to stay at
home for a month after childbirth. An excellent law, she comments,
that has reduced the mortality rate of new mothers. But it makes no
sense to provide for a leave of absence without also giving economic
assistance. "The men who make the laws boast of their having said
to the new mother: take a rest! But how can you rest when you are
hungry? Despite their bodies crying out with the need for rest, these
women are forced to hurry back to work."[44]

She doesn't neglect her new job as a physician, and before leaving
Berlin she goes to visit the city's great pediatric hospital. Back in
Rome, she discovers the large number of articles the press has devoted to her. The young delegate Montessori is a big hit with the
Italian correspondents. All the attention annoys her, especially because what they talk about most is her appearance. "Her loveliness
won over all the pens—or perhaps we should say the hearts of the
journalists,"[45] one article reads. Another ups the ante: "Her voice,
her dark tresses, her penetrating gaze, the gloves worn with such elegance."[46] Maria is irritated by such praise. She knows well that those
who speak of her beauty see the woman in her, not the physician. For
her part, she is determined to escape from the trap of the female condition. What she wants is to leave her mark on the world. "Nobody
will dare sing the praises again of my so-called beauty," she declares
to her parents. "I am going to work seriously!"[47]

A Woman on the Ward

She divides her time between work, her feminist commitment, and volunteering. By now she has her degree in medicine and a professional position, albeit unpaid. Actually, she has more than one, because she is an assistant at the Hospital of the Holy Spirit and an intern at the Institute of Hygiene. Her presence on the ward is noted. At that time, the only women who work in the large salons of hospitals are nuns, hidden under their veils. Seeing Maria go by, with her decisive air and rebellious black curls, causes a stir. Her presence during the night shift is actually a problem. The only place for her to sleep is on a cot next to her male colleague on the shift. It's the nun in charge of the department who shows her the shared room with an ironic smile, almost as if to say: "So you wanted to be a doctor?"[48] Only after presenting a petition to the director's office does Maria succeed in getting her own room to sleep in.

Every day, when she gets off work in the hospitals, she continues with her volunteering for the city's disinherited. Together with the ladies of Roman high society, she participates in the philanthropic activities of the Union for Good in the working-class San Lorenzo neighborhood. With her physician colleagues, she lends her services in the dispensaries, where sick children line up every day. Her interest in childhood is kindled here, in the face of these poor children, the most fragile members of society. The infant mortality rate in those times is frighteningly high. Only one child out of two makes it to age five, and those who do are immediately put out to work to help support the family. The little ones are sent out into the streets to beg, into the countryside to pick vegetables in the fields, leased out by the season to work as chimney sweeps. Maria Montessori is scandalized by what she sees. Very soon she will put her indignation to work in the service of pedagogy. In a world where in the first years of life a child essentially must try not to die, she will propose a primary education that begins before compulsory school age and that will nurture those little minds that nobody cares about.

She devotes herself to the little ones as a physician, too, and often finds it difficult to keep her role as doctor distinct from that of a nurse. "If a severely ill child needed a hot bath and a clean bed," a journalist would write years later, "she knew it made no sense to ask that of the poor mother who lived in one of Rome's deprived neighborhoods, so she had the child taken to her own home for the needed time and saw to it herself, combining the roles of doctor, nurse, and benefactress."[49] Sometimes, to help the unemployed parents of one of her little patients, she invented jobs to be done at her house, paying for them herself. Many of them write to thank her, brief, ungrammatical, and moving letters. One of them is from the parents of a little girl whom Maria cured of pneumonia, spending an entire day at her home. Another is from a mother who seemed condemned not to survive the difficult birth of her twins. Knowing that the family was too poor to afford a nurse, Maria ordered the woman to stay in bed, remained with her at the house the whole day, made a fire in the fireplace, and prepared a hot bath for the newborns.

She learned the lesson from her professors, who in those years of social activism are more akin to missionaries than physicians. "They were true benefactors of humanity," a woman of the time observed. "For them there was no patient too modest, no case not interesting enough, no patient to whom they devoted a less than meticulously attentive examination, for whose recovery they left some option untried, to whom they did not address a kind, encouraging word."[50] Among these colleagues, Maria had noted some time ago a young man named Giuseppe Montesano.

Giuseppe Montesano

W̲e don't know exactly when they met. Perhaps as early as 1895 at the Institute of Hygiene, where she was a student intern and he a young doctor. Perhaps even before then, through his brother, a classmate of Maria's. What is certain is that it was a meeting charged with future. Giuseppe Montesano is Maria's only known love. Her relationship with him never puts her career in question. But it marks her life with a secret drama.

He is a very handsome man, with a sharply chiseled face and an intense gaze. Two years her senior, he was born in Potenza to a wealthy family of Jewish origins. He was a brilliant and precocious student. At seventeen, he was already enrolled in Medicine and accumulating awards and scholarships. Even before taking his degree, he won two competitions that gave him the chance to do clinical work in the hospital. He seems to be Maria's kindred spirit: the same devotion to work, but opposite in character. "She, so extraordinary, determined, creative, impetuous; he dispassionate, refined, with a discriminating analytical mind. Both ingenious, they fell in love and she found in Montesano's sweetness the complement to her forcefulness," a student of his recalled. "She socialist, in a certain sense, he instead biblical, with that precise, individual, Jewish mentality. Sure, he was not a practicing Jew, but he had that medieval Jewish ethic, that rigorous moral sense. Their very diversity cemented their relationship and allowed them to do great things in different fields."[51]

Maria speaks to no one about what she is experiencing. Matrimony has no place in her plans, and all she can offer her lover is a sort of free, clandestine union, something quite transgressive for the time. In 1897, they are working together at the Royal Psychiatric Clinic, where she is the lone woman among many male colleagues. The university archives conserve the ministerial authorization to appoint her as a voluntary assistant. In the document her name is written as Mario Montessori, an error revealing of the prejudices then. If it was difficult at the time to think of a female doctor on the hospital staff, imagining one in the psychiatric ward was almost impossible.

The two lovers are inseparable. Maria convinces Giuseppe to become a member of the feminist Association for Women and to accompany her to the evening meetings. He works with her on a long research study, which is then published in a scientific journal. When he is named chief physician of the asylum in Rome, she accompanies him on his first explorations. That is how she enters that secret place, deep inside a huge building on the via della Lungara. She discovers what were once the "straw rooms," downright stalls, where the more violent inmates were left in isolation for days, completely naked, with just a little straw to absorb their excrement. She gazes out through the large, barred windows overlooking the boulevard, where until just a few years before, the people of Rome went to "have fun with the crazies" and throw them pieces of food as though they were animals at the zoo.

The appointment of Giuseppe Montesano coincides with a moment of transformation at the asylum. Doctors are gradually replacing priests and nuns, bringing with them a scientific organization where before there was only repression and the intimate conviction that insanity was a divine punishment. It is a difficult process that requires a lot of patience. In the meantime, the building in via della Lungara remains a dangerous place. Just three years before, one of the administrators was killed by a patient during an inspection. When Maria enters the women's pavilion, Giuseppe always makes sure that she is accompanied.

It is during one of these visits that she discovers the children of the asylum. They are the so-called phrenasthenics, commonly referred to at the time as "feeble-minded," or "idiots." It is a very broad category, since, apart from mental illness, it includes cases of blindness, muteness, deafness, epilepsy, paralysis, autism, rickets, character disorders, dementia, and malnutrition. Considered incurable, and therefore committed for life, dressed in burlap aprons, dirty, unruly, they are perhaps the most horrifying element of that terrible place.

Maria realizes that she has found something she can devote herself to. As often happens in her life, everything comes together in an illumination. One day, one of the orderlies who accompanies her to the children's pavilion tells her that the children are filthy and gluttonous. Maria stops and, staring her up and down, asks her to explain herself better. The woman, happy to vent her resentment, recounts: "As soon as they've finished eating, they throw themselves on the ground, gather up all the bread crumbs and eat them."[52] Maria looks around. The large room is completely empty, a vast space, bare and cold. And if it wasn't hunger, but the desire to be able to interact with something? After all, those crumbs are the only "things" at their disposal. Maybe it's not hunger for food, Maria reflects, but for experience.

This incident marks a fundamental step in her life. Up to that time, Maria Montessori had been a young physician, with a strong social and feminist commitment. From that moment on, she starts down a road that will take her on a long journey, all the way around the world as the prophet of a new concept of the child. In that ward of the asylum in Rome, she intuits that the little "phrenasthenics" are in need of a special treatment to stimulate them and prompt them to reach higher. She asks Giuseppe for permission to take some of them out for experiments. She audits some courses in pedagogy at the university. She reads everything there is about the education of intellectually disabled children.

That is how she discovers the work of Édouard Séguin, a Frenchman who half a century earlier had developed a system of special education with surprising results. She becomes a passionate disciple of the message of this highly original figure, ostracized in his own country, forced into exile in America, who died in New York when she was a child. "The voice of Séguin seemed to me even then that of the precursor shouting in the desert, and my mind grasped the immense importance of a work that wished to do nothing less than reform child rearing and children's education."[53] Séguin is the great inspiration of Maria Montessori, and the creator of teaching materials which will be her starting point in the elaboration of her method. His forgotten story deserves to be recalled.

The Boy Savage

Born in Auxerre and come to Paris to seek his fortune, in 1837 Édouard Séguin is a young law graduate with a big need for money. He accepts a post as assistant to Jean Marc Gaspard Itard, an elderly physician who became famous many years earlier for having attempted to educate the "savage of Aveyron," a young boy captured in the woods by a group of hunters and brought to the capital to be studied. The boy appears to be an animal. He doesn't speak, doesn't look people in the eye, sleeps on the ground. Itard is given permission to look after him and for five years he offers him hospitality in his home and devotes all of his time to him, with the help of a governess, Madame Guerin. It is the beginning of an extraordinary educational drama, which changes forever the history of pedagogy.

To try to educate the young boy, whom he has renamed Victor, Itard develops a method based entirely on the study of his student. He observes Victor day and night, taking note of every detail. He recounts how the boy sits for hours looking out the window at the landscape during the day and observing the moon at night, as though he were homesick for his woods. When it snows, he rushes outside to roll on the ground, eating handfuls of snow. When he goes outside for a walk, he runs in bursts like an animal, and Itard runs beside him. Tireless and patient, the doctor begins to make progress. Victor starts to sleep in regular cycles, to control his eating habits, to develop a sensation of hot and cold. Curiously, he also begins to catch colds, to which he previously seemed immune.

Itard invents all kinds of exercises for him. He hides objects under cups turned upside down, to develop his concentration. He has him exercise his sense of touch with bags containing different objects. He shows him the different dimensions by placing before him objects of the same shape but in different sizes. He teaches him to recognize geometric shapes using figures cut from wood, which the boy has to replace inside same-shaped spaces. At the cost of enormous effort, he obtains some results, but he cannot overcome the apparent impossibility of teaching the boy to read and write. After months of trying, he has to give in to the obvious reality: Victor cannot grasp the symbolic system of writing. Discouraged, Itard gives up on the enterprise and takes the boy to the Paris institute for deaf-mutes. From then on, Victor will live in a house annexed to the institute, supported by a pension and cared for by Madame Guerin, and he will die in 1828, around the age of forty.

Itard believes he has not accomplished his objective. He does not know that his splendid failure is about to give birth to a new pedagogy. By the time Séguin starts working for him, Itard is very old but he still has time to transmit his legacy to Séguin. Together, they take care of a phrenasthenic boy whose parents have entrusted him to Itard. Séguin is impressed and inspired by the old doctor and his experimental method, where patient observation is combined with great creativity. After the doctor's death, Séguin continues to work with the boy, obtaining extraordinary results, which attract the attention of the authorities.

Let Them Shout and They Will Talk

So it is that, in 1840, Séguin is put in charge of what is probably the first special education class in history, a group of intellectually disabled children taken from the Paris asylum: "Here I am, right in the middle of them. Some are waving their arms wildly, others are screaming at the top of their lungs, others are on the ground in stupefied immobility. The first one I speak to runs away laughing maniacally, the second starts saluting me repeatedly until I forcefully block his arm, the third makes the sign of the cross and kisses my hand, the fourth lies down on the ground."[54]

Full of enthusiasm, Séguin works night and day trying to communicate with his charges. He has decided to create a complete education, something systematic that starts with training the senses, to then broaden out to the development of ideas and abstract concepts. First, he teaches the children to remain still and silent, then to move in a coordinated way. To do this he invents a lot of different materials: blocks to guide their feet in their first steps, a tilted table for learning how to stand up and sit down, a series of ropes and balls for training their arm movements. The classroom thus becomes a sort of obstacle course, where the pupils work on their muscles and brains: "To walk among so many difficulties is to think,"[55] he repeats.

Once they have acquired control over their bodies, he turns to manual skills. He stimulates their hands with feathers, immersing them in hot and cold liquids, in bags filled with seashells, peas, flour, and bearing balls. To better develop their sense of touch he blindfolds the children so that they see with their hands rather than their eyes, convinced that the hand is a person's biggest help, the best translator of thoughts. With a marvelous capacity for invention, he puts together a complete set of materials to guide the children from the recognition of very simple concepts all the way to very complex concepts. He has them work with geometric jigsaw puzzles, graduated poles, towers of cubes, movable superimposable letters. Each time, he repeats his lessons tirelessly in three stages, slow and solemn as a ritual, with which he has learned to capture the attention of his little pupils: "1st. we say *bread*, he must show the bread and appose it to its written name. 2nd. We show a piece of bread, he must say *bread* and put the word bread on the piece. 3rd. We show him the written name, he must show us the piece and give the name, etc."[56]

In 1842 he is appointed teacher in Bicêtre. The doctors at the institution attack him from the very first day, hostile toward that youth who is not even a colleague and challenges them on their own terrain, demonstrating that intellectually disabled children—the ones that they define as "incurable idiots"—can in fact be cured. Over the span of just a few months, Séguin comes into open conflict with the administration and is expelled, accused of insubordination and unspecified "opprobrious things," probably sexual abuse of his pupils.

He doesn't give up and opens a private school in Pigalle, where he continues to apply his method to the children who are brought to him by their families. Most of all, he works on a book which in 1846 sums up his experience. When he realizes that the French medical establishment doesn't want to have anything to do with him, he emigrates to the United States. He lives the rest of his life there, taking his degree in medicine and creating special schools where, with his optimistic vision, he changes forever the education of intellectually diabled children. Let them move and they will work, he seems to say, let them shout and they will talk.

Before his death in 1880, he manages to publish a second book where he proposes to extend his method to the education of healthy children. In France, his name has been forgotten. Many years later, a doctor, Désiré-Magloire Bourneville, rediscovers his teaching material in the storerooms of Bicêtre and decides to carry on his work, in order to make up for the injustice that the great visionary had suffered during his life. It is thanks to the articles by Bourneville, conserved in the library of the Psychiatric Clinic in Rome, that the name of Séguin comes to be known by Maria Montessori.

The Secret Son

▪

While she is immersed in her research on Séguin, Maria realizes that she is pregnant. Her maternity catches her by surprise. In those years, and in her social environment, an out-of-wedlock pregnancy would destroy her reputation and her career. She, who is usually so determined in her decisions, is nearly paralyzed. In the end, it is her mother who takes the situation in hand and goes to meet with the parents of Giuseppe Montesano, worried as much as she is about the risk of a scandal. The two families are allies in hiding the incident. Renilde arranges for Maria to spend the last months of her pregnancy far away from meddlesome eyes, with the pretext of a journey. She gives birth at home on March 31, 1898.

A midwife sees to the recording of the event. The birth certificate declares that the little one was born to an unknown father and mother and gives him the name of Mario and an invented surname, Pipilli. The municipal functionary concludes the entry in the registry of births as follows: "The declarant, having petitioned me to leave said child with her promising in the presence of the above-named witnesses to take upon herself the nursing and custody of the same and to give an accounting upon any request of the authorities and finding nothing in opposition to such petition, I have approved it and left to the petitioner said child."[57] The newborn is then entrusted to a wet nurse, who lives with her husband and three children in Vico-varo, forty-five kilometers from Rome.

It is Renilde who makes all the arrangements, as recounted by her granddaughter: "I believe that the mother had projected all of her ambitions onto her daughter. She would say to her: 'You have done what no other woman has ever done in Italy. You are a scientist, a doctor, you are everything, now because of a baby you could lose everything.'"[58] In any case, a reparatory marriage is out of the question for Maria, who has a highly negative opinion of the institution. Years later, a student of hers will recall that she didn't know how to announce to her that she was engaged: "I didn't have the courage to tell her. Imagine that! A bourgeois marriage!"[59]

In those times the condition of a married woman is not compatible with working outside the home. The legal system still sanctions the juridical doctrine of marital authorization, according to which a wife needs her husband's permission to do anything. One descendant sums up the memories handed down in the family like this:

> Montessori then faced an impossible choice: she could either marry Montesano and by doing so give up her career—for in those days women were not allowed to work once they were married; or she would have to renounce her son. There was no alternative. Even in Catholic Italy there were couples that lived together without being married, but they were artists, writers, painters, leading progressive, bohemian lives. Montessori, however, was a doctor and a scientist. If the fact that she had a child out of wedlock were to become public knowledge, it would have meant the end of her career. At the age of 28 she had made a name for herself despite the many difficulties she had encountered and she was already quite well known

in Italy, as a female doctor working in a Roman hospital with mentally and physically retarded children, and as a feminist. [...] Wishing to continue her work without renouncing her son, but without getting married either, Montessori went along with her mother's wishes.[60]

If she had strongly desired it, perhaps she could have tried to combine working with motherhood, but the price to be paid would have been enormously high. Surely she would have had to give up her hospital career, and therefore also her work with the children in the asylum. Her only chance to work as a doctor would have been as a private practitioner. We know of other women who in those years find themselves in the same situation. One example is Anna Kulischioff, who does not hide her daughter born of her union with her socialist comrade, and for her whole life, even when she finds emotional stability with Filippo Turati, she refuses matrimony. Because of the scandal, she is denied a hospital staff position and she falls back on private practice, becoming the physician of the poor in the working-class sections of Milan.

Anna Kuliscioff, however, is a socialist activist, a foreigner whose mere presence is scandalous, who smokes cigars in public and preaches revolution, who challenges head-on the norms of the bourgeoisie. Those who want to retain a place in respectable society have to be more diplomatic. The writer and journalist Olga Lodi, Maria's feminist comrade, found herself in a similar situation a few years earlier. Having gotten pregnant with a married man, she gave birth to her son in secret and entrusted him to a nanny. She managed, however, to bring him back to live with her when he was two, making use of a stratagem. During an outbreak of cholera in Naples in 1884 she volunteers to care for the sick and saves a little orphan boy. She declares to the press that she has adopted him, then she secretly gives him back to his parents and takes her natural child home with her in his place. "We won't give the same publicity to the restitution that was given to the adoption," she writes to her mother. "I succeeded, by risking my life, in securing my right to be a mother and now I no longer need anyone else."[61]

Maria Montessori accepts her mother's decision and separates from her newborn son. The bond between the two women wins out over everything. "They held each other in true adoration. Something bigger than the love that commonly unites mother and daughter,"[62] Maria's son will say as an adult. We know nothing of Maria's thoughts during this dramatic transition. She never talked about it. Only many years later she will confide that, from the day her son was born, she entrusted him to God every night with a prayer: "Give all the sorrows to me and leave all the joys to him. Amen."[63] Weakened by child-birth, pressured by her mother, she doesn't know what she wants. She feels all the weight of the decision to abandon her newborn child, but she also knows that she has to do it if she wants to carry on with her work on Séguin's method, of which she is beginning to sense the revolutionary implications. Moreover, she knows that the scandal would break her mother's heart after she had bet everything she had on Maria and suffered through endless family arguments in order to allow her to study and become a doctor.

So she grits her teeth, confirms her severe vision of life—"reality is made of struggle, pain, hard work, and that is all life is"[64]—and she continues to work as a doctor, concealing her situation from every-one. As for her relationship with Giuseppe Montesano, she imme-diately lays down her conditions: care of their son at a distance and a promise never to marry. He tries to go along with her and hold everything together, in keeping with his meek character. His motto is "Look for the harmonies,"[65] a student of his recalls. But his family is already pressuring him to find a wife and put an end to the relation-ship with his overly emancipated colleague.

A Pioneering Speech

Six months after giving birth, in September 1898, Maria Montessori makes her first public appearance, at the Pedagogical Congress in Turin. She is invited to present Séguin's physiological education, of which she is by now the most authoritative expert in Italy. Two days after the opening of the congress, a breaking news story fills the front pages of all the papers. Elisabeth of Austria is assassinated during a secret visit to Geneva. She is boarding a ferry with her lady in waiting when a man attacks her and stabs her in the heart with a file. He is arrested and turns out to be an Italian, Luigi Lucheni. When the police ask him why he attacked the empress, he responds, "Because I'm an anarchist. Because I'm poor. Because I love the workers and wish death on the rich."[66] Politicized late in life and very confused, Lucheni wants above all to avenge his childhood abuse suffered in violent foster families and in infamous orphanages.

At the congress, Maria refers to this episode to argue for the importance of creating special schools for children with special needs. She explains that neglecting children in difficulty, abandoning them in the streets, or worse, in reformatories and asylums, lays the foundation for one day having maladapted adults and criminals. She recounts how in the United States and England, where Séguin's ideas have been known for some time, institutions for special needs children turn out manual workers who can be useful to society. She invites Italy to apply Séguin's method too, concluding her speech with words that move the audience: "No one who refuses to support this program has the right to be called a civilized person today. This is not sentiment or rhetoric but wisdom and science."[67]

It is a pioneering speech, delivered before three thousand educators. Until that moment, the problem of special needs children was studied by a few physicians but was ignored by the pedagogues. But Maria is increasingly convinced that it is more than anything else a problem of education. That is why she wants to talk to teachers. The reaction to her speech goes well beyond her expectations. Her motion, which asks the national government to create special classes in elementary schools and establish courses to train specialized teachers, is the central decision of the congress, approved by a unanimous vote. The minister of public instruction to whom it is presented is Guido Baccelli—the same man who, years earlier, as dean of the Medical School, had tried to convince her not to enroll in medicine—who in the meantime has become one of her great admirers.

She also gets a lot of support from women of high society, feminist comrades, and philanthropists. Often they are the wives of influential political leaders and therefore precious for obtaining support in Parliament. Rome at the time is a very small world, where everyone knows one another, and it is here that Maria Montessori begins her struggle to spread the ideas of Séguin. Minister Baccelli commissions her to give lectures on special needs pedagogy in the teachers colleges of the capital. On the day of her introductory lecture, the hall is packed to overflowing. All the newspapers write about this woman doctor "admirably sure of herself,"[68] who has decided to become the leader of a crusade on behalf of children.

She gathers around herself political radicals but also many religious. When she has her heart set on something, she seeks support from everyone, with no political prerequisites. "Her advisors, the men who support her initiatives are—as is widely known—freemasons, who proclaim humanitarian ideals, but her prestige is so lofty that even people of the Church sustain her,"[69] writes one observer at the time. The circles she moves in are those of the traditional political left and the freemasonry and, through their wives, those of the enlightened philanthropy of high society. At the same time, she tries to win over to the cause the high prelates of the Vatican. In a letter to Olga Lodi, she writes: "Gracious friend, would you like to come to a little party at my school for the mentally deficient on the Corso? By exclusive invitation: a few gentleladies, among them, Countess Taverna, the Princess of Venosa, Lady Giacinta Martini, the Marquise Nobili, the Vitelleschi, etc. Perhaps the Mayor and Prince Borghese with their respective wives, *perhaps* Boselli: *certainly* (something which won't often happen to you) you'll find a *cardinal* who is coming to bless a small oratory for the religious education of the children."[70]

To publicize her ideas she begins a collaboration with a journal of pedagogy. One of her outstanding early contributions is an article about children expelled from school, who end up roaming the streets and turn into delinquents. The article is an act of accusal against the government, which thinks it can resolve the problem of troubled youth by hiding it from view. Maria finds this policy doubly unacceptable, ethically and scientifically. She knows that science by now makes it possible to fashion measures that do not consider mental illness to be a question of fate. Above all, she cannot forget the children of the asylum in Rome, abandoned to their beds of straw. Now that she has brought a child into the world, the thought of that tragedy is even more unbearable.

A New Woman

$\int$ he knows that the waiting times in politics are long, but she's not willing to wait. In January 1899 she decides to create, with Giuseppe Montesano and their other colleagues at the Psychiatric Clinic, an association that starts to raise funds and open special schools. The name chosen for the association is the League for the Protection of Mentally Deficient Children. Maria Montessori is the spokesperson and a member of the executive committee. Clodomiro Bonfigli, her former university professor, now a member of Parliament, is named president.

Armed with her notoriety, Maria leaves for a long series of lectures in the major cities of Italy, to sensitize public opinion and raise funds. Hosted by feminist organizations and cultural associations, she wins over her audiences with her fiery speeches. At the end of each evening's lecture, she hands out sign-up sheets and collects membership dues. The proceeds from the lecture ticket sales also flow into the coffers of the League. In late nineteenth-century Italy, so unused to women who are also public figures, Maria Montessori quickly becomes a celebrity. "The easy, full, clear words—as clear as her ideas, her self-assurance, and her argument—evidently comes to her from having mastered the issue that she addresses,"[71] one newspaper comments.

Reading those speeches today, one appreciates all of her ability as an orator. In Milan, she gives a lecture on the theme of the "new woman," during which she dismantles the idea, sustained by the great scientists of the era, that the female brain is less developed than its male counterpart: "It's really true that men lose their heads on the subject of women."[72] She also ridicules the theory according to which women who study risk sterility, and she does it talking about a foreign scientist who upon hearing this affirmation at a congress, stood up and exclaimed: "Dear friends and colleagues, please try to refute my nine children." She proclaims her dream of maternity that is finally free, where women are independent and competent to decide. "The woman of the future will marry and have children by choice, not because marriage and maternity are imposed on her." As she pronounces these words, she also thinks of her own situation, of her maternity experienced as something shameful, of her son raised in secret to avoid scandal; above all, of the double moral standard. She knows well that, if the existence of little Mario became known, all of the social disapproval would fall on her, not on Giuseppe.

Each time she speaks about the new woman in her public speeches she also talks a little about herself, of her living in a nowhere land, in the transition between an old world, which continues to impose its rules, and the new world, which does not yet exist: "In this waiting period, what we see today is not the new woman, but a woman in transition. The woman who is emerging from the home today enters society without preparation. She has to demonstrate exceptional strength. She is an anomaly, not yet a new woman but a pioneer opening up new roads. She has lost the rights that were given her by her supposed weakness but she has still not earned her position in society."[73] Her audiences are enthused by her tone. At the end of her lectures, many women stand up with tears in their eyes, shouting, "Brava! Brava!"

She combines her feminist arguments with her thoughts on pedagogy, illustrating the special education inaugurated by Séguin. For all children classified by science as mentally deficient and excluded from the school system, she proposes a new approach: start special education in the very first years of school, rehabilitate those who can be saved, isolate only those who are shown to be extreme and incurable cases. She emphasizes that all of this must not be the work of a few charitable souls but an obligation of the state. Giuseppe Montesano follows all of her lectures at a distance, writing to her from the league headquarters and sending her the funds necessary for her travel and expenses. He is impressed by her capacity for work and he writes about it in the newspapers, underlining how the results of her lectures, in terms of both membership recruiting and fund raising, have far exceeded all their expectations.

In every city where she speaks, Maria also visits the local hospitals, clinics, asylums, and university departments. The press follows her with attention, at times with some criticism. She is accused of being naive, of having a lot of experience in science and not very much in life. Or else, as usual, she is reduced to her appearance: "Doctor Maria Montessori has a nice little head, teeming with high and sublime ideas."[74] When she is leaving Genoa, the last stop on her lecture tour, on her way back home, she finds her train compartment full of flowers. Back in Rome, her work as a private practitioner awaits her, along with her experimental work with the children in the asylum, and the activities of the League, but also much else. She participates actively in the creation of an association to defend the rights of teachers in rural school districts, young women who live alone and who are often accused of immorality or become the victims of attacks. And then there is her son, who is now one year old and is growing up far away from her. As soon as she can, she hops into a carriage and goes to see him at the farm in Vicovaro. But the time she has to do so is always too little.

A Niagara of Words

H er sideline as a lecturer also takes her abroad. Her first stop is London, where in the summer of 1899 she goes to represent Italy at an International Feminist Congress. It is a big event. Five hundred speeches, two hundred reports, a "Niagara of words,"[75] the newspapers call it, against a vividly colorful background, where "the Indian scarves and the wide Chinese sleeves were right next to the silk and wool skirts of the European women."[76] Maria delivers three speeches, devoted respectively to Italian feminism, in her view still insufficiently developed; to the condition of elementary school teachers in Italy, underpaid and still less appreciated; and to child labor in the mines, for which she proposes a law prohibiting the employment of children under fourteen.

At the congress, she represents the moderate wing of feminism. Her training and experience have instilled in her an absolute faith in the future. She is convinced that the new world is on the march: "Progress leads to the invention of machines that substitute for women's work: sewing machines, washing machines, etc. Therefore, women must apply their energies differently. How will they apply them? By studying. Instead of speaking with their hearts, they will speak with their brains; they will participate in discussions because the world now is positivism, and positivism can only be understood with your brain."[77] That is why we must encourage girls to study the sciences, overcoming the prejudices of the time: "I hope that all women will be enamored of scientific reason, which does not suffocate the voice of the heart but rather explains the reasons of the heart and supports it."[78]

Her participation at the congress is criticized by members of the socialist fringe of Italian feminism, who accuse her of being the representative of a group of society ladies from Rome and a protégée of the minister, because her appointment as a delegate was made by Guido Baccelli and by Countess Taverna, president of the National Council of Italian Women. Maria responds with an article in which she defends the minister and her Roman sponsors, nobles, yes, she admits, but active in the clinics for children, in the sanatoriums for victims of tuberculosis, and in the craft workshops for poor mothers.

While she is in London, she tries to procure Séguin's second book by meeting with all the physicians specialized in special education, but the volume seems to be unavailable. She also visits several schools that use the method of her French mentor. At the end of her stay in London, she goes to Paris, where she wants to meet Bourneville, the doctor who discovered Séguin. She is finally able to see in person what is left of Séguin's original material. The treasure trove of equipment invented half a century before opens up before her eyes: the little dressing frames for finger exercises, for opening and closing buttons, strings, ribbons (which she will make more elegant and varied), the wooden bases for the insertion of geometric shapes (which she will organize in stackable drawers), blocks for the dovetailing of three-dimensional shapes (which will be inspiration for her cylindrical insets), the metrical rods (which she will make easier to use by coloring the notches), the numerical columns with movable numbers (which even today in the Montessori method are called "Séguin boards").

Back in Italy, she returns to her work at the League with renewed energy. She goes to view the premises to rent for the opening of her first special class. She contacts artisans to produce the teaching equipment. The association archives conserve the list of all the expenditures: translation of Séguin's books, purchase of a piano, classroom aprons for the pupils. The Italian newspapers continue to follow her activities. Maria is a new kind of woman, galvanizing, devoted to a mission, and she is very popular with the public.

A journalist who interviews her on her return from her sojourn abroad describes her like this, as usual highlighting her beauty above all:

> the fine oval visage, the thick ebony ringlets of her hair, the eyes of a gazelle—black, deep, scrutinizing, a perpetual smile on her lips, symbol of the treasure of affection harbored in her bosom, of the good will that she radiates, of the purity of her candor. But one could feel in her an indomitable will, a spasm, I would almost say, of volitional energy; the constant movement of her eyes, her razor-sharp phrasing, her resolute gestures, made one realize that hers was a nature of tempered steel, cold-blooded and endowed with tenacity.[79]

Maria does not neglect her medical practice. In December 1899 she wins an award for her work in the hospitals. A month later she attends a continuing education course in public health, to broaden her medical skills to inspection and evaluation, and she passes the exam with honors.

But all of her energies are addressed to the crusade for special education. She tries to involve the Opera Pia of the Nursery Schools of Rome, managed by the Roman nobility, which at the time is a powerful force in the city, with nine nursery schools and two breast-feeding shelters in the working-class neighborhoods of Testaccio and San Lorenzo. She writes to the president of the Opera, asking to create some special classes in their schools where she can bring some special needs children from the asylum. When he stalls for time, she insists that she be allowed at least to talk directly with the school principals, even asking Minister Baccelli for his support, but in the end she has to give up: there seems to be no place for her ideas in the nursery schools of Rome.

The Lesson of Things

In April 1900 Maria inaugurates, with the other league members, the Orthophrenic School of Rome. It is the only institution of its kind in Italy, conceived for the training of special education teachers. Maria is the director, together with Giuseppe Montesano and the Hygiene professor. Her teaching position is unpaid, as are those of her colleagues. Even though it has been four years since she graduated from medical school, she still does not have a regular salary and depends on her father's pension to make ends meet. For the moment, she is unconcerned about that, absorbed as she is in her endeavor to put into action the ideas of Séguin. Beyond that, she knows that her parents will support her, always and no matter what.

The children imprisoned in the asylum have become her obsession. The first thing she does when her course begins is to take her students to see them. Many of them end the visit in tears. "This is what our work is about," Maria explains, enunciating her words clearly as they are leaving the building, before accompanying them back to class. The students follow her down the sunlit sidewalk along the Tiber, struggling to keep up with her march-step pace.

The courses also include practical exercises. For this purpose, the League establishes a Medical-Pedagogical Institute annexed to the school, where they welcome a pilot group of fifty children taken from the asylum. It is with these little ones finally freed from their prison that Maria becomes an educator. She constructs her materials based on Séguin's indications and repeats each exercise designed by her French mentor. She verifies with her own eyes that what Séguin writes is true: after working, the children are "warmed up, bright-eyed, tired but not exhausted."[80] She proceeds by trial and error and above all by direct observation. Each time a child gets stuck on some point, she stops with them, to understand what is wrong with the materials, and to make small adjustments. Thanks to Séguin, who taught her to adapt the materials to the pupil, she works differently than most pedagogists, who start from philosophical, or worse, ideological schemes. When she is in the classroom with her little charges, she considers herself a scientist sitting in her laboratory.

She transcribes by hand the six hundred pages of Séguin's book, so she is able to reach a deep understanding of it. She reflects on every sentence, focusing on the principles of the master's approach, which will then flow into her own. Respect for the individuality of every student: "There are as many beginnings as there are children."[81] The need for the adult to be quiet to let the child work: "The lessons of things will present themselves on their own."[82] The centrality of love in every educative activity: "Making the child feel that they are loved, and pushing them to love in turn, is the end of our teaching just as it was the beginning."[83] The patience to respect the child's pace of learning: "The slowness of this procedure is inevitable. Like seeds, ideas grow slowly, and the slower they grow the longer their product will last and the farther it will go."[84] Séguin's suggestion that teachers should conduct themselves as actors awakens memories for her of when she wanted to be an actress: "He would like them to be beautiful, with charming voices, and that they take meticulous care of themselves, to make themselves completely attractive. Their gestures and the modulations of their voice should be prepared with the same care with which the great dramatic artists prepare their scenes."[85]

After multiple searches, she tracks down Séguin's second book in the private library of an American physician, and she has it sent to Rome. The volume arrives in such poor condition that her father insists that it first be disinfected. Maria does not know English and has to ask for help from one of her students: "Two or three evenings a week, I took her some pages I had translated and we read them together and talked about them," the young woman recalled. "We would sit next to each other at the writing desk, where papers and books, graphs and charts were scattered all around. The door to the room always had to be kept open because in the adjacent dining room a monumental matron, her mother, read, smoked, or admired her, waiting patiently for her Maria—I having left late in the evening—finally to go get some rest."[86] Renilde always keeps a close watch on her daughter. She knows too well that sudden and mysterious illnesses can force her to bed for days. She is the only one who knows that this woman, famous in all of Italy, who appears to be so triumphant, is hiding the wound of her secret son and often walking on the edge of a nervous breakdown.

Maria publishes her lectures in pamphlets, in which she explains how she is developing an educational itinerary that goes from muscle training to social-emotional learning, and then intellectual and moral education. Like Séguin before her, she begins to preach that all education, even education for healthy children, must be reconceived on this new basis. There is no lack of criticism, starting in those very first years. One colleague, Sante De Sanctis, he too very active in the education of mentally deficient children, feels that Maria is a little too free in passing off Séguin's material as though it were her own, and he does not hesitate to say so. In a long response, she tries to explain and justify herself: "Your bitter and impetuous letter brought me considerable displeasure. But I hope that everything that seems so serious will dissipate with reciprocal explanations. Now I am too tired to respond exhaustively to all the words you address to me, to your accusations [. . .] When you think that I am not only interested in the ownership of my method—that this is not a question of individual morality—then everything, I hope, will be clarified for you. [. . .] You do not know my situation and so my demonstrations surprise and offend you."[87]

On August 31, 1900, Maria turns thirty. As a birthday present, her father gives her a large bound volume engraved with the title *Memories*. It is a collection of all the articles that mention her, starting from her years at the university. On the first page he has written:

Dear daughter, over the last few years a pile of newspaper clippings has grown up, here in our house, sent by some of your friends and admirers. Those clippings contained memories as dear to me as they are to you, because they demonstrated the uncommon explication of your talent and your activity. But kept in such disorderly fashion as they were, it would have been almost useless to conserve them. I thought it would be good to reunite those memories in a "Volume," now completed, and on the occasion of your thirtieth birthday I now present them to you, with the hope that it will please you. Your father.[88]

The new century begins. Maria's life is about to take a new, dramatic turn.

A Different Teacher

Everything she does for the League is on a voluntary basis, but that cannot go on indefinitely. Maria has to construct for herself a more solid professional position. She knows that a university career in her time is almost impossible for a woman, so she starts activating her contacts to obtain a faculty position at the Teachers College, which is a middle road between high school and university. Giacinta Marescotti Martini, a comrade of feminist struggles and the wife of an influential politician, writes to Minister Baccelli, underlining the urgency of the situation: her protégée is living on her father's pension and she needs a salary of her own. A couple of months later, Clodomiro Bonfigli also writes to the minister in support of her candidacy.

Maria herself sends a letter to the director of the Teachers College, in which she explains why she feels her candidacy is appropriate, thanks to her experience obtained at the Orthophrenic School. The management rejects her application on the grounds that her qualifications are insufficient. It's possible that they do not welcome her candidacy because it is supported from on high, but also because

Maria is known as an exponent of progressive culture. The Teachers College is a conservative institution and somewhat bigoted—"a safe harbor for overage professors who had done so much to merit an honorable resting place,"[89] it was defined by a student of the time—which requires those who enroll to provide a certificate of morality, and when selecting faculty considers, in accordance with its bylaws, the applicant's deportment and moral character. With her image as a feminist activist and freethinker, Maria doesn't fit the bill. Beyond that, there are rumors of a child born out of wedlock, who is being raised out in the country, far away from indiscreet eyes. In the end, Minister Baccelli acts on his own authority and, in January 1900, assigns her the chair in Hygiene and Anthropology.

Her arrival at the Teachers College is a breath of fresh air. This famous woman, who participates in feminist congresses, who works in clinics for the poor, who refuses to marry and who always says what she thinks, energizes the students. She is different from the other teachers. She teaches her lessons in a new way, bringing together anthropology, science, and pedagogy. She organizes visits to public latrines, to disinfestation offices, and, above all, to the children's pavilion at the asylum, her obsession. Each of her lessons is awaited as though it were an event. "She always comes alone," writes one student. "Advancing boldly, at a slow pace, absorbed in her thoughts. While the intellectuals, the feminists, show off their unkempt masculine look, she adorns her feminine figure with grace, often with a fluttering of veils."[90]

Given that her students are supposed to become teachers, she insists on taking them to schools, overcoming the initial resistance of many principals who do not want strangers in class. During the visits she shows them everything that in her view is wrong: the compulsory silence, the immobility of the children, "butterflies stuck with pins, fixed in their places."[91] She explains that the whole system must be changed, because its premises are mistaken. The very idea of the child to whom something must be taught must be contested. "In each class there is a teacher-intermediary who pours the knowledge into the heads of the pupils," she will write years later. "Essential to the success of this work is the discipline of immobility, the compulsory attention of the pupils; and it is advantageous for the teacher to distribute with largesse rewards and punishments, so as to force the right attitude on those who are compelled to be the listening audience."[92]

Her lessons still resound with the tone of the volunteer committed to helping the least of society. She urges her students not to cling to appearances in judging children. "Even an aesthetically pleasing body is a class privilege," she admonishes them, looking at them one by one. "Even in school, the poor child is a pariah. Less attractive and less genteel, they do not draw to themselves that friendliness that the teacher so easily grants to the courteous grace of happy children. Less intelligent and bereft of help from likely illiterate families, they do not benefit from the encouragement that praise and good grades lavish on the stronger kids, who have no need to be encouraged. So the oppressed of society are also the oppressed of school."[93]

At the same time she continues her work with the learning-disabled children at the Orthophrenic School. In the summer of 1900, at the end of the school year, she organizes a demonstration in the presence of Minister Baccelli and various dignitaries. She gives a speech and responds to questions from the audience, then she lets the pupils show what they have learned. The results are extraordinary, putting them on the same level as nondisabled children. Some of them pass exams in the public schools, eliciting astonishment and surprise. Maria, for her part, asks herself: "While they were all in admiration of the progress made by my little idiots, I was trying to understand the reasons why the healthy children of the regular schools could be kept at such a low level that they could be reached in the tests of intelligence by my unfortunate pupils!"[94]

She would like to undertake a reform of the regular schools, move quickly, revolutionize the whole education system. But those prepared to listen to such radical ideas are few. She is met with thousands of questions and reasons to take it slow. "I am desperate, it's useless, they're deaf, deaf, deaf. They call me a visionary. The times are not ripe, it makes me want to cry. What am I to do?"[95] she vents in a letter to Giuseppe Montesano. He responds with the serenity that endears him to her: "You need to recognize what is possible, overcoming their resistance, do, do, seeds always bear fruit." He is one of the few—along with Renilde—who is able to stand up to her authoritarian character and get her to see reason. Maria does not know that he is about to break their secret pact and put her in an impossible situation.

More Painful than
Losing the Man You Love

W hat exactly happened next has always remained a bit of a mystery," recounts one descendant. "Montesano may only have gone along with the initial plan not to marry and to raise Mario from a distance, in hopes that Montessori would consent to marry him at a later date. When this did not happen, their relationship started to suffer."[96] The tension was also fueled by pressure from his family, who urged him to find a good wife. Signs of the crisis also appeared in their work. In August 1901, Maria is supposed to give the keynote address to the National Pedagogical Congress in Naples, but her presence is in doubt up to the last minute, and Giuseppe Montesano is indicated as a possible substitute. In the end they both participate. In October, at a congress in Ancona, it will be Giuseppe, rather than Maria, who presents the journals kept by the teachers in Maria's internship class because in the meantime she has resigned from all her assignments in the League and in the Ortho-phrenic School.

Everything falls apart in just a few weeks. On September 29, 1901, Giuseppe legally recognizes his paternity of their son, through a lawyer sent to the Office of Vital Statistics, though still leaving him with a nanny at the farm in Vicovaro. A few days later, on October 6, he marries a girl named Maria Aprile. "Deeply hurt by Montesano's betrayal and afraid that her carefully kept secret would become known, Montessori broke off all relations. She gave up her psychiatric work and all other activities connected with Montesano,"[97] a descendant recounts. The few memories of those who are close to her speak of a terrible moment, in which Maria remains lying on the floor crying for days. She will never speak of Giuseppe again, but a student remembers a confidence she heard some years later: "'There is something more painful than losing the man you love,' she told me, 'it is having to convince yourself that he is totally different from what you believed. Having to despise him is atrocious.' Her gaze turned hard, the contracted visage of someone who has to swallow a bitter pill. She changed the subject immediately."[98]

She sends a letter of resignation to the League and never sets foot again in the Orthphrenic School that she founded with Giuseppe. It is not possible for her to go on working at his side. As she always does in life, she makes an impulsive decision, burning her bridges behind her. This way of doing things—"the ability to abandon instantly the things to which I seemed most attached, for which I had even made heroic sacrifices"[99]—is typical of her character. We have no details on the breakup of the romance, but considering the character of the two lovers—"Montessori very charming, beautiful, intelligent, overbearing: a firebrand! Montesano gentle, delicate"[100]—it's easy to imagine that it was Maria who did not want to see him anymore. "In a creature so strongly armed for life, love and hate must have been terrible,"[101] one student commented. Giuseppe Montesano writes her a long letter where he urges her to change her mind and not to throw away all the work they had done together.

With her choice, Maria Montessori loses everything she had done for special education, the mission for which she had given up her son at birth and fought for so long, against everything and everyone.

She was also pushed to the breaking point by the fact that, despite her commitment and hard work, the League had not produced the hoped-for results. Local resistance, especially in the big cities of the North, had kept the League from becoming a true national coordinating center. Nor had the Medical-Pedagogical Institute been able to get off the ground. The asylum schools for learning-disabled children created by Sante De Sanctis—the colleague who had criticized her over the question of Séguin's material—were much more successful. The one he opened in via Rubattino has become a model in the city of Rome. Maria senses that the experiment begun with the League is not going as she had hoped. Her intuition, borrowed from Séguin, that physiological education can be applied to everyone, not only to learning-disabled children, is an idea that will never leave her. If she really wants to change things, it is this to which she must devote herself.

From that moment on, the roads of the two lovers are divided. For Maria Montessori it is the start of a long journey through the desert, at the end of which she will have a clear idea of her mission: something that will send her traveling the world as a theorist of a new vision of the child. Giuseppe Montesano stays on to work with the little ones with learning disabilities, spending his entire career in Rome, between the asylum and the Orthophrenetic School. He will die on August 9, 1961, after a life spent on his first project created with her, without ever forgetting her. A student who met him when he was very old has no doubt: "When Montesano spoke of Montessori it was something that still hurt him."[102]

PART TWO

Discovering Her Mission

(1901-1907)

I do not feel the outside work so much,

but what I am fully conscious of are its

origins, the hidden spiritual work from

which it derives, the communication

with God[1]

A Great Faith

I n 1901, Maria Montessori has cut all ties with the past and is as though immersed in a profound silence. It is a time of great crisis. "Sudden farewells, hasty getaways, instantaneous changes, true complete breaks, inevitable destruction that no one and nothing could remedy,"[2] she writes in a notebook. From a professional point of view she has lost all of the work done with the League for the Protection of Mentally Deficient Children. In her personal life, Giuseppe's legal recognition of their son has eliminated any chance of her seeing her child, over which she has no legal rights. Every once in a while, she goes to Vicovaro in secret, to look at him from afar. For little Mario, she is a mysterious apparition, a "beautiful lady"[3] who arrives in a carriage and sits there in silence looking at him while he plays in the barnyard with his milk siblings. She does not approach, does not take him in her arms. After each visit, when she goes back to Rome, Maria takes to her bed, in her room with the shutters closed.

This "crushing experience of pain"[4] pushes her increasingly to search for comfort in religion. The Catholic faith, which up to that time had been simply a part of her culture, becomes a refuge and a new way of looking at life, something that explains and illuminates everything. She starts participating in long spiritual retreats. She is particularly drawn to the Handmaids of the Sacred Heart, a women's religious congregation founded a few decades before by two Spanish sisters to combine contemplation with dedication to the instruction of poor girls. She applies to be accepted as a novice. Mother Maria del Patrocinio, née Carmona Diaz, superior of the Roman house of the congregation, examining the spirit of that unusual postulant, seems instead to be more farsighted than Maria, and she urges her to devote herself to her mission as a scientist of education, which is tantamount to a vocation and can be lived as such. "This method is the work the Lord wants from you,"[5] she tells her, encouraging her not to stop working.

Starting all over again isn't easy. This period of religious fervor also helps her prepare to do that, to contain her pain and gather her energies. For a long time, she lives "a life of absolute self-recollection"[6] as though separated from everything and everyone. She is convinced that God wants something from her. She clings to the idea that her pain over the loss of her son is part of a mysterious design. Along this narrow divide—uniting her pedagogical intuition and her Catholic faith—she will walk for years, concealing her faith from her lay and anticlerical supporters. On the outside, almost nothing will transpire. Everyone will always admire in her only an almost metaphysical tenacity, a capacity to confront any difficulty, and to persevere in a kind of intimate conviction. "A great faith inspired me," she will recall years later, "although I didn't know if I would ever be able to experience the truth of my idea, I left every other occupation to pursue it, almost preparing myself for an unknown mission."[7]

Very quickly, driven by her willful character, she stops imagining herself as a postulant in a religious order and sees herself instead as the founder of a congregation all her own, formed by teachers who work in the world without any outward sign, to be able to reach any environment. Over the course of the years, she will try several times to present her project to the pope, through the priests and nuns who are friends, but her history as an activist and a scientist will always work against her. Yet again, as with her engagement annulled when she was a young girl, as with the refused reparatory marriage after the discovery of her pregnancy, this will be a boon for her life story, which can thus continue.

Back to University

In those first days of isolation and silence, she tries to give herself new goals. In September 1902 she presents an application to obtain a license to teach anthropology at the university level. Her idea is to teach a course that applies anthropology to education, founding a pedagogy that is truly scientific. At the center of it all, a revolutionary concept—the classroom as a laboratory of observation—borrowed from Giuseppe Sergi, who was her professor at the university and is very influential in the Rome school of anthropology. Sergi is an ex-Garibaldian volunteer and a positivist scientist, a member of the Società del Libero Pensiero (Society of Free Thought) and a fiery anticlericalist. In other words, someone as far removed as one can imagine from Maria's Catholic faith. But he doesn't know this hidden side of his student and he supports her enthusiastically.

Owing to a series of misunderstandings, delays, and withdrawals, the appointment of the commission that is supposed to examine her candidacy is continually postponed. Maria waits, in silence. Except, every so often, she vents in a letter to a friend: "How bitter and cold is this solitude of mine!"[8] While waiting to be called before the commission, which takes more than a year, she can't stand not doing anything.

On January 4, 1903, she initiates the process for enrolling as a student in Letters and Philosophy. She asks to be admitted to the third year (of five) and to be exonerated from the literary exams, in recognition of her scientific merit. She relies on her notoriety and on the support of the minister of public instruction, but the department rejects her application, noting that she lacks a classical diploma, a prerequisite for admission. "One day they said they didn't believe me cultivated enough to admit me to the exam, the next day others made up the excuse that as a woman I already knew too much and should content myself,"[9] she writes to a friend. "A woman... who cares? Today you give it to her, tomorrow you take it away; today you make her a promise, tomorrow you fail to keep your word, she asks for justice and you laugh in her face."[10] In the end, it will once more be Minister Baccelli who intervenes on his own authority to force her admission to the third year.

Going back to sitting at a desk at the university is not easy for Maria, who by now is over thirty. She is a student again where many of her former classmates are now professors, and she feels "the shame that a rich man fallen into poverty must feel."[11] One consolation are her encounters with extraordinary professors, like Antonio Labriola, a Marxist philosopher famous for his audacious lectures, and Luigi Credaro, a radical politician and education reformer, who delivers crowded lectures on pedagogy.

From time to time, news from the Orthophrenic School reaches her like a dagger: "I heard talk at the university about the inauguration of the new quarters of the Orthophrenic School. The girls spoke about refreshments, verses, a party. Indeed, I bought a newspaper and found the attached report. You, too, can read about the triumph of my enemies. Everything smiles at them: the young sing their praises and the beneficent authorities provide them new quarters, sums of money and protection. Who even remembers me anymore?"[12] She has heard that to replace her as director of the school, Giuseppe Montesano has called his sister-in-law, Maria Levi della Vida. The idea that someone else is managing her work fills her with bitterness: "In that school, it is forbidden to pronounce my name, the name of an enemy. In that school, they have destroyed everything that could remind people of me. They've even taken apart or burned the equipment that I had made for the children's education with so much enthusiasm and love, so that it can't be said that something of mine might still be useful."

Thanks to a recommendation from Giuseppe Sergi, she is called to teach some courses in a new avant-garde school in Crevalcore, near Bologna, founded by the physician Ugo Pizzoli to train elementary school teachers. She teaches there for two summers, in 1903 and 1904, presenting an anthropology course based on the study and measurement of the children's bodies. In the laboratory, she has at her disposal all of the discoveries of anthropology applied to pedagogy. In front of those complicated and cumbersome machines she feels a strong sense of nostalgia for the materials designed by Séguin. Simple and immediate, because conceived for learning-disabled children, characterized by a profound essentiality, which is almost a form of philosophical purity, those materials continue to beckon to her like a lost treasure.

A Partisan of Free Love

H er lectures at the summer school in Crevalcore are very well received. In his report to the minister of public instruction, Ugo Pizzoli writes that Dr. Montessori has enriched her course in anthropology with many references to social problems and current events. He recounts that she has also spoken about the women's question, emphasizing how women's liberation is part of the triumph of socialism. This topic elicits much interest from the audience, the majority of whom are schoolteachers, and at the end of the course Maria is asked to address the issue in a series of lectures. In the chronicles conserved in the archives, a handwritten note reads: "Montessori shows herself to be a partisan of free love."[13]

Maria in those years is all of this: a socialist sympathizer and a woman who theorizes liberation from the prison of matrimony. At the same time, in private, she is a devout Catholic who has decided to devote herself to education in the same way that others join a religious order, and who cultivates the dream of creating a lay congregation of consecrated schoolteachers. While she is in Crevalcore, she tries to meet the archbishop of Bologna, noted for his liberal views.

She does not succeed, but from the letter that he sends her to apologize for the missed meeting, it is clear that she presented him her plan for a "nascent association,"[14] asking for support from the Vatican. A letter that the prelate writes two years later continues the discussion of the idea: "The project you outline is arduous, but magnificent. If I were in Rome, I would gladly assist you for the holy aim of generous and beneficent charity to which you intend to consecrate yourself, but I understand that from far away I can do nothing more than offer the contribution of my prayers."[15]

At the end of the courses at Crevalcore, Maria is exhausted. "I worked and endured too much, lost all notion of time and things, ruined my health,"[16] she writes to a friend. She then adds, "I was oppressed by work, and all my pain." After three years, her break with her lover is still an open wound, and the sadness of not being able to see her son is a torment that will not pass. She writes to her friend: "I live (live?) alone and on the outer edge without acquaintances, without even the simplest conversation, bent over the work of which I have willfully made myself a bit of a victim." Alone in her personal life, isolated in her professional activities, she doesn't know what to make of her future. She attends classes at the university, waits for the convocation of the commission for authorization to teach anthropology, clings to the intuitions she has arrived at thanks to Séguin. Everything is possible and impossible at the same time. She remains immobile, absorbed in study and in a form of essentiality that very much resembles meditation. "I am searching within myself and by myself for the strength to get back to work again and overcome my desperation."[17]

Sorceress, Witch, Enchantress of the Young

After a wait of nearly a year, she is notified that the commission to examine her candidacy as an anthropology teacher has been named. Actually, all the delays have been useful for her because she has had time to prepare herself. She has enrolled as an honorary member of the Anthropology Society, done research at the Rome Institute of Anthropology, directed by Giuseppe Sergi, and published two articles on anthropology applied to education, based on her studies of hundreds of students and interviews with their teachers. As always, she stands out for her originality and her straight talk. In the first article, she addresses a new topic: how environmental factors influence intelligence, emphasizing a principle—epigenetics—that will not emerge in the discipline until many decades later. In the second article, she criticizes the schools, which instead of helping socially disadvantaged students, reinforce their exclusion. Personally, she dreams of a new anthropology allied with pedagogy, which does not limit itself to measuring the bodies of students, in a certain sense sanctioning intellectual and social inequalities, but works to eliminate them.

When the commission gives her a research assignment on the physical characteristics of the population of the region of Lazio, she gets right down to work. She asks for help from the staff at the Hospital of Saint John, where she had done her first internship in medicine. Gathering the data is not easy. Frequently the nuns have to put down proper rebellions, when patients refuse to let themselves be measured. The nuns of Mary Help of Christians open the doors of the female recreation center (*ricreatorio*) in the Trastevere neighborhood, where working women meet on Sundays. Maria has at her side, acting as her assistant, a young student, Elisabetta Ballerini, who is amiable, delicate, and a fervent Catholic. She calls her Bettina and she loves her tenderly, as though she were her daughter.

She also takes her along with her when she goes out into the countryside south of Rome. The lovely women of Ciociara, a favorite subject of painters, are less wary of her measuring, but as soon as Maria puts her camera on its tripod, they run off, protesting that "photographs go round the world."[18] She measures cheekbones, breasts, feet, hands, necks, noses, and ears. She compares skin and eye color. Their hair, most of all, amazes her. Many of the working-class women, when they undo their long tresses, wrap them around themselves down to their feet, like the gowns in fables.

Her research takes her all the way out to the Ager Romanus. She had already worked there as a volunteer and she knows the living conditions of the local population. She also knows that her presence will elicit diffidence and hostility.

My incomprehensible question dumbfounded them. Doctor, because I was looking for beautiful, young, healthy women? No. Sorceress, witch, enchantress of the young for the gallows, a spy for the jails, a maker of illustrated postcards—that's what I became at times in their eyes befogged by the prejudice of ignorance. And as such, as an enemy and an exploiter, they treated me in their often brutal hostility. So many times I had to leave half-done the measuring of a woman because there appeared before me a surly man to interrogate me in a threatening manner, and, unable to provide adequate justification for what I was doing, I was sent away in a flurry of invective.

In June 1904, she is convened to present her findings, and she is given a mark of 40 out of 50. Then she draws two topics for lectures to be delivered in public and chooses the one on craniology and comparative craniometry. Once she has passed the examination, she is declared eligible to start teaching anthropology as an adjunct teacher in the School of Sciences, the same one where she began her university studies. On the day of her inaugural lecture, her comrades in the feminist struggle send her an enormous bunch of white flowers. Maria Montessori has succeeded in entering the male citadel of the university, albeit as an adjunct professor, that is, paid by the students enrolled in her course and not by the department. From the outside, she seems like a woman of success. Only a very few know the truth of her life, marked by the tragedy of her lost son.

He Who Possesses Love Is a God

I n 1905, at the age of seven, Mario is sent by his father to a boarding school in Castiglion Fiorentino, near Arezzo. Now he is really far away, and Maria has no chance of seeing him. She can only, every now and again, get information through the few who know her secret. A priest who has some contacts in Vicovaro gets information from the family of the nanny who receives letters regularly from the boy. A friend who has a son in the same school often asks how little Montesano is doing. The news is always good. The little boy is healthy, doing well in school, and is well liked by everybody. In his letters to his father, he constantly asks for information about his unknown mother. Each time Giuseppe responds that she is a very famous woman and very busy, and that someday she will contact him.

At the other end of this taut string, Maria, concentrated and severe, lives only for her studies. "Every communication of mine with other people was as though suspended, even with the closest members of my family, the dearest to me,"[19] she will write about that period. When she is not studying, she prays. She goes on spiritual retreats near Bologna, with the Jesuits, and in the Roman hills, at a convent of Franciscan nuns. She is wearied by her pain, but not broken. She believes in providence, sees in every difficulty a seed that will bear fruit. She feels that what seems to be an end is in reality a moment of passage, almost of rebirth, as demonstrated by a dream recounted to a student: "She dreamed that she was dying. She was dead. Then she regained consciousness in a half-open coffin, brimming, overflowing with books, books that were oppressing and suffocating her. But she grabbed onto those books desperately, managed to pull herself up, felt herself come back to life. The woman, lover and beloved, was dead. She was rising again in the study of science."[20]

Slowly, her efforts to fashion an academic position for herself produce their first results. In 1906 she is called by Luigi Credaro, one of her professors in the Philosophy Department, to teach in the School of Pedagogy, which he himself has recently founded in Rome. It is not a proper university department, but an intermediary institution, for the continuing education of graduates of the Teachers College. In the course assigned to her, entitled Pedagogical Anthropology, Maria continues to illustrate her ideas about primary education—the laboratory classroom, the child at the center, the teacher scientist who observes—adding as a personal note a touch of spirituality: "What really makes a teacher is love for the child. Because it is love that transforms the social duty of the educator into the consciousness of a mission."[21]

These are new words that inspire her students. One in particular has the impression of having found what she has been seeking for years. Her name is Anna Maria Maccheroni. She studied to become a schoolteacher but refused an excellent position because school as it is currently organized does not satisfy her. To support herself, she gives private lessons and works in an after-school program. Listening to Maria, she feels rising up inside her the enthusiasm of a convert. She is not the only one to be deeply moved. Many of her classmates confide to her, "These lectures make us feel the desire to be good."[22]

One day, she goes to Montessori's home. When the professor asks her what she wants, she replies, "That's exactly what I don't know."[23] Maria looks at her with intense attention and invites her to come in. Sitting on a couch, they talk for hours. Anna Maria Maccheroni recounts her frustration with the schools. Maria Montessori tells her about her past work at the Orthophrenic School. She explains that Séguin's new approach to the child is the key to changing the schools. She encourages Anna Maria to get the books of the French thinker and to go do volunteer work with the mentally deficient. "The state in which you find yourself is a beautiful sign of predestination: I can't tell you how much it interests me," Maria writes to her a few weeks later.

> Gathering one's own energies for a purpose, even when it seems that those energies are being dispersed—and when the purpose is obscure—is a great act, the fruits and comfort of which will sooner or later make themselves felt. Be steadfast, because that is our primary duty, the most beautiful thing we can accomplish. Summon your courage and make the effort, it doesn't matter in what; have faith that you will succeed, it doesn't matter in what, and you will certainly succeed in some useful work, and find your place in the world and your peace of mind.

During the course, she takes Anna Maria Maccheroni and her other students to visit the Rome reformatory, which she finds as scandalous as the asylum. In that prison, treated as miscreants and left at the mercy of violent and ignorant personnel, there are many children who have been locked up because they are mentally disabled, or because they were arrested for crimes of which they were really the victims, such as vagrancy or prostitution. According to the rules, a woman such as herself can only look at them from a distance: "In the background, behind a gate, like a cargo hold, from where they shouted vulgar greetings, mingled with threats from the guards."[24] But when she wants something, Maria is unstoppable. She soon succeeds in gaining entry to the reformatory and organizes courses of instruction in practical work skills inspired by Séguin's method.

She becomes attached to each of those little disinherited urchins and writes about them in a series of articles. When they are offered love and attention, she explains to her readers, those apparently lost youngsters are transformed in surprising ways: "As soon as you *make them understand*, touch their hearts with a tenuous ray of affection, they respond ebulliently, with a vivacity that we are not used to ever seeing in *good* kids. Their faces emanate a moving expression of amazement and appreciation."[25] As always in her reflections, the theme of social inequalities comes to the fore. "How infinitely rich we are! And why don't *we give*, why don't we feel shame at our knowing how to think and to love so much in the midst of people enclosed in the dense darkness of ignorance? Why know, why love, if we are not to *disseminate* to these outcasts and to these children, and to all of humanity, our knowledge and our love?"

Among these youngsters, she finds confirmation of what she has been saying now for some time: that education is a creative skill of love. This, too, is an intuition that will remain with her always. She explains that love redeems not only the youngsters shut inside the reformatory but also those who go to help them. "He who possesses love is a God,"[26] she says, citing Tolstoy. One episode in particular moves her. As she is leading a group of noble ladies on a visit to the reformatory, a little boy performs a song full of melancholy, in which a little chimney sweep cries out to his far-off mother. One of the ladies asks him: "So you love your mother very much?" He responds, "Mother? I don't know, I've never had one." Maria can't manage to hold back her tears. The wound of her lost son is always ready to reopen inside her. At the end of the academic year, the youngsters make her a gift of a photograph, taken at the institute and printed on cardboard. Maria is wearing a severe dress, closed up to her neck. On the back of the picture, the dedications says: "Photo taken by the minors of St. Michael's Reformatory in Rome. To their mother."

All Women, Rise Up!

In this period of transition, Maria Montessori does not forget her feminist commitment. She is also in the front lines in the struggle for women's suffrage. In 1904 she founds an association which she baptizes with a name inspired by Giuseppe Mazzini: Pensiero e Azione (Thought and Action). She directs it with an iron fist, convincing many of her students to join. Shortly thereafter, half of the members resign, frightened by her extremist and anticlerical ideas. Maria always says what she thinks, even if this means going against the Church. When a strike is organized in Italy to protest against the arrest of Francisco Ferrer, the Catalan anarchist and pedagogist accused of terrorism, she signs on to the initiative and writes a bellicose press release in which she denounces "the war of the Jesuits against the light of progress."[27]

In 1906 the Italian suffragists decide to launch a test of strength against the government. The idea is to organize a massive voter registration campaign, since the law doesn't formally prohibit woman from registering. Maria is one of the first to try it, bringing along with her a group of her students. Then she publishes in the newspaper a proclamation inviting all Italian women to join the initiative. It is a long, vibrant text that begins with these words: "All women, rise up! Your first duty in this social moment is to demand the vote."[28] One detail gives us an idea of her notoriety. She signs the proclamation with her name and then she writes to the editor of the newspaper to ask her to change the formulation to avoid irritating her comrades: "Put at the bottom under my name, in small print, honorary member, because such is what I am in the association Pensiero e Azione, which is childishly sensitive to *form*. It does not want to be *suspected* of having a *president*, that is, a mistress: at such a price it would quash the proclamation and the undersigned along with it."[29]

Huge numbers of women respond to the appeal, despite knowing that the electoral commissions will try to stop them from registering. Unexpectedly, however, some commissions accept the requests. The minister of internal affairs, taken by surprise, hurries to file an appeal. At the second level, the competent courts of appeal invalidate the registration lists; all except one, the one in Ancona, presided over by one of the best-known jurists of the time, Ludovico Mortara, who recognizes the registration of a group of ten schoolteachers in the Marches. It is an historic moment. For the first time, some Italian women are registered as voters, even though they will be for less than a year, the time it takes for the judiciary to block their little revolution with a decision of the Court of Cassation.

During the proceeding in Cassation, Maria is sitting in the audience with her comrades in arms, and she recounts it all in an article. She describes the activists listening to the closing arguments of their counsel, "impassive, as though those who have no rights must not have any enthusiasms."[30] She reserves a sarcastic comment for the government lawyer who spoke against women's right to vote on grounds of custom: "If the mafia created custom in Sicily, should that officially constitute Sicilian law?" She keeps working for the cause. She gathers signatures for a petition that is presented in Parliament in February 1907. Once again—at the moment of the floor debate on the document—she is in the audience and looks on at the failure of the initiative. The government, in fact, creates a commission whose work will drag on for years, effectively shelving the issue.

The Communion of Sins

M aria Montessori's feminist activism is also expressed in her work as a teacher. She writes an article denouncing how the young women who come from other cities to study at the Teachers College are not offered any housing by the public authorities and are forced to turn to convents, places with an antiquated and narrow worldview. These words demonstrate, yet again, her intellectual liberty. She is a devout Catholic, but she is also a liberated woman who always says what she thinks. The teacher who criticizes publicly the convent and its outmoded spirit is the same person who, in the summer, goes on spiritual retreats with Franciscan nuns. Everything cohabits in her: a deep religious sensibility, an idea of personal mission, feminist activism, an openly progressive and continuously indignant consciousness, and a mind curious about all new ideas.

Her public image in those years is without doubt that of a radical thinker. She writes articles in feminist reviews that emphasize her sensitivity to justice and her social commitment. "The only escape route for individuals is that all of humanity is saved,"[31] she proclaims.

In class, she explains to her students that the misdeeds of criminals are not to be considered errors committed by individuals, but by society as a whole. Some are born poor and excluded and some are born rich and favored, she says, adopting Marxist categories. She does not hesitate to use spiritual language as well—in a blend of socialism and Christianity—to urge participation in the struggle against inequality. She speaks of the "communion of sins"[32] and of solidarity in shared guilt, which is "the scientific form of forgiveness." And she gives her own personal version of eternal life: "The religious say that God records in eternity all the great and small sins for which we will have to pay, and records as well all the great and small virtues for which we will be compensated. Well, there it is, eternal life, the big ledger where all of our works are recorded: our posterity."[33]

Her last public involvement as a feminist activist is her participation at the National Congress of Italian Women in 1908, where she delivers a speech entitled "Sexual Morality in Education." It is a scandalous topic for the time. Few address these issues publicly, but she is used to doing it with her students. Her speech spares no one. She criticizes the secular middle-class men who frequent brothels: "When the little boy becomes an adolescent, his mother says, 'A young man has to sow his oats' and that means seducing, committing adultery, going to the whorehouse."[34] She criticizes the Catholics, who avoid talking about sex: "Believers in God the Creator, what better blasphemy could they pronounce against their God than that of having created things of which the mere mention makes the forehead turn red?" Above all, she denounces the absurdity of prohibiting women, who bring children into the world, to speak about such things.

She also proposes practical solutions, for example, stop talking about storks and cabbages, or hiding the expectant mother's belly from children. As always, the school has a central role in her vision: it is above all in the classroom that one must talk about sexual education. Today, this sounds like a modest proposal, but at the time it was something revolutionary. The Jesuit review, La Civiltà Cattolica (Catholic Civilization), reports the news in scandalous tones, speaking of a "lack of modesty"[35] and of "perverse fanaticism." With this transgressive finale, Maria brings her feminist activism to a close. It is 1908. Her life is about to change, yet again, thanks to a social experiment inaugurated in San Lorenzo.

San Lorenzo

In the first decade of the twentieth century, the San Lorenzo area, situated between the Aurelian walls, the Termini station, and the Verano monumental cemetery, is one of Rome's most disreputable neighborhoods, a sort of no-man's-land where the police are reluctant to set foot. Maria Montessori knows it well. She started working there as a student, with the women of the Unione del Bene (Union of Good) and the doctors of the poor people's clinics. This is where she opened the Medical-Pedagogical Institute of the League, to receive the first children released from the asylum. It is also here that for years she has been going to provide home care to poor patients and teach free courses for working people at the School of Civic Education.

She knows what lurks in its entryways and dark alleys. She is used to the spectacle of disheveled women, their bulky bodies wrapped in torn blouses, and men with menacing looks on their faces. The children of San Lorenzo, above all, elicit her compassion: barefoot, defenseless, victims of all kinds of abuse. Another activist working in the neighborhood in those years described one of them like this:

One day a little fruit vendor friend of mine was in via San Lorenzo. Despite the rain that was coming down thick and ceaselessly, he went about composing in perfect order on the sidewalk his piles of tangerines, which the passersby paid no attention to as they rushed to find shelter. I went over to him and suggested that he go home. "I'd rather stay here, Miss," he responded. "At home I can't leave my room, because the kitchen is rented out, and when we kids go in there, *some want to beat us, some want to cut our throats*. I prefer to stay here," he concluded, looking at me with his big smiling eyes.[36]

In San Lorenzo, the poor often live inside of hollowed-out buildings, the ruins of real estate speculation schemes by companies that launch development projects for the capital only to abandon them when they lose their financing. The whole neighborhood looks like a ghost town. Foundations excavated and left uncovered turned into plots of weeds. Apartment buildings interrupted after two floors still sticking up into the sky like cavity-riven teeth. Windows boarded up and nailed shut.

In 1904, the Istituto Romano di Beni Stabili (Real Property Institute of Rome), an agency created to improve the real estate situation in the capital, decides to take action. It carries out a reclamation project for the entire neighborhood, completes construction of unfinished buildings, and installs shared bathrooms with running water and washtubs for washing clothes. It assigns apartments to families, creating a system of incentives to reward those who keep them in good repair. During the day, when the adults are at work and the children in school, the buildings are left in the hands of preschoolers. Left unsupervised, the rascals rove in bands and do damage everywhere, breaking windows, scrawling on walls. On market days, they entertain themselves by picking up rotten fruit and vegetables left by the vendors and throwing them from the windows at people passing below.

Eduardo Talamo, the director of the institute, attempts to resolve the problem by creating a system of block kindergartens to keep children until their parents have come home from work or older siblings from school. It is a very ambitious project, which very quickly spreads into dozens of buildings. There is need for a program director who can coordinate the whole operation. Someone proposes Maria Montessori, whom Talamo knows from her time at the League. When she is presented with the official request, she stalls for time. Devoting herself to kindergartens for poor children in the most disreputable neighborhood in the city might seem like a step down, especially just when she's starting to build an academic career. On the other hand, the work of pedagogy has been taking on more and more importance in her vision of things: more than medicine, more than feminist or social activism. She has understood that changing the world starts with children, possibly with poor children. She consults with one of her former professors, who urges her not to lower the prestige of the category of physicians by becoming a kindergarten director. She also confides with a Franciscan nun, who is a very close friend. Maria explains to her that this offer calls her in a mysterious way. She senses that it is something that will very quickly fill up all of her space, taking every bit of her energy. "Maria, if that's what you're thinking, then you have to do it,"[37] is the nun's response.

Thy Light Is Come

S he tells Talamo that she accepts the job, on condition that they give her complete freedom. She wants to transform the challenge of San Lorenzo into a chance to test out her ideas on kids who still haven't entered the school system. She sees the institute's lack of funds almost as an advantage. There isn't any money, so the structure is not organized as a traditional school. No teacher's desk, no rows of desks for the children, no licensed teachers who implement the rules they learned at Teachers College. It will be something new, where she will be able to set up everything the way she wants. She has decided to apply the lesson of Séguin to healthy children and see what happens.

In a few weeks, she gets the project off the ground. She gets support from everyone: the queen, the nobility, the feminists, the radicals, the masons. Only *La Civiltà Cattolica* criticizes the experiment, finding it too socialist. On January 6, 1907, Maria inaugurates the first kindergarten in an apartment building in via dei Marsi. The children—fifty or so, aged two to six—cling to one another like a herd of sheep, scared and weeping. The audience gazes at them with looks that go from tenderness to puzzlement. Maria stands in the middle of the room with the air of a chieftain. What looks to the others like the makings of a disaster looks to her like a great opportunity. "They were exactly like a group of savage children. Sure, they hadn't lived, like the little savage Aveyron, in a forest full of animals, but rather in a forest of lost people and beyond the confines of civil society."[38]

After a speech by Talamo, Maria delivers some brief remarks, then pulls out of her purse a breviary and reads a passage for that day, which in the Catholic liturgy celebrates the Epiphany: "Rise and shine; because thy light is come, and the glory of the Lord is risen upon thee."[39] She looks around the room, satisfied, while many of the politicians present turn up their noses at these religious references. Years later, she will comment: "I don't know what happened to me, but I had a vision and, inspired by it, I caught fire and said that the work we were starting would prove to be very important and that one day people would come from all over the world to see it."[40]

The kindergarten, on the ground floor of the building, is made up of a large room, a bathroom, and a courtyard. At the beginning, the furniture is secondhand—a few big tables, some unmatched chairs— but very soon Maria commissions some child-size furniture. On the wall near the entrance she hangs a reproduction of Raphael's *Madonna of the Chair*, as a spiritual protectress of her work. She has instruments installed in the bathroom to weigh the children, keeping a diary of their growth, along with child-size sinks and mirrors, so they can wash themselves. These are all new things for these children of the poor, who have never had a bathroom at home. Every detail is designed for their autonomy: aprons with buttons on the front, so they can fasten and unfasten them by themselves, sandals that are easy to put on and take off. The furnishings are small and above all light, so they can be moved without help. Her friend Olga Lodi, invited to visit the school, exclaims in delight, "But it's a children's house!"[41] Thus is born a name that in just a few years will be heard around the world and become a synonym for the Montessori method.

The Children's House

As the teacher, she chooses the daughter of the building custodian. She tells her to just keep an eye on things and report everything to her. She wants everything that happens in that pedagogical laboratory to be revealed naturally, without outside interference. The children have to have total freedom of movement. They must be allowed, if they want, to lie on the floor or sit under the table. The girl tells her that when she sweeps the floor, the children follow behind her and want to help her. They seem to be attracted more by the idea of doing the cleaning with her than by the toys donated by the wealthy ladies who support the kindergarten. Maria is very impressed. She writes it down in her notebook, so she can take some time to think about it at home.

She spends all of her free time at the Children's House. Each time she focuses on some new element, following her observations and her instinct. One morning, struck by the sight of a baby girl in the courtyard, smiling and peaceful in her mother's arms, Maria takes her into class and shows her to the children. When she challenges them to be equally silent, the little scamps take her very seriously and instantly fall silent, almost holding their breath. This is the start of the silence exercise, which over time is enriched by new elements and becomes a regular moment of every day at the Children's House. It is a moment very similar to meditation, something that Maria considers important for the children's preparation for their work in the class.

During the exercise, the children sit in absolute silence, their eyes closed, and wait until Maria—from the next room—calls them. She pronounces each name in a low voice, elongating the vowels, as though she were calling them from far away, and each of the children stands up without making noise and joins her, happy to have been chosen. "After those exercises, it seemed as though they loved me more: certainly they became more obedient, more sweetly meek. In fact, we had isolated ourselves from the world and we had spent some minutes united to each other: I desiring them and calling them, and they receiving, in the most profound silence, the voice that personally addressed each of them, judging him or her in that moment to be the best of them all."[42] Even in the most ritualized situations like this one, her scientist nature cannot be denied. Years afterward, a student will recall: "During the lesson of silence, a girl came in jumping and making noise. I stopped her. The doctor looked at me askance. At the house, they never pointed out our mistakes, but this was serious. She asked me: 'Why did you stop her? It would have been interesting to see what she was going to do.'"[43]

Another time, she comes into class with a bad cold and, when she pulls a handkerchief out of her purse, she notices that the children are crowding around her. So she improvises a little lesson on how to blow your nose. At the end of the demonstration, the children explode into a thousand thank-yous. At first Maria is surprised, then she understands. Until that time, adults had yelled at them or scorned them, but no one had treated them like equals.

She never raises her voice in class. She doesn't impose her authority. She sits there and waits for the children to come to her. She repeats the need to respect everything about the children, even the confines of their little bodies. "People have so little consideration of the child that they feel it their duty to caress them and it is the children's duty to let themselves be caressed and kissed. A person comes in and says, 'Pretty baby, give me a kiss.' The child pulls back, but his mother intervenes, 'Come on, don't be nasty, don't be shy.' If a stranger were to enter—handsome or ugly, it doesn't matter—and kiss the mother, she would feel offended and would react with indignation."[44]

At the Children's House, the body is not only respected but appreciated. The little ones can move tables and chairs on their own and move around the classroom at their own pace. This is something revolutionary in an era when the body has no place in school and even the desks are designed to cage it and isolate it. One of Maria's intuitions, which will be confirmed a century later by the cognitive sciences, is that movement is part of the learning process. Children learn by moving, she says.

Blocks, Clay, and Pencils

To reproduce the Séguin materials that she had at the Ortho-phrenic School, she has to start from scratch, search out arti-sans one by one, and explain all the details of what she wants from them. She wants the best materials and the most harmonious shapes. She has always been scandalized that schools use objects of poor quality and shoddy workmanship. She says over and over that to speak to the child's soul things have to be beautiful. A student describes her dealing with an artisan:

> I remember the scene very well: the young man, tall, thin, smart; the Doctor with the drawings spread out on the table in front of her. "Make them out of cardboard!" the young man says by way of conclusion. I was standing there, off to the side, and I saw the Doctor remain pensive for a minute. But then she started explaining to the young man how that learning material is used, the equivalences, the equalities, the move-ments. The young man's face became attentive, interested. It was a hands-on lesson. Now they were both smiling. The

young man headed off carrying the drawings with him. "I'll make them, don't you worry!"[45]

It's the first time she uses the teaching material with healthy children. With the little "phrenasthenics" she had to explain every single thing, help them with every gesture. The healthy children, instead, work by themselves. It is in this passage that she makes the first, fundamental innovation in relation to her French master. Séguin taught intellectually disabled children, constructing an activity appropriate for each one of them. He was capable of spending hours holding a child between his knees, to get him to look him in the eye. Maria, working with healthy children, has more room to maneuver, and right from the start, she takes a different approach, almost that of an outside observer. This allows her to see the big picture, to rethink her way of interacting with the children. It is a crucial passage, which will take her a long way beyond Séguin; all the way to creating a new vision of the child's mind.

She shows the children the material and how it works, then she lets them work while she observes, or better—as she likes to say—meditates. For her there are no established truths, no received basic concepts. Everything is open and possible. Slowly, the first elements of what in future years will become her method begin to take shape. Already, in a lecture delivered after just a few months of activity in San Lorenzo, she illustrates the two central elements of the didactic approach that is being invented in the Children's House: the different nature of the teacher, who directs without imposing ("The adult must not remain on high, issuing judgments and grades. The adult must humbly get down among the pupils");[46] and the different nature of the child, who works without tiring ("Study does not consume, does not weary, on the contrary, it nurtures and sustains").

Every day in San Lorenzo she tries out new things. She wants everything in the class to be aimed at making a true home for the children. When the little ones arrive in the morning, they are checked for cleanliness. Their hair is combed to search for lice. By turns, some of them are given a complete bath, while the others wash only their face and hands. Together with the learning materials, the children are given what Maria calls "practical life skills." The children practice with dressing frames to fasten and unfasten buttons, with vases for pouring water, rags for cleaning the table. Each of them is responsible for the care of the classroom. For Maria this is fundamental. She often says that each person, even the richest, should begin each day by making his own bed.

She also proposes lots of other activities: with paper, clay, blocks, and colored pencils. Only with time, after verifying the children's response, does she discard those that don't work; for example, all activities where the children are supposed to copy something. She realizes very quickly that the children love to put things in order. One day, when the custodian's daughter drops a box of papers, the children rush to pick them all up, putting them back in perfect order. Another time, the teacher comes in late and discovers that they've already taken the materials from the shelves. "The teacher judged this behavior to be an instinct to engage in theft. Children who steal, who lack respect for the school and the teacher, demonstrate, according to her, a need for severity and moral education. I preferred the interpretation that the children knew the objects so well by now that they were able to choose them on their own. And that's how it was."[47] From then on, Maria establishes that the children can take on their own initiative the objects they want to work with, asking them only to put them back in their place once they have finished.

In the years to come, she will also introduce a common meal, where the little ones take turns serving. The plates and tableware will always be of glass and ceramics, because the children must be given complete confidence by the adults. The surprise is that the children show themselves to be capable of great care and do everything with caution and responsibility. Maria, as usual, observes and interprets, "Peppinella (just four years old), after putting the heavy soup tureen down on the table, leaned on the tabletop with her hands and did a little hop with her feet. She immediately reassumed her dignified mien of the little waitress and waited for the moment to take the tureen to the next table, where she repeated her little hop. The on-lookers laughed. The Dottoressa said to me, under her breath, 'That little hop is a sign of her relief after the effort of carrying the heavy soup tureen.'"[48]

The Immense Work

Maria is an extraordinary observer. She watches the children for hours, recording every detail. From the very first day, she is struck by how intensely they work with the learning materials: "The normal child, attracted by the object, intensely fixed all of his attention on it, and kept on working and working without pause, with marvelous concentration."[49] She devotes a lot of time to studying this behavior. She realizes that children, traditionally thought to be agitated and voluble, demonstrate a capacity for attention far superior to that of adults. They concentrate on every step, repeat every exercise until they are completely satisfied, and—when they work this way—nothing can distract them.

One episode in particular strikes her as an epiphany. One day she sees a little girl of three working with a pegboard, placing and replacing the little pegs in their holes. She looks deeply absorbed, as though nothing could get her attention. Maria takes the little chair the girl is sitting on and puts it on top of a little table, but the girl grabs the pegboard, puts it on her knees, and keeps working on it up there on the table. Then Maria asks the other children to sing and dance in a circle around the table. Once again, the little girl gives no sign of hearing or seeing anything. She goes on sticking the pegs in their holes again and again—forty-four times Maria counts—then she suddenly stops working and looks up, finally taking a look around her. It's as though something had happened inside her, but what?

Maria devotes a lot of time to this phenomenon. She studies other children, takes notes. She is confronted with something that, in reality, has always been staring everyone in the face. Who has never seen how children, when watching something that really interests them, seem almost hypnotized, deaf to any behest? Her discovery lies in isolating this behavior and making it the starting point for the development of her method. "This was the first crack that opened up in the profound, unexplored infantile soul,"[50] she will say years later. She senses that children have an enormous hidden capacity for attention that emerges as soon as they are placed in an environment created for them and not for adults. Thanks to this particular state of mind—that she will call "polarization of attention" and that will be confirmed a century later by the neurosciences in terms of "experiences of flow" or "the flow state"—children learn in a way that is more profound and definitive.

Maria becomes convinced that this is the fundamental point of education: helping children to reveal their true nature, usually hidden because oppressed by a school conceived for adults, that is, for the teachers and their work of instruction. In reality, the oppression starts even earlier, in the family. Many years later, in a lecture, she will compare children starting preschool to warriors, who have already been subjected to repression and who, therefore, have grown in a deformed way, forced to defend themselves and to hide their true nature.

Another of her intuitions is that children are dedicated workers. They don't play, they learn. They are born for this, to do what she will call in her lectures—using an expression from alchemy—the *gran lavoro*[51] (the immense work). After concentrating for hours on the learning materials, as though isolated from the world, they raise their serene faces toward her. Instead of being tired, they are full of energy. Instead of wanting to move and run around, they seem pacified. They have been doing what they came into the world to do. They have achieved the aim of their existence. If they are allowed to work in this way, they become different children, transformed from the inside.

This is what, in the coming years, Maria will call "normalization," a phenomenon that she does not hesitate to define as a second birth. Children, placed in the right environment, provided with the right materials, soon stop being agitated and noisy and are transformed into quiet creatures, calm, happy to work. A century later, once again, the neurosciences will confirm her observations, identifying some "executive functions"[52]—inhibitory control (remaining concentrated), working memory (retaining information), cognitive flexibility (creative thinking)—which are the biological bases of learning. If children are enabled to develop these functions early on, their behavior is modified in extraordinary ways. When children learn in this way, they are also better at social interaction, because they are better able to achieve harmony with others. Above all, they are children that nobody has to force to pay attention in class. "When you have resolved the problem of controlling the child's attention you have resolved the whole problem of education,"[53] Maria will write years later.

Normalized children have almost no more need of a teacher. They do everything on their own, enacting what Maria will soon call self-education. She is very impressed by the surprised response of a little boy at San Lorenzo when asked who had taught him something: "Who taught me? Nobody taught me. I learned."[54] What she sees surprises even her. "It took some time for me to be convinced that these were not illusions. With each new experience, I would say to myself: 'I don't believe it, wait till the next time.'"[55] She reprimands the teacher who reports things to her that don't seem possible. Every day, she observes the little ones at work, in silence and totally concentrated, like creatures from another world: "The children seemed inspired by angels. Finally, one day, standing in front of the children, she said to me, 'Who are you? Have I met children here who are in the arms of Christ?'"

Speaking of those first experiences at San Lorenzo, she often uses spiritual language. There are always two spirits that coexist in her—the scientific and the religious—separate but not contradictory, held together by a curious mind, especially sensitive to intuitions, and to everything that is truly new. Her metaphysical conception of life passes immediately into her vision of the child, a spiritual being par excellence, but also into the attitude that she herself has in the classroom. When she is among the children it is as though she is in mediation, an observer open to any surprise, capable of intuitions and epiphanies that sometimes seem psychic. She sees details that many others are unable to grasp. Many years later, toward the end of her life, she will say: "A discovery, if it is really that, must contain something new. And the something new is an open door for whoever has the courage to pass through it, a door that gives access to fields still unexplored; therefore, a fantastic door, wondrous, that should strike the imagination."[56]

The Marvelous Fact

The newspapers write increasingly more often about what they call the miracle of San Lorenzo. The children, who in the early days were a shapeless mass of scared street urchins, are now calm and orderly. When someone arrives, they stand, greet them, and offer them a chair before getting back to work. If they receive a donation of some toys, they accept them politely, but then they set them aside and go back to their school materials. One day, some visitors put a bag full of geometric pastries on the table, but none of the children thinks to eat them. They are too involved in telling each other, Look, a triangle; I have a circle; I found a rectangle. The guests are left speechless. The only one in the room who is not surprised is Maria: "That's the marvelous fact: the child works on his own, and after having worked he is stronger, mentally healthier."[57]

She is sure that this result can be repeated. You have to create the right environment. The rest comes by itself: "The children found no obstacles in the way of their development. They had nothing to hide, nothing to fear, nothing to shun. It was as simple as that."[58]

To those afraid of anarchy, she responds that she believes in order, but the order that comes from within, not the order that is imposed from outside. She will write years afterward: "In our system, we have a different concept of *discipline*; discipline, too, must be *active*. It is not necessarily the case that someone is disciplined only if they have artificially been made as quiet as a mute and as immobile as a paralytic. That person has been annihilated, not disciplined. We call disciplined an individual who is his own master and, therefore, can decide for himself when and where it is necessary to follow a rule of life."[59] At the Children's House, no grades are assigned and no prizes are given. Maria became convinced very early on that the little ones are not interested in the cardboard medals that are given out in traditional schools to reward the most diligent. What interests them is learning. So the only form of punishment allowed is inactivity. Those who misbehave are treated as though they are sick and told to rest. Usually, the child, once isolated, "is cured" quickly, because he is so keen on going back to work with his classmates.

Very soon, Maria opens a second Children's House. To supervise the new kindergarten she chooses a young schoolteacher. She doesn't like this term, preferring instead "directress," which reminds her of her experiences on spiritual retreats.

With my methods, the teacher teaches very little, observes a lot, and, above all, has the task of supervising the psychic activities of the children and their physiological development. That's why I changed the title of teacher to directress. At first, this title was met with smiles, because everyone asked themselves who that teacher was supposed to direct, since she had no subordinates and was supposed to leave her little pupils their freedom. But her direction is much more profound and important than what is commonly understood by that term, because this teacher directs lives and souls.[60]

She asks the directress to go live in the same building where school is held, so that her culture and her ways can provide an example for those poor families. In her conception of education, the directress is a sort of lay missionary: "Among these people, in these houses, where nobody goes at night unless they are armed, there goes, to live *their same life*, a genteel woman, highly cultured, an educator by profession, who devotes all of her time and her life to education. True missionary and moral queen among the people, she, if she has enough tact and enough heart, will gather admirable fruits of goodness from her social work."[61]

This religious element of her thought does not appear on the outside. For all of her supporters, Maria remains the militant feminist and radical she has always been. In her inaugural address for the second Children's House she reminds everyone that the block kindergartens are an element of liberation for working women: "We come, therefore, to socialize a 'maternal function,' a female function, in the home. Here is the practical solution of some feminist issues that many thought were unresolvable."[62] She imagines a future where it will be possible to collectivize the infirmary and the kitchen as well. Her dream is that one day, poor mothers will be able to say, like wealthy mothers: I left my child with the governess and the nurse. Maria Montessori is a revolutionary thinker, not least because she thinks as a woman, bringing her female mentality to a field, pedagogy, dominated, up to that moment, by men.

Sandpaper Letters

I n the first Children's Houses, she did not take into consideration reading and writing because they were subjects taught in elementary school. It is the children of San Lorenzo themselves, who, after the first few months working with the sensorial materials, ask for more. Raised in a world of illiterates, they sense that written words are the key to the future. Maria decides to try after the summer vacation.

She doesn't want to use alphabets and notebooks like those used in schools, and returns instead to using Séguin's movable letters. She would like to make them of wood and enamel paint like the ones she had seen at Bicêtre, but she doesn't have sufficient funds. In the end, she resorts to doing it herself, at home. She takes some paper and uses glue to stick on some letters cut out of sandpaper to create a contrasting rough surface. Once again, it is the paucity of means that stimulates innovation. "It was only *after* having fashioned these simple things that I realized the great superiority of this alphabet over the one for the retarded, on which I had wasted two months: if I had been rich, I would have kept forever the superb but sterile alphabet of the past. We *want* the old because we cannot know the new, and we always look for the grandiosity, which lies in things that are already passé, without recognizing in the humble simplicity of new beginnings the germ that will have to develop in the future."[63]

The paper alphabet has the big advantage of being easily reproduced. Plus, it has a special feature. The sandpaper letters are not a guide for the eye but for the hand. The children don't have to reproduce the outline of the metal letters with a pencil, as in Séguin's materials. All they have to do is feel the sandpaper letter with their finger, and by doing so they learn the gesture of writing it even before they know what it means. This is a fundamental innovation over Séguin's alphabet. Later, Maria will invent two further innovations: a rod on the back of the letters to indicate the right way to hold them and a cardboard filing cabinet for storage. They are simple objects that will later become classics of Montessori materials. "I still have that filing cabinet, made out of the old cardboard of a broken box that was found in the custodian's room, and roughly sewn together with white thread,"[64] she will recall years later, when she is famous all over the world.

The children in San Lorenzo are enthusiastic about the sandpaper letters. As always, Maria leaves them free to use the material at their own pace. One day, she is holding on her knees a little boy of two and half who has got his hands in the letter boxes. He takes them off the shelves and shows them to his mates, who call out the names of each letter. The game goes on for almost an hour and, in the end, he knows how to recognize the letters, too. Another time, Maria comes into the classroom and surprises the children as they are making a lot of noise, walking around in a sort of procession. Some of them are holding the letters over their heads. The directress, a bit embarrassed, is standing off to the side, unable to contain that collective enthusiasm for the alphabet.

The children spend entire days on the cardboard letters. They work thoughtfully, concentrated, tracing over the sandpaper lines with their fingers, murmuring the sounds, putting the letters next to one another. Maria realizes that they are metabolizing the letters, even before being able to read. "When I went over to one of the children and, to celebrate, read out loud the word that he had just composed, the child looked at me in amazement, as if to say: 'How do you know that? How did you guess that I was thinking of that word?' In effect, the phenomenon of reading was extraneous to this curious exercise."[65]

The Explosion of Writing

■

Two months after starting to work with the sandpaper letters,
something happens. It is Christmas of 1907, and in San Lorenzo
it is the time of what Maria will call the "explosion of writing":

It was a winter's day in December, bright with sunlight, and
we went up on the terrace with the children. They were running around, playing freely; some of them were around me.
I was sitting next to a chimney stack, and I said to the five-
year-old boy near me, offering him a piece of chalk: "Draw
this chimney." Obedient, he squatted on the ground and drew
the chimney on the pavement, reproducing it in recognizable
fashion. So, as is my way with the little ones, I burst into ex-
clamations of praise. The boy looked at me, smiled, waited for
a minute as though ready to explode in some act of joy, then
shouted, "I can write! I can write!" and sat stooped over on the
ground and wrote *mano* (hand), then, excited, wrote again:
camino (chimney), then *tetto* (roof). As he was writing, he
kept on shouting out loud: "I can write! I know how to write!'

so loud that the other children heard him and came over to stand around him in a circle, looking at him in amazement. Two or three of them said to me, shaking: "Give me the chalk, I want to write, too," and in fact they wrote out various words: *mamma, mano, gino, camino, ada*. None of them had ever held chalk or any other writing instrument in hand; it was the *first time* they wrote; and they traced out a whole word, as though the first time they spoke they said a whole word.[66]

Reading comes afterward. Maria does nothing to encourage it, because she starts from the idea that to read is to understand. She thinks it is useless to have children mechanically repeat sounds, if they don't grasp the meaning of what they are doing. She lets every-thing happen for each of them with their own timing. As always, she invents and improvises. One day, she writes on the blackboard, "If you know how to read this, come up and hug me,"[67] then she sits as always in a corner, letting the children work freely. At first, nobody seems to notice the sentence, many of them forget it. Then, suddenly, after a few days, the turning point: "A minuscule little girl, as tall as a cheese penny, comes over my way and says, 'Here I am,' and she hugs me."

Another day, she puts all the class toys out on the table. She writes the name of each toy on a piece of paper that she puts in a box. The children each draw a name by lot, read the name silently, then go in front of the table, say the name out loud, and in exchange are given the toy. When they have finished, Maria offers to give something to the children who still can't read. To her great surprise, they refuse the gifts and instead ask to draw a card and participate in the exercise. Maria understands that they are not interested in getting a toy. Their reward is learning. "I looked at them, trying to explore the enigma of their soul, which had remained unknown to us, and I sat there, almost meditating, to contemplate them, while the discovery that children love *knowledge* by human instinct and not *play* devoid of meaning struck me with wonder and made me think of the greatness of the human spirit."[68] One of the teachers remembers Maria sitting with a long box full of strips of paper and children around picking them and reading them, and saying to her at the end of the day, "You won't believe this, I've been here for more than an hour, and they are still not satisfied."[69]

On reading and writing, Maria Montessori innovates with respect to Séguin. She finds his use of block letters too rigid, preferring cursive. Moreover, she does not share his idea that writing is based on the visual recognition of the letters. Rather, she believes that it starts from the gesture training of the hand. Her inspiration for this comes from her internship with the intellectually disabled children. Years earlier, at the Orthophrenic school, she had worked for a long time with a little girl who couldn't manage to sew. To help her, she had her practice on a loom, inserting a strip of paper crosswise between two others, attaining in a short time the hoped-for result, with a needle and thread. "I realized that the necessary hand movement had been *prepared* for sewing without *sewing*; and that what's really needed is to find a way to *teach before having them execute*."[70]

The explosion of writing is the element of the Montessori method that attracts the world's attention and, in just a few years, transforms the system applied in a poor neighborhood of Rome into a global phenomenon. Actually, Maria will always try to explain that precocious writing is only the emergent part of something much bigger: the revelation of children's natural capacity for self-education, when placed in the right environment. The sandpaper letters are not the secret, she will keep on saying to those who want to listen to her. Movable letters have existed since the time of Quintilian in ancient Rome, but, despite that, we have no news of processions through the streets of the Roman Empire with people carrying letters over their heads, as the children of San Lorenzo did. The secret is not in the materials but in the children, she will say, thinking back on those first experiments. "Nobody back then managed to admit it. That prejudice of 'not believing in the extraordinary,' the shame of appearing naive if one wants to uphold one's dignity and cultural superiority, is common; and it is one of the obstacles that conceal the 'new' and stifle discovery."[71]

The reality is that in San Lorenzo a revolution was begun. Up to that time, children were considered passive beings, who needed only food, sleep, and play to pass the time and become, preferably in a hurry, adults. Maria Montessori, instead, is convinced by now that children are special creatures, different from adults and in many respects superior. This is one of her many intuitions that will be confirmed a century later by the neurosciences. Today, we know that in the first three years of life the brain has a capacity for creation of synapses incomparably superior to that of the adult brain. A being so potent, Maria explains, must be treated as such, and placed in a suitable environment—"prepared," she will soon say—which is not the school, but a new place. Here, left free to express their potential, children learn almost without adult intervention. The experiment has only just begun. Anything is possible. Maria Montessori has discovered the child, and there opens up before her an unexplored continent.

PART THREE

The First Disciples

(1908-1913)

What a miracle to find souls that bond
with us to help us on the arduous way
of construction! Who give up everything
and who are no longer anything
but our followers![1]

An Angelic Baroness

The results obtained by Maria Montessori in San Lorenzo attract, almost immediately, the attention of an American, Alice Hallgarten, who lives in Rome, where she is married to the baron and senator Leopoldo Franchetti. A little younger than Maria, Alice is an angelic creature who devotes all of her energy to an ideal of universal love. She has been working for years in the Unione del Bene, doing volunteer work in San Lorenzo. She hates high society and, whenever she can, takes refuge at the family's country estate Montesca, near Città di Castello in Umbria. She has a great passion for Francis of Assisi and a profound love of nature. In case of illness or melancholy, she prescribes as therapy long walks in the gardens of the estate, of which she knows every tree.

She dreams of turning Montesca into a refuge for the tenant farmers from the surrounding area. She creates two rural schools, a kindergarten for orphans, a medical clinic, and a textile workshop with a canteen and redistribution of the profits among the female workforce. Every day she visits the poorest family, taking them food and medicine. The farmers venerate her as a saint and frequently baptize their firstborn daughter with her name. Leopoldo Franchetti, passionately in love with her, finances all of her initiatives. But every so often he sighs, "We're going to end up in misery."[2]

Alice is always on the lookout for new pedagogical ideas for her rural schools. She takes advantage of her travels abroad to meet the most active educators of the time, with a predilection for the women among them. She appoints the German Felicitas Buchner to direct the girls' vocational school at Montesca and invites Lucy R. Latter, the English theorist of the garden school, to the estate after commissioning an Italian translation of one of her books. When she visits one of the Children's Houses in San Lorenzo for the first time, she is impressed. More than that, a friend of hers will say, "enraptured."[3] From that moment on, she has but one thought: to help Maria Montessori transform elementary education. She finances the fabrication of materials and spends entire days discussing pedagogy with her. She also promises her political support, but to deliver on her promise she needs help from her husband. She organizes a visit for him to one of the Children's Houses in San Lorenzo. "The Doctor remained off to the side, so the Baron could see for himself how things proceeded," one witness recounts. "The Baron watched in silence. Finally, the Doctor approached him and asked him what he thought. 'Have you written a book?' he asked, brusquely. 'A book?...No.' 'But you could die and all of this would be lost.'"[4]

Leopoldo Franchetti is a man of action. He organizes everything very quickly. He makes an agreement with an important publisher in Rome so that he will be ready to print the book. He invites Maria to come stay at his residence in the city, Villa Wolkonsky, where a quiet office and the gardens, considered some of the most beautiful in Rome, are put at her disposal so she can work with no distractions. Helped by her student, Elisabetta Ballerini, Maria writes the book in less than a month. During her brief stay at his home, Leopoldo Franchetti comes to know Maria's imperious character. He understands that she will not easily accept the requests of a large publisher, who might demand cuts and corrections. So, when he is presented with the manuscript, wrapped in tissue paper and bound with a white ribbon, instead of taking it to the Rome publisher, he takes a train to Città di Castello and delivers it to a local printer, whom he orders to reproduce it in its entirety, without changing so much as a comma. Maria has chosen a long and complicated title—*The Method of Scientific Pedagogy Applied to Infantile Education in the Children's Houses.* She is determined to emphasize that the method is not her invention but the application of the scientific observation of children. From the start, however, everyone calls it *The Montessori Method,* and, with that title, it will be translated around the world, transforming Maria into a celebrity.

It will be a meteoric explosion of notoriety, at a time when communication and news travel slowly, and it will change her life yet again. But for the moment she knows nothing about all this. She still thinks that her future will be in Rome, and she hopes to remain at the university, to disseminate from there her pedagogical ideas. When her teaching position at the Teachers College is opened to an official public hiring process, with the risk that it might be assigned to another candidate, she moves her highly placed friends. "It wouldn't be bad if Minister Rava were besieged with strong recommendations and manifestations of interest so I could *quickly* have this post assured through the hiring competition."[5]

New People Who Speak in Us

I n the summer of 1909, Alice Franchetti invites Maria to present
her method at the School of Home Economics, which is held every
year at Montesca to train local teachers. Maria's course is one of
the many offered by the summer school, but it attracts all the attention. Her opening day speech is very inspired: "I am not the one
who has created something new in the art of educating. Rather, it is
the soul of the child that has revealed itself to me, and that I have
contemplated in its true manifestation. This, which is truly great in
the new method, this voice of the child's soul, of the new people who
speak in us, this and this alone has brought us to make our way here.
Like a great internal fire, it has pushed us to move beyond material
life and elevate ourselves to a higher spirituality,"[6] she proclaims. She
then acknowledges the fundamental support she has received from
Alice. "Many have visited the Children's House to restore themselves
in that bath of the spirit; but only the angelic Baroness Franchetti
has understood that those waters would reinvigorate humanity. Here
today, we see its first actuation."[7]

The students are enthused by her revolutionary message. "During the lessons, it happened that many of the attendees wept, so much so that it seemed a rather sad course. And I would say, 'What is it that you find so sad in the things I'm saying to you?' They responded, 'We can feel our consciousness coming to life inside us.'"[8] During breaks, they go for walks in the gardens of the villa or listen to Alice, who plays music on the terrace with an exotic instrument sounded by the wind. Maria is her guest for the duration of the course, showered with care and attention. The baroness insists that she take a nap in the afternoons in a large quiet room. She clears the room of books, closes the shutters, and orders, "Get some rest!"[9]

Talking for hours in the torrid August heat is draining. Maria has to explain her intuitions for the first time in public. "I didn't only do lessons, but I isolated myself from the world, remaining in meditation an entire month, speaking every morning according to the ideas I put together the evening before," she writes in a letter. "In the end, I was exhausted."[10] In September, a commission composed of all the teachers examines the students for their final grade. One of them remembers the day like this: "I have just sat for the exam which came down to a spirited conversation and I am now waiting for the Doctor to come out to bid her a last farewell. The group and the whole thing is very nice. Tenerani always approves and laughs with his blue eyes, while his mouth remains motionless; Chiaraviglio asks questions and more questions and enjoys hearing responses that are in agreement with her ideas. Montessori is always smiling, everything is all right with her."[11] At the ceremony for the conferral of the diplomas, Alice is by Maria's side. Dressed in white, with wildflowers in her hair, she looks like a young girl. Nobody imagines the tragedy that is brewing.

Immediately following the course, Alice leaves for the United States, determined to speak about the Montessori method to everyone who will listen to her. Through her contacts in the world of education, she alerts the main English-language pedagogical journals.

During the journey, she starts having recurring symptoms of illness. She's always tired, loses weight. She spends a period of rest in a German sanatorium, but in August 1910, she is already on her way to Brussels, where she presents her rural schools to the World's Fair, winning a gold medal. When Maria speaks in Rome, she is in the front row to applaud and support her. "Yesterday, I attended the Doctor's beautiful lecture," she writes to her collaborators at Montesca. "She is rising ever higher, how I wish all of you could hear her inspiring words."[12]

Her health continues to decline. In April 1911, the diagnosis arrives, like a death sentence: tuberculosis. Six months later, Alice dies in a Swiss sanatorium, after writing a letter of farewell to all her loved ones: "Praised be the Lord for our corporeal death. Before going on to meet our dear sister Death I want to send you my words of love, peace, and farewell."[13] Leopoldo Franchetti is nearly mad with suffering. He walks the empty rooms of Montesca for days and days. "Where are you, Alice? Why don't you answer me?"[14] He tries to carry on with his wife's work, in the rural schools and in her commitment to spreading the Montessori method in the southern regions of Italy. But a few years later, in 1917, he commits suicide. In his last will and testament he forgives all the debts of his tenant farmers, leaving them their land, and he has a last thought for the trees that Alice loved so much. "It is my will that in the gardens of Montesca a living and healthy tree shall never be cut down."[15]

Just Three Darling Girls

My darling girls are bound to me and I to them, for all our lives, for an endeavor to which we have devoted ourselves. It seems like a small thing but it is extraordinary!"[16] Maria Montessori speaks this way about the first young women who follow her in her work, and who are, in her eyes, disciples, assistants, and adopted daughters. Elisabetta Ballerini, called Bettina, the first to sign on, and Anna Maria Maccheroni, her student at the Teachers College, are soon joined by Anna Fedeli, a comrade in feminist struggles.

The three young women leave everything to follow her, putting their savings together to offer them to the cause. Their families are worried about such a radical choice. Anna Maria Maccheroni recalls the early days when, after turning down a position as a teacher in a regular school, she was working with intellectually disabled children, and in the evenings she would construct her Séguin materials with a saw, wood, enamel paint, and turpentine, right before the astonished eyes of her family: "It's only natural that my family thought I had lost my head. They had already disapproved when I didn't go to teach in secondary school, now they saw me sawing wood."[17]

Maria is about to turn forty, at the time an advanced age for a woman. The thin-waisted young psychiatrist, immortalized by the newspapers in the days of her work with the League for the Protection of Mentally Deficient Children, has been replaced by a heavily built, mature woman, who is still living with her elderly parents. Her lost son, who is now eleven, is growing up in a distant boarding school. Intense, severe, always dressed in dark colors, she lives as though immersed in a sort of spiritual and scientific retreat. Soon she takes her three students in the house, transforming the apartment into a small feminine commune, where everyone lives for the dream of developing a new conception of the child. Maria asks her disciples for total devotion—"Those who devote themselves to my endeavor have to leave all others, sacrifice themselves, and follow me,"[18] she says in a letter, paraphrasing the Gospel—but in exchange she offers them an ideal to which they can devote their lives.

Together with them, she confronts the growing interest in her method. After the publication of her book and the course at Montesca, everything takes off. Invitations arrive from everywhere. A kindergarten in Perugia commissions her to open up a Montessori section. The directress of the kindergartens in Bellinzona asks her to give some lectures in Switzerland. The worldly things are swelling up, she writes, worried, in a letter. For legal questions, she turns to a lawyer in Rome, whose office is soon invaded with correspondence on the Montessori method.

By nature, Maria is not well suited to organization—"I can do some things but not everything. I don't know how to organize"[19]— and even less so to financial management. As long as she can, she leaves the treasury in the hands of her mother, who has always taken care of the accounting at home, a black satin purse hanging from her belt and an accounts notebook in hand. "She paid the workers who had done some job immediately. 'You might need this money,' she would say,"[20] one of Maria's students recalls. But expenses are multiplying rapidly and they go well beyond simple family management.

"All of this immense work that is growing like a tempest, like something far beyond our energies, something overwhelming! What will become of us?"[21] Maria writes in a letter to Donna Maraini, a noblewoman who has supported her for some time. Rich, well known to the royal court, married to a member of the Senate, she is a precious contact with the political world of Rome and with the queen mother. She raises her children according to the Montessori method, and dreams of opening another Children's House at the family estate in Palidano, near Mantua. Her husband, annoyed by her devotion, complains, "If we leave our automobile unattended, it goes on its own to the Montessori house."[22]

Maria can confide in her friend about everything, for example, the tensions that arise every now and again with Renilde. The balance in her life is changing. She is less and less daughter and increasingly more mother, or even more so, a Mother Superior of a small group of disciples who have sworn fidelity to her mission and who help her to care for the wound of her secret maternity. When she has time, she cooks for them. She is a good cook and loves to eat. She also loves household chores. She says they help her think. When she has to resolve some complicated question, she takes her wooden clogs and a bucket of water and gets down to work, carefully washing the floors.

The Martyred Saint of the Movement

The follower that Maria loves most tenderly is Bettina. She feels that she has a special talent with children and a strong spiritual nature that recalls the "characters of the angelic saints."[23] She met her at the nursery-kindergarten for "phrenasthenic" children in via Rubattino, where Bettina, who had studied to become a school-teacher, was a volunteer. Maria invited her to enroll in her course at the Teachers College, and from that moment on she has always kept her by her side.

When a strange illness forces Bettina to take to her bed, Maria thinks it is a problem of fatigue: "She became ill after all the running around that I made her do, and she obeyed me tenderly, even if I told her to go somewhere and die. I am filled with remorse!,"[24] Maria writes to Donna Maraini. In reality, Bettina is suffering from the first symptoms of tuberculosis. Maria's friend intervenes with solicitude, paying for the young woman to be treated in the best sanatoriums. She knows Maria's secret. She knows what that girl means to her. "My heart had adopted Bettina like a daughter and, with her, it had filled its emptiness," Maria confesses in a letter.

For a while, Bettina is admitted to a sanatorium run by the nuns in Nettuno, where she writes angelic letters devoted exclusively to Maria: "Time passes quickly for me, contemplating the sea while I think of my revered Mama and of the future that awaits her great work."[25] With her fatalist nature and her religious vision, Maria tries to accept this terrible blow for what it is, but at times she lets herself be overwhelmed by her distress. "I realize that I placed in that young woman the last relic of my egotism," she writes to Donna Maraini, "presuming to have in her a sweet relief that would give me courage and strength forever. And taken together, this is what in life is called affection. Something   it's true!   that I couldn't allow myself, because I believe (and now even more so!) that I must not become attached to anyone. That is the price of my mission."[26]

Very soon the situation looks desperate. Maria insists that Bettina spend some time with her at home, almost a leave of absence. She has her stay with her, ignoring the risk of contagion. By now the young woman is extremely weak, but still thinks she can be saved. She spends entire days in bed, talking constantly, as though in a fever, about future plans, the development of the method, the things that they will do together. Maria periodically withdraws into another room to cry. Her most beloved student is dying, and there's nothing she can do, beyond lamenting her loss in letters to Donna Maraini: "Good as my beloved daughter, devoted as she, consecrated in every part of herself to our work, no one, no one else can be so."[27] Bettina will live her last years in and out of sanatoriums and she will die in 1914. Maria will always remember her as a sort of martyred saint of the movement. "A 'sponsa Christi' pure even in spirit as a lily, and placed at the foot of the altar."[28]

Anna Maria Maccheroni also suffers from strange illnesses that prevent her from walking for long periods of time. To keep her energy up, she keeps raw eggs in her purse and from time to time she takes one out, pierces the shell with a pin, and drinks it. Maria considers herself her mother in all respects and acts accordingly. When Anna

Maria has to have an operation for a uterine fibroma, Maria makes the decision of what to do without consulting the girl's parents and accompanies her in the operating room. Because of the operation, Anna Maria will not be able to have children, and Maria interprets this as a divine sign: a sacrifice and an oblation, necessary to the cause, she says in a letter.

Maria has not abandoned her project for a lay congregation. In 1910 she pronounces a solemn promise with her students in front of the altar, in a sort of private rite of consecration. To preserve the memory of the event, she writes a brief note in her diary: "On Christmas night 1910—he was born and remained—with us."[29] From that moment on, she considers herself united to her students by a sacred and indissoluble bond. Years later, she will recall that Bettina died while repeating her religious vows and that Anna Fedeli, at the time housed in a sanatorium, wrote her letters that were a "continuous *invocation* to the work before us—a constant exhortation to me that I *act* and obey the order of the Lord."[30]

Anna Fedeli will also come down with tuberculosis, and she will die in 1920, felled like Bettina by the malady of the century. At the time, Maria is abroad, but she arranges for her student to be buried in Rome, in the Montessori family tomb. Anna Maria Maccheroni will ask to be buried there too, in 1965, after working up to her last day for the method. "I can't even imagine what my life would have been like without this work," she will write in old age. "I was looking for a form of love not bound by family ties, personal friendships or interests. To have found it has been my peace."[31]

The Humanitarian Society of Milan

The first city in Italy to reproduce the San Lorenzo experiment is Milan. In 1908, the Humanitarian Society, a socialist-inspired organization very active in the city, proposes to Maria Montessori that she open Children's Houses in its model working-class neighborhoods. She accepts with enthusiasm and obtains permission from Eduardo Talamo to be away from Rome for a few months to lead the project. She inaugurates a first house on October 18, 1908, in via Solari, and, immediately after that, a second, under the respective leadership of Anna Maria Maccheroni and Anna Fedeli.

As soon as she can, she goes to visit her two students, even though the train trip from Rome takes an entire day. She enjoys walking in the big Lombard city, where everything seems new to her: "I go out early in the morning. I go to do shopping for the children, walking in the rain. I buy some lovely prints to bring cheer to their eyes and get them used to beauty. I buy toys, little furniture, linens, choose the decorative figures for their aprons and organize the work."[32] As always, she oversees every aspect of the environment, which she calls "clothing for the soul."[33] She wants everything around the children to express beauty and simplicity. She even takes care of decorating her students' houses, with the help of the workers of the Humanitarian Society. Everything is very spartan: an iron bed, a wool blanket, a table, a chair. As required by Maria, the young women live in poverty, in the same buildings where the workers live, and devote their whole lives to teaching.

When she is in Milan, Maria spends a lot of time in the classroom assisting her students. "Seeing her with the children helped me more than reading her books," says Anna Maria Maccheroni. "I saw, felt, her interior dispositions, even though on the outside they didn't do anything extraordinary. It's the 'tone,' it's the whole of her person, that expresses itself with great simplicity."[34] While the children are working with the materials, Maria stays off to the side, to demonstrate the art of withdrawal, something that is hard for adults who are used to "teaching" the lesson. She observes each child with great attention, as though she were in front of a laboratory experiment. "Many of those who haven't understood me," she will say one day, "believe I'm a sentimentalist, a romantic, who dreams only of seeing the children, kissing them, telling them fairy tales, and who has to visit all the schools in order to contemplate them, spoil them, and give them candy. Generally, they weary me! I am a rigorous scientific observer, not a literary idealist like Rousseau, and I try to discover the man in the child, to see in him the true spirit of the man, the design of the Creator: the scientific and religious truth."[35]

While Séguin was her starting point, she is now proceeding rapidly on her own road and developing concepts that in the following decades will become part of standard pedagogy and common ways of thinking: the child-sized environment, attention for the individual, free experience. Today, these are principles accepted by everyone, but for the time they were revolutionary. Other concepts, such as self-education and the value of error, remain even today specific features of her method.

Error has a central place in her vision. She doesn't consider it a failure, but a passage toward progress, the other side of learning: "Why correct the child? When the child makes a mistake, we have every reason to believe that he is not ready, at least for the moment, to grasp the psychic association that we want to provoke in him. If we correct him, and we say to him, 'That's not right, you made a mistake,' these words of reprimand strike him much more than others and remain in his memory, taking the place of the things he was supposed to understand. Instead, the silence that follows the error leaves the field of consciousness intact."[36]

Give the Child Exactness

In the Children's Houses, Maria continues using Séguin's materials, which have by now become Montessori materials. Already in 1908, with the help of Leopoldo Franchetti, she had registered the patent in Paris, New York, and London, making herself the legal owner. She added new elements for writing and reading. She tested each piece, made many modifications, and defined, once and for all, measurements, raw materials, and colors. Every measurement, every color, every gradation have to be those indicated by her. In other words, every piece has to be exact. "We had forgotten to give the child exactness," she will say one day. "There is a failure to understand the importance of this detail, which is at the center of everything. That is where joy, diligence, improvement, and freedom come from."[37]

The material, she says repeatedly, must have precise characteristics. It has to be beautiful, in order to attract the children. It must isolate a single concept, so that it teaches by the simple fact of being manipulated. It must lend itself to the correction of errors on the part of the child, who realizes on his own when he makes a mistake and keeps trying until reaching the goal. The adults must simply demonstrate how to use it and then let the children go to work. This is the hardest thing, because adults are naturally inclined to intervene, help, explain. Instead, Maria theorizes a sort of Zen for teachers. One of her students recalls, "She knew how to observe and she emptied herself of everything she knew. She wanted to see. One day she said, speaking in a low voice to herself, 'I empty myself—I empty myself—I empty myself.' To see, the eye must be uncluttered."[38] To summarize her method, Maria herself says, "Wait, observing."[39]

She warns against overstimulation, because she believes that too much material can be confusing. She doesn't like toys, because she considers them a diversion. They suggest that the child has to distract himself, while she wants to facilitate concentration. In the first Children's Houses there are lots of toys, because visitors bring them constantly, convinced that poor children are hungry for them. Maria notes that the pupils really don't seem interested. To activate them, she starts playing with the toys herself. The children sit next to her and for a while they join in, more to please her than themselves. As soon as they can, however, they go back to their activities with the learning materials. "That's when I understood that perhaps play was something inferior in the lives of children and that they resorted to it for lack of anything better to do. But there was something greater that undoubtedly prevailed in the souls of children over all futile things," Maria says, to then comment, "So we might think this about ourselves: playing chess or bridge is something pleasant in moments of idleness, but it would no longer be so if we were obliged to do nothing else in life. When you are occupied in something that is elevated and urgent, you forget about playing bridge; and children always have something elevated before them, and urgent."[40]

Producing the Material

P art of the Humanitarian Society in Milan is a House of Labor for young artisans. It is here that production of the materials begins. The solid pegboards with their rows of cylindrical pegs in descending order, the pink tower of wooden cubes, the series of brown prisms of equal length but different sections, the graduated rods, the geometrical-shaped puzzles, the color spools, the sound boxes; all of the rich educational materials that Maria Montessori has designed and patented are produced and shipped on request. She is allotted a percentage on every article sold. The first year for which there are official accounting records is 1913, when the Humanitarian Society pays her 1,300 lire. For the prices of the materials, there is a price list from 1916, with a cost of 650 lire for a complete set.

If we consider that at the time the annual salary of an Italian public employee was three thousand lire, these figures tell us two things: that the cost of the materials is very high and that Maria has a strong financial interest in its production. This is a fundamental detail, given that one of the recurring criticisms of the Montessori method is that it was also an economic enterprise. From the very beginning,

Maria lives on her method. She patents the materials and makes agreements with various companies—first in Italy, then abroad—for their production and sale. Every inauguration of a new Children's House brings with it new orders for learning materials and thus economic support for Maria. The same is true for job applications for new teachers, which rapidly give rise to fee-based training courses.

Her critics point out that in the same years, another woman scientist, Marie Curie, elaborates her method for isolating radium but decides not to patent it, leaving it in free use to science. It must also be remembered, however, that after the death of her husband, Marie Curie inherits his chaired professorship at the Sorbonne. Maria Montessori, on the contrary, has no permanent employment. Indeed, she gives up teaching very early on to devote herself to her method. In the letters written to her by politicians and members of the Italian royal court, she is always and only "Signorina Montessori," a woman with no husband, no job, and no official position. When Marie Curie is mentioned, what strikes one most is another detail. While the Children's Houses are being opened in Italy, the French scientist creates with some of her friends a home school to educate their children outside of the official school system. She is scandalized by what she sees in the schoolrooms of Paris and cannot bear to think of sending her two daughters to those schools: "At times I have the impression that it would be better to drown our children rather than shut them up in the schools of our time."[41]

A Thorny Individual

Maria Montessori continues to work in Rome as the directress of the Children's House service created by the Real Property Institute of Rome. She soon opens four new schools in the San Lorenzo neighborhood. Eduardo Talamo, the director of the institute, is also very active in the project. He is particularly concerned with discipline and works out a detailed set of rules, which he posts at the entrance to each of the schools. The relationship between him and Maria soon grows very tense. She struggles to put up with his frequent interventions, while he is annoyed by her excessive notoriety. The idea of the school in the house is his, but by now everyone talks only about her. It is not long before things come to a head. In a letter to a mutual friend, Talamo complains:

> Montessori and I are in heavy seas; she writes to me not accepting my proposals, letting on that she wants to sue (?) and threatening to impede the use of her method in our schools. It seems to me that she's completely off the rails and badly advised. As far as withdrawing her methods, she can do what

she wants, she's the one who loses when they say that the Real Property Institute banned them from its Children's Houses. All the same, I don't see how her methods can be withdrawn, when the teaching materials are sold by the Humanitarian Society, which hands over to their inventor 20 percent of the price.[42]

Her conflict with Eduardo Talamo is marked by a contradiction that will repeat itself all the way to the end. On the one hand, she wants to disseminate her ideas; on the other, she wants to control every step along the way and remain the sole proprietor of her material. During her increasingly tense meetings with Talamo, she asks for assurances that everything she is developing at San Lorenzo will not be reproduced elsewhere without providing her some compensation. Talamo is reluctant to commit himself to this. He has a whole city neighborhood to fill with Children's Houses, and in a hurry, and he wants to do it without excessive costs. Exasperated, he describes the situation like this:

It's the same as someone who, having published a book on the history of grammar which is on sale in bookstores, demands that those who study it have to take the author as their teacher, otherwise they can't study it. In this case, Montessori is even worse because I tell her to go ahead and teach all you want, but discipline in the schools is up to me, and she responds (as she writes to me) that discipline cannot be separated from teaching, and I protest, and I'm going to leave, and I'm going to sue. The mad are getting madder all the time, even worse when they become famous, not even the Good Lord can keep them down.[43]

Maria, too, in a letter to Donna Maraini, mentions the growing tension between them: "This morning Talamo called me with the usual aggressive tone, how is it possible to put up with him? Suppose you write to this thorny individual that he should try to come to an agreement with me and treat me better?"[44]

The break comes in 1910. From one day to the next, the custodians in San Lorenzo are given the order not to let her enter the Children's Houses again. This brusque ending of her collaboration with Talamo deprives her of the pedagogic laboratory of the neighborhood schools, but it also allows her story to go on. Without this break, Maria could have remained confined within the framework of social assistance in Rome. Instead, she takes a much more cosmopolitan direction, which will take her very far. As had already happened in the past, this apparent defeat turns out to be laden with promise. Every time, aided by her decisive and almost unstoppable character, Maria leaves the others behind her, without looking back. "Closed doors are providential. They are always fonts of progress,"[45] she will say many years later, looking back on her journey.

But San Lorenzo will not be forgotten. Until the end of her life, Maria will revisit her memories of the first manifestations of the mind of the child that she experienced in Rome and she will continue to work on this intuition for half a century and through two world wars. She knows that San Lorenzo is the origin, the moment when she came to understand the immense potential of children. "For thousands and thousands of years, humanity had passed right by children, remaining totally insensitive to this miracle of nature that is the formation of an intellect, of a human personality."[46] Every year, on January 6, she celebrates the anniversary of the inauguration of the first Children's House. In 1932, for the twenty-fifth, a sort of silver anniversary, she lights twenty-five large candles and arranges them around the perimeter of the room, remaining in meditation at the center of the circle of light.

After the break with Talamo, she has to start all over again, but she doesn't despair. By now she knows the road to follow—observe the child—and that's where she lands throughout her entire life:

"The method can't be seen, *what you see is the child.* You see the soul of the child that, free of obstacles, acts according to his nature. The child-like qualities that we glimpse simply belong *to life*, just like the colors of birds and the fragrance of flowers; they are not at all the consequence of a "method of education."[47]

Like Flies in Summer

At first, she sets out to retrace the path of her experience in Rome. She goes back to knock on the doors of the Charitable Institute of the Kindergartens of Rome to convince the directors to assign her some classes where she can continue to apply the insights developed in San Lorenzo. Again, she comes up empty-handed. In the end, she finds a new potential sponsor in Ernesto Nathan, the city's first progressive mayor, elected with the support of a coalition of republicans, liberals, radicals, and socialists. Nathan is a convinced anticlericalist, and the centerpiece of his program is the reform of primary education, which he wants to remove from the control of the Catholic Church. It is only logical that he should take an interest in the pedagogical work of Maria, whom he also knows personally, because he, too, had been one of the original supporters of the activities of the League for the Protection of Mentally Deficient Children and because his wife had been one of Maria's feminist comrades.

In October 1910, the city inaugurates a Children's House in via Sant'Angelo in Pescheria, a working-class district in the old Jewish ghetto. In December 1911, a group of women from the National Council of Italian Women open a house for the children of the well-off in the area of the Pincian Hill. The city provides the space and advances the seed money, but from then on the school is financed by tuition paid by the families. It is an elegant school, where foreign languages are also taught and the children are accompanied back home by a horse-driven omnibus.

Up to now, the Children's Houses have served the kindergarten age-group, but Maria Montessori is looking ahead, toward elementary school, encouraged by her friend Donna Maraini, who has raised her children with the method and wants them to continue their education in the same way. Maria is frequently her guest at Palidano. There she enters into contact with a family of artisans, the Bassoli family, who start producing her materials in association with the Humanitarian Society. It all happens quite by chance. During a carriage ride around the little town, they pass by a small shop and the noblewoman turns to Maria, exclaiming, "But weren't you looking for a good carpenter for your materials?"[48]

Mayor Nathan also presses her to move ahead with the method into elementary schools. He wants to take it into the public schools, and he needs to train teachers. He asks Maria Montessori to teach a four-month course at the Fuà Fusinato Normal School. She accepts the assignment for 1910, and repeats it the next year. Right from the start, however, she is bothered by the fact that the City of Rome is moving fast, without consulting her. City functionaries open some Montessori classes in some of the public schools, eliciting her protests. Only she, she tells them, can open up new Montessori classes and decide who will teach them.

These are the first skirmishes in what will soon become an open conflict. Maria complains about the bureaucrats who want to rush things and keep bombarding her with a thousand projects, "like flies in summer."[49] She can't accept seeing her method managed by the City Council as though it were just another of the capital's many public affairs. Besides, she suspects that the interest in her method is based only on the rapidity of learning reading and writing, and this embitters her. She has long repeated that the precocious writing that attracts so much attention is not really the main point. She wants to reform education down to the roots, not provide shortcuts for quick scholastic success. She becomes increasingly cautious, determined to protect her work, especially the learning materials that she is preparing for elementary schools. In a letter to Donna Maraini, she explains that in Rome she feels like she's working in an environment she can't trust. "You can be sure that in that school not only will I not do experiments, but I'll be very careful not to reveal my ideas, because there are some indelicate people who are capable of using them to publish them on their own account, misrepresenting them, and thus doing even more harm to the advancement of my work."[50]

The application of the method will carry on in the Rome public schools with ups and downs until the First World War. The city archives conserve the minutes of heated discussions between the factions of the favorable, who praise above all the rapid learning of reading and writing, and the opponents, who point their fingers at the high cost of the materials. Even the personal relationship between Maria Montessori and Ernesto Nathan goes sour in a hurry, and in the span of just a few years, the two stop speaking to each other. The same thing happens with Luigi Credaro, once a great supporter, who in 1914, as minister of public instruction, prefers to introduce in the public kindergartens the nursery school method created by two pedagogists from Brescia, Rosa and Carolina Agazzi. In his view, their method has the advantage of not requiring the purchase of teaching materials and using instead what its supporters call, in a dig at Maria Montessori, "bric-a-brac without a patent."[51] Inspired by a vision of the nursery school as an extension of the family, the Agazzi method is also more homespun and reassuring.

The Year of Farewells

Maria Montessori's radicalism is scary. Hers is a method that does not allow half measures. It requires specialized training and a generalized rethinking of the way to organize a school. Consider for a moment the abolition of rewards and punishments, an innovation that provokes resistance from teachers everywhere, who protest and claim they cannot work without them. "Punishment! I hadn't realized that they were an indispensable institution, dominant over the lives of all humanity's children," Maria comments. "All people have been raised under this humiliation."[52] Her method asks adults to work deeply on themselves, and to have the humility to recognize that they are not the engine of learning. Development cannot be taught, Maria explains, and nobody can grow in the child's place. "Whoever creates the child, it is certainly not us,"[53] she will declare years later, with one of her lightning-bolt phrases. Adults can facilitate, remove obstacles. At that point, placed in the right situation, the child does it himself.

Maria is alone again, but that doesn't stop her. She works it all out, on endless days, where "even at night thoughts impose themselves on sleep."[54] Every so often she has a nervous collapse, provoked by fatigue and by her secret pain for her faraway son, and she has to withdraw for a few weeks. She writes to her friend Olga Lodi during one of these forced vacations: "I'm in the country—*exhausted from fatigue*—almost ill from fatigue."[55] When she is too weak to write, it is her students who send her news to her friends and supporters. Anna Fedeli tells Donna Maraini, after visiting her mistress in retreat at the motherhouse of the nuns in Grottaferrata: "She needs calm. All of the movement that goes on around her in her name, in her favor, passes through her soul and leaves her anything but unfazed."[56]

In theory, she still has her work as a physician and a teacher, but in reality she neglects all other activities. Her personal dossier in the university archive is full of medical certificates with which she requests periods of absence for illness and long periods of leave, always extended. Her doctors state that "she suffers from headaches, insomnia, and from other symptoms obviously related to fatigue,"[57] and that she needs a pause from "all mental work for a period of time that cannot be established with precision."[58]

Maria understands that she cannot keep everything together anymore. She has to make some choices. She stops practicing as a doctor, resigns from the Pedagogy School, and asks for a leave of absence from her role as anthropology professor at the university. At first, she hopes to hold on to at least her teaching post at the Teachers College, but she soon begins requesting there, too, a series of long leaves of absence, abandoning active teaching. It is really a leap in the dark. She has no assurance that her method can sustain her economically in the years to come.

Still, in 1910 she publishes her second book, *Pedagogical Anthropology*, which is her farewell to her academic career. Dedicated to her parents, the volume gathers together the lectures that Maria delivered in her four years at the Pedagogy School, trying to change the vision of school in the academic world, too. At the time, anthropology is still very much influenced by measuring and classification techniques, but she has gone well beyond these technical aspects. In many of her lectures, she describes the pupil's biographical chart, which in her view must replace report cards and registers, throw light on the causes of the child's difficulties, and map his improvement. For this purpose, she suggests that it also contain information on the child's family and social environment, on his behavior in class, so that it will become a document capable of serving as a guide in his further self-education.

Her student Anna Maria Maccheroni recalls this year of transition like this: "I had the impression that she was like a young dove, leaving known terrain to go on her way to an unknown destination. She gave everything she had, standing on her own two feet looking out into the face of the unknown, alone. In all the world, there were just a few Montessori classes. That was all."[59]

The School in the Convent

Her Catholic devotion, very discreet up until this moment, moves now into a public phase through the collaboration with the sisters of the Franciscan Missionaries of Mary. Like the Handmaidens of the Sacred Heart, who had attracted her in the past, this too is a young order, founded a few decades earlier on the initiative of a French noblewoman. Some sisters from this order in the convent of Grottaferrata, where Maria goes for spiritual retreats in the summer, work as teachers, and they become enthusiastic about her method. Sometime before, at their convent on via Giusti in Rome, the order had welcomed a group of orphans who survived the earthquake in Messina, and the method could be a new idea for managing the traumatized children. The sisters suggest to Maria that she request an audience with the Mother Superior.

Maria is very impressed by Marie de la Rédemption, born Jeanne de Geslin de Bourgogne, an aristocratic Frenchwoman who is ten years her senior and has the comportment of an old-time princess. She appreciates nobility—she writes in a letter—that when it is lived deep down possesses the grace of the spiritual life. She falls immediately in love with the grand elegant salons and the shaded flower-filled cloister, and with the self-possessed silence of the nuns. She proposes to hold a training course in the convent, for the nuns and for high-society women, opening an internal Children's House for the practical exercises, which will then become a stable school.

The Children's House is organized quickly, with the patronage of Queen Margherita, who finances the expenses, and a promotion committee, which brings together the crème de la crème of the capital. The children are the orphans of the earthquake in Messina, all of them deeply traumatized: "Their names were unknown, as was their social condition. A tremendous shock had rendered them all more or less the same: beaten down, mute, absent; it was hard even to get them to eat and sleep. During the night they could be heard shouting and crying."[60] A delightful environment is created for them, with elegant, light-hued furniture, ceramic tableware and crystal glasses on the tables, and flowers everywhere. "The sisters taught the children good manners with careful attention that improved from day to day," Maria will recall years later. "There were a lot of sisters in the order who came from aristocratic circles, and they practiced the extremely finicky rules of the social life they had left, recalling them to memory from their old habits. The children seemed like they couldn't get enough of those refinements. They learned to conduct themselves at table like princes, and they also learned to serve at table like highly trained attendants."

The training course in the convent is inaugurated in April 1910. For eight months, the students follow the lessons in theory and the practical exercises in class. To keep them from disturbing her didactic work, Maria puts up signs on the wall that say: DON'T TALK TO THE CHILDREN.[61] Anna Maria Maccheroni remembers how severe she was on this point. "When a child went to the materials closet, student-teachers and visitors would ask him, 'What are you going to get?' Or 'What do you like to do? Why?' The small child doesn't think; he simply does what corresponds to his current state of development. He obeys a guiding instinct. He needs to be left alone, do not disturb him."

Maria also runs a small experimental class in her house, with a group of children between the ages of six and nine, to study how to extend her method to elementary schools. They are children of friends and supporters, so all from fine families. One day, one of them tells his parents that the food at the Montessori house is better. This information leaves them dumbfounded, given that they have at their service one of the best-known cooks in the city. In reality, what their son appreciated is not so much the food but the experience of the meal, the fact of being involved in preparing the table and serving himself. Maria, who in that period is experiencing the first tensions with the City of Rome, also appreciates the time spent with her pupils: "This is a rest—being with little children with whom there are no arguments."[62]

Whether at school or at home, her research activity goes forward each day, like an uninterrupted interior workshop. Thanks to her eclectic training, Maria observes the children from various points of view—medical, physiological, anthropological, pedagogical, and religious—which complement one another. The object of her research, on the other hand, is always one and the same: the mind of the child. She keeps going round and round the fascinating paradox of the first years of life, which are central to personal development but which are also a period that often leaves no memories. This is the "secret of childhood" that she will talk about all her life, with a form of admiring reverence. "I don't intend to guess, nor do I wish to scrutinize the thoughts of the children I educate. That the child's intelligence, and the rules that regulate it, are mysterious and difficult to penetrate, all educators recognize, but I go further than that, and I say: let's respect the secret, let's give up on penetrating it."[63]

Taking Religion to the People

M aria also tells the Mother Superior of the convent in via
Giusti about her project for a lay congregation. Marie de
la Rédemption knows well that Maria's past as a feminist
and scientist, like her collaboration with the Masonic and anticlerical
politicians of the City of Rome and with the socialists of the Humanitarian Society in Milan, make her suspect to the Catholic hierarchy.
But she tries to help her anyway. She invites her to participate with her
students in the training course for novices, and she gathers together all
the useful elements to support her cause. In the archives of the order
there is an entire dossier on this topic. One of the documents in the
dossier reads: "The sisters positively know that Montessori is now a
practicing Christian, that she leads a most pious life, that she often
goes to Mass and receives Communion, and they fervently hope that
she will be one more scientist that the study of science has brought to
the faith."[64] In a letter from the provincial vicar to the Superior, we
discover a surprising detail: "At the Montessori home they are about to
build a chapel, with a secret entrance for a priest who can go there to
say Mass. Nothing must be known about this presence, not even by the

servants. Montessori's father is opposed to religion, the mother became religious only after her daughter did."[65]

The archive conserves a long account that one of the sisters sends to the Mother Superior after having a meeting with Anna Fedeli, during which Maria's student explained how the method can be considered a way for bringing religion to the people:

> The education of children has an important role in her plan, there is no doubt about it. But the main purpose is that the children's teacher be for the adults (the parents of her pupils and the whole neighborhood) a reformer of their ideas, an elevating element, a moralizer, an agent of truth. This rare bird must be fundamentally Christian, conduct a pure and serious life, live in the midst of crudity and be delicate, in the midst of vice and be virtuous. She must, without directly approving atheist and revolutionary theories, let on that she is on their side, in order to obtain first their trust, and little by little lead them back to the road of discipline, of obedience to divine and human laws, finally to Christianity. It is science itself [says Signora Fedeli] that will lead us to Christianity, but we must, in order to penetrate the environment of the ignorant working classes, make them believe first that we seek the good, without saying that this good comes to us from Catholicism.[66]

This idea might appear to be the fruit of Anna Fedeli's imagination. But Maria Montessori herself, in a letter to Donna Maraini, makes this comment on her days at the Children's Houses of the Humanitarian Society: "Here it is so interesting to listen to the needs of the souls of the people: they thirst for spirituality, and they have nothing to drink...What great work it is to quench their thirst! To indicate the way to elevation and peace!"[67]

The archive also conserves a document entitled *Rules*, which describes Maria's project. She has in mind a lay order of women who take vows of chastity, poverty, and obedience and are organized in small communities of teachers. True missionaries to the periphery, they will work among the people without outward signs of their status, with the attitude "of those who are *learning*, not of those who teach; of those who *depend*, not of those who *command*."[68] After the ceremony of private vows pronounced with her disciples, Maria considers that she has offered her life entirely to God, and she reiterates this in her letters to Donna Maraini. She also does promotional work by going in person to various Catholic women's orders in Rome and taking them materials illustrative of her method.

Through her protectresses, she tries to obtain an audience with the pope, but without success. It is not only her past that makes her suspect to Catholic traditionalists. There are also strong theoretical differences, because her method contrasts with the traditional pedagogy of the Church, based on the concept of authority. Furthermore, many Catholic commentators fear the acceptance of the idea that children can do without any outside teaching at all, including that of priests. The initiative to abolish rewards and punishments also scandalizes the theologians, given that Catholic morality is constructed around the concept of Heaven and Hell.

To make things worse, these are the years of the Catholic Church's struggle against the modernists, that is, the many who are trying to renew the faith from within, in the name of freedom of thought and science. Modernism must be fought as heretical, its main proponents excommunicated, and if clerics, suspended. Maria's ideas are defined by *La Civiltà Cattolica* as "pedagogic modernism." The director of the traditionalist daily *Unità Cattolica* (Catholic Unity) places the Montessori method on the list of novelties that are threatening the Church, next to "female sports, the law on the precedence of civil marriage, the tango, pacifist congresses, and freemasonry."[69]

In this tense climate, her collaboration with the sisters of the convent in via Giusti is short-lived. Already in 1912 the annual training course is interrupted. The internal Children's House is taken away from Anna Maria Maccheroni and assigned to a religious, to then be closed in 1914. When she receives the news, Maria is abroad, and she writes a heartfelt letter to the Mother Superior:

When we heard that the school in via Giusti was closed we felt a cruel blow to the heart! It was our support and, in the eyes of the public, the only sign of public love and of the open approval of the Church. [. . .] Dear Mother, I do not understand what has happened, but I still allow myself to recall all of the good I received from you! The comfort that came to me from your goodness to us. And if you have decided to reject without explanation or notice those who confided in you, those to whom you had shown such benevolence, it must be because God has so disposed. Perhaps in the future, light and compensation will also come from this humiliation.[70]

A Pilgrimage

R ome, perennially an obligatory stop on the Grand Tour, is home to a lot of foreigners, and this helps in the dissemination of the method abroad. On their return home from the Eternal City, travelers talk about the Children's Houses, eliciting interest on the part of their fellow nationals. Very soon, people from virtually all walks of life show up at Maria Montessori's home to meet her: professors, journalists, doctors, public officials, aristocrats, religious leaders, and philanthropists. "A pilgrimage from every part of the Earth, with all the characteristics of a pilgrimage: the faith, the fervor,"[71] as one of them will describe the phenomenon. Often the crowd is so numerous that the visitors wait for entire days to speak with her.

Those who can't come in person write, and the house is overrun with letters asking for information on how to open a school, on where to buy the teaching materials, on how to find a teacher trained in the new method. "Among the many letters, I remember very well one that came from China," one student recalls.

It was stuffed and puffy like a cushion. It contained a strip of white satin hand-embroidered with figures of Chinamen. Their costume said that it was very old embroidery. It was precious. The letter was not registered, the envelope was quite common and ordinary, very lightweight paper and, I remember well, light blue. But it arrived intact. The letter was in English and said this, more or less: They say I'm crazy because I have always been convinced that school has to be changed completely. And now your book translated into Chinese tells me I'm right, that my conviction is not crazy after all.[72]

Maria's students collect all the letters in big cardboard boxes. Periodically, one of them proposes to reorder them, but there is never time to do it. Every so often, Maria picks one of them and reads it out loud to her mother, who is frequently ill and bedridden.

In 1911, Maria decides it's time to look for a new home. She wants something bigger, where she can host a class for experimentation and a permanent study center to develop her method. She dreams of a place where everybody can feel at home: parents, her disciples, visitors, the children of the model classes, students in training. She chooses a large apartment in via Principessa Clotilde, with big terraces overlooking Piazza del Popolo. Maria is completely taken with it from her very first visit: "Oh, what a beautiful house! How grand, sweet, white, new, just like a virgin. At the same time robust, magnificent. Full of air, light, adorned with terraces like a bride with her jewels."[73]

She activates all of her contacts to convince the owners to rent it to her. The cost comes to twelve thousand lire per year, an enormous sum. To pay it, she asks for help from her sponsors among Rome's aristocracy. She is good at fund raising; she's been at it since the time of feminism and the League: "You know the story of Saint Philip Neri, who importuned an avaricious gentleman to help an unfortunate family, until the gentleman, tired of Neri's constant pestering, slapped the saint in the face. And Saint Philip said: 'That's for me, but for the poor family?'"[74] Finally, some of her supporters agree to cover a part of the rent. Queen Margherita takes care of the rest. Maria's is a risky choice, considering that she has no certainty of finding the necessary funds even in the years to come, but that's the way she is. "The source of my strength is not the outside world,"[75] she says.

The interest that her ideas are eliciting abroad encourages her to continue. By nature, she is an optimist and trusts in the future, and she says so frequently in her letters: "It's all so beautiful, so wonderful, so promising."[76] Every now and again she has moments of discouragement, in which the enterprise to which she has devoted her whole life seems too difficult. She is alone with few students and fewer means, faced with an amount of work that just keeps on growing. She has no office, no administrative staff. She hates managing money and she complains about the bills that "jump up her nose" unexpectedly. She has a head full of ideas but she doesn't always have the peace she needs to work. In a letter to her friend Olga Lodi, she writes: "By now I can never find a minute of rest and relaxation in my life! I have accumulated work in a manner that's crazy! And I feel like I'm a porter of ideas!"[77]

She is constantly besieged by visitors in search of news. Some of them, awestruck by Maria, leave everything to devote themselves to her method as though on a divine mission. Others write to her to suggest ways of managing the development of the movement. All of them are driven by an overwhelming enthusiasm, like carriers of a new spiritual message. An English Anglican pastor writes her a long letter to explain that she has to organize a vast international movement, where she will be the leader and her trusted friends her vicars in every country.

Montessori, Rome

An excellent information campaign for foreigners is conducted by the British ambassador to Italy, who opens a Children's House in his embassy in Rome. The pupils are all children of diplomats and they speak different languages, but this, a visiting American journalist highlights, does not impede the proper functioning of the method. "Confusion reigned at first; but before a month has passed, [the teacher had converted] this Tower of Babel into a community of happy and busy children."[78]

The discussion in the specialized English-language press is opened by an article in the *Journal of Education*, published in London in September 1909, and then in the American review the *Kindergarten-Primary Magazine*, where a pedagogue named Jenny Merrill writes a series of articles starting in December of the same year. In that period, kindergartens are the center of attention in American education. Convincing their theorists of the quality of the new method means winning over the whole country. In her articles, Jenny Merrill explains that something new is happening in Rome, something that could change the concept of nursery school forever. She recounts the explosions of writing, the work performed with great concentration and in silence, the transformation of the children. She also expresses some reservations, for example, that work prevails over play. But she declares herself certain that the subject must decidedly be studied in depth, and if possible on site, because the Montessori schools must be seen in person. Merrill concludes her series of articles with the "hope that our traveling kindergarteners will endeavor to visit these new institutions in Italy."[79] She has no idea just how many of her colleagues would welcome this suggestion.

Dozens of American school administrators get on ships and go to Rome to meet Maria Montessori. The country's major universities send their teachers as observers. One journalist describes the situation as follows: "Public school teachers in Carolina write to their cousins on vacation in Europe to be sure to pass through Rome to see the Montessori schools. Mothers from Oregon and Maine write, addressing their letters, 'Montessori, Rome,' and make demands for enlightenment, urgent, pressing, and blamelessly peremptory; since they conceive of a possibility that their children, their own children, the most important human beings in the world, may be missing something valuable."[80]

Among the first to arrive in Rome is Anne George, a thirty-one-year-old teacher, alerted by a friend who lives in Italy. Her story describes well how the method spreads in those early years, thanks to the enthusiasm of foreign visitors. Anne George arrives in Rome in the spring of 1909 and goes immediately to the Montessori home. Maria does not speak English, Anne knows only a few words of French. Communication is not easy: "I managed to say that I was a teacher, then we sat looking at each other in silence for what seemed like an eternity,"[81] Anne George recalls. Despite the difficulties posed by the language barrier, she is deeply impressed by Maria Montessori. "As we looked at each other, I knew that this woman dealt with the real soul of things and that her work was big, sincere, and reverent. I shall never forget the smile with which she welcomed me then; nor the beautiful sincerity with which she talked to me of her work and her hopes." These words express something that all those who have met Maria Montessori have emphasized: her great charisma, her uncommon personality, and a kind of serene strength that makes her almost invincible.

When she is seen in action with the children, the impression is even stronger: "The simplicity of Dr. Montessori was a revelation. Every time we entered a class-room, I distinctly felt that a new and sweeter spirit pervaded the place, and that the children were, in an indescribable way, set free."[82] Here, Anne George describes another fundamental point: Maria's way of being in the classroom, which is different from the way of adults, especially at the time. In her training courses, Maria will try to transmit this attitude to her students, asking them to be, before all else, people transformed, capable of approaching children in a new way.

Those who want to teach with the Montessori method must work deeply on themselves. That is the only way for them to become what Maria dreams of: a new kind of adult, who knows how to use silence better than words, the capacity of observation more than authority. She presents her students with a list of suggestions—prepare the environment, explain how to use the materials, observe the child—but the golden rule is always abstention. Adults, who by definition are in a position of strength, have to do all they can to withdraw and leave room for the children, traditionally thought to be weaker. The adults have to overcome the temptation to help the children, letting them use their own resources, letting them make mistakes and correct them as many times as necessary, without trying to accelerate the process. This lofty, almost utopian idea is one of Maria's fundamental contributions to pedagogy, but at the same time it is one of the reasons why her method encounters so much resistance. Heeding it, for the adults that run the schools, means questioning their own ideas and behavior from the bottom up. And few are prepared to do that.

Anne George is one of them. Impressed by what she sees, she remains in Italy for the whole summer, then she returns to the United States, taking with her a copy of Maria's book and a complete set of teaching materials. Back home, she sets out to learn Italian so she can read the book. The next year she returns to Italy to improve her Italian and enrolls in a training course taught by Maria in her home for a few select students. Upon her return to the United States, George starts a school in Tarrytown, a suburb of New York City. It is the first Montessori school in the United States; a private school, financed by the president of the National Bank of New York. All of the pupils come from families of the city's financial elite.

An American Impresario

U p to that time, in America, news of the Montessori method was restricted to the world of education and pedagogy. For the news to reach a wider audience, it will take the entrance on the scene of a very picturesque character, Samuel McClure, who will orchestrate a huge publicity campaign around Maria Montessori. Born to a family of poor Irish immigrants, McClure is the incarnation of the myth of the self-made American. As a young man, he began working as a journalist for a cycling magazine without ever riding a bike, and in just a few years he became a legendary publisher, inventing a new concept—commissioning articles and serialized books to be sold to multiple newspapers—that became a trend.

Indefatigable and enthusiastic, he alternates periods of depression and moments of creativity in which he dreams of creating a McClure bank, a McClure insurance company, a McClure publishing house, even a McClure ideal city. In 1893 he founded a review, *McClure's Magazine*, that was an instant success. One of his strong points is the discovery of new personalities. For this purpose, McClure keeps correspondents in numerous American states and an office in London, which has the task of keeping him informed on events and new trends in Europe.

When the London office sends him the proposal of an American writer, Josephine Tozier, who, on a trip to Italy, had interviewed Maria Montessori, he senses that the story has something. That European woman who preaches a new way of looking at children is the perfect incarnation of what he calls the McClure ideal: a strong personality, a pioneer who will change the world. He commissions an article, against the advice of the editorial board, who do not understand how an unknown Italian woman doctor, who, to boot, collaborates with a convent of Catholic nuns, could be interesting to an American readership.

The article comes out in May 1911. Josephine Tozier recounts her visits to two schools in Rome, the private one in via Giusti and the public school in via Sant'Angelo in Pescheria. One has large rooms, gardens full of roses, and, according to the journalist, an excessive dose of religion. The other is situated in one of the poorest neighborhoods of Rome, in the Jewish ghetto, but the children at work in the classroom, serene and quiet, seem to her much different from the urchins running through the nearby streets. Only the pallor of malnutrition reminds her that they, too, come from the neighborhood of the disinherited.

Josephine Tozier describes the most important elements of the method through nicely crafted anecdotes. For example, the importance of always letting the children take the initiative. One pupil can't manage to see some material because a group of taller classmates is standing in front of him, and he is about to climb up on a chair. Just then, the teacher picks him up by the arms, without realizing, as the journalist explains, that by doing so she has interrupted something precious and has deprived the child of a joy greater than that of seeing the material: finding a way to do it on his own.

To explain the great order in freedom that she admires in the Children's Houses, the journalist cites Maria Montessori:

The first idea that the child must acquire, in order to be actively disciplined, is that of the difference between good and evil; and the task of the educator lies in seeing that the child does not confound good with immobility and evil with activity, as often happens in the case of the old-time discipline. And all this because our aim is to discipline for activity, for work, for good, not for immobility, not for passivity, not for obedience. A room in which all the children move about usefully, intelligently, and voluntarily, without committing any rough or rude act, would seem to me a classroom disciplined very well indeed.[83]

The article lists all of the main points of the method: an environment made to the measure of children; the use of learning materials; the freedom to work, with the only limitation being to put everything back in its place when finished; classes with children of different ages; the absence of rewards or punishments; the teacher's marginal position.

The issue of the magazine featuring the article is such a success that it has to be reprinted immediately. "It seemed that everyone was waiting for Maria Montessori's message,"[84] McClure will write in his memoirs. The publisher commissions Josephine Tozier to write more articles, but the readers want even more and write thousands of letters. Very soon a new regular feature is created under the title "The Montessori Movement." A group of journalist on the magazine staff acts as an information office on the progress of the method in America. The readers, especially female readers, want to know when Maria Montessori's book will be translated into English, if someone is already selling the teaching materials in the United States, if there are plans to open Children's Houses. Many letters make it all the way to Rome.

In the face of this explosion of interest, Maria Montessori is flattered but also anxious, divided between the desire to make her method known in that great, distant land, and the fear that it will be applied in a rushed and inexact manner. For the moment, everything is characterized by happenstance and improvisation. Another American journalist writes:

When they reach Rome, most of them quite unable to express themselves in Italian or even in French, what do they find, all these tourists and letters of inquiry, and adventuring school-mistresses? They find a dead wall. They have an unformulated idea that they are probably going to a highly organized institution of some sort, like our huge "model schools," attached to our normal colleges, through the classrooms of which an unending file of observers is allowed to pass. And they have no idea whatever of the inevitability *with which Italians speak Italian*. They find—if they are relentlessly persistent enough to pierce through the protection her friends try to throw about her—only Dr. Montessori herself, a private individual, phenomenally busy with important work, who does not speak or understand a word of English, who has neither money, time, or strength enough single-handed to cope with the flood of inquiries and inquirers about her ideas.[85]

Soon McClure goes to see her in Rome, to propose himself as her impresario. He knows all the secrets of communications and he is sure he can create a true Montessori movement in America. Since he knows French, he can talk with Maria without an interpreter. It is the beginning of an improbable collaboration, between two people of opposite character—she quiet and concentrated, he enthusiastic and voluble—who come together on the basis of a great misunderstanding. Maria thinks that he is a disciple accustomed to her same level of devotion to the cause, while McClure is a businessman, who sees in her above all else a source of profit. Despite everything, her meeting with McClure is a fundamental passage. It is thanks to him that Maria becomes an international celebrity and begins her nomadic life, traveling the world following what she will soon define as her "calling."[86] But before confronting this new change, she will have to close a wound left open too long.

The Refound Son

On December 20, 1912, Renilde Montessori dies following a long illness. Maria takes care of her to the very end. She almost never leaves her bedside, doesn't eat for days, and, when someone insists, she responds, "I can't."[87] During the funeral, she sits next to her father, surrounded by her students. To her black dress, her customary apparel for years now, she has added a black veil to cover her head, where her white locks are visible. When the coffin is placed in its vault in the cemetery in Verano, she sticks her head into the darkness, resting it on the wood for a good while. When the ceremony is over, she accompanies her father and some students to the seashore, not far from Rome. She always finds immense comfort in nature.

Now that her mother is gone, the main obstacle to her secret maternity has been removed. "Maria found Mario again when Renilde died, because her mother just did not want to acknowledge that child. For Maria's family her son did not exist. It was a tragedy, a silence about which no one ever talked,"[88] one descendant has recalled. Maria decides to send a signal to her distant son. Through the father of one of his boarding school classmates she sends him her name and address.

She wants to leave the initiative to the boy. She doesn't know what to expect. Her son might hate her for that long abandonment and refuse to speak to her. Maria, usually such a fatalist and imperturbable, is shaky this time, and confides in Donna Maraini: "It seems like the sun has set on a period of my life and the dark night has fallen."[89] As soon as he receives the message, Mario reacts with great enthusiasm. He writes her a long letter, calling her "Mamma," and explaining that he has been waiting for this moment for years.

It is the beginning of an exchange of emotional letters, where the sentiments repressed for too long can finally be liberated. No reproach from the son, no fear on the part of the mother, only the happiness of finally being able to talk, like two heroes of a fable separated for years by a spell. They want to skip all the preliminaries and try to see each other as soon as possible. Maria arranges a meeting during the school holidays for Carnival. Mario goes on a school trip to Arezzo and there he finds Maria, who has come to the appointment by car, waiting for him. They leave together on February 1, 1913. Before getting back on the road to Rome, Maria sends Donna Maraini a telegram with just one word: "*Arriviamo*"[90] (We're on our way).

It is a sort of kidnapping, as in an action film. Possibly agreed upon in advance in every detail, it was more likely improvised, as recounted by Maria's first American biographer, who was able to interview Mario as an adult: "Mario Montessori's memory is of a spring day in 1913 when he was about fifteen, seeing on a school outing the lady whose visits have punctuated his childhood and been explained in his fantasies. A car stopped where he was resting; she got out and he went up to her and said simply, 'I know you are my mother,' and told her he wanted to go with her. She made no objection, he got into the car with her..."[91]

By taking home a minor who by law is not her son, Maria runs a big risk. If the boy's father were to decide to denounce her, it would

mean a scandal. But Giuseppe Montesano knows that he cannot oppose what is happening, now that Mario has made his choice. Between the two onetime lovers it is not a true reconciliation, but rather
the end of a long period of silent tension. She takes back what has
too long been denied her, he acknowledges defeat. It is a decision
which, in a certain sense, is an act of liberation for both of them. "I
remember hearing her say that someone who is offended is like someone who has been wounded and still has the knife in the wound. If
they forgive, the knife falls out and the wound closes over,"[92] a former
student recalls.

From that moment, Maria keeps her son with her, introducing
him to everyone as her nephew. Few actually know the truth. One of
her disciples, interviewed years later, will explain that it was a topic
that Maria did not like to face. All she said, speaking of the boy, was
"You know Mario had a difficult childhood."[93] Everybody who meets
him in that period describes him as an extroverted and cheerful boy,
robust, in excellent health, who adapts incredibly fast to his new situation. He studies at home with a tutor. He never leaves his mother,
as though he were afraid to lose her again. He has decided, once and
for all, that his place is by her side.

Until that day, Maria accepted the separation with great stoicism,
trying to put all her energy into her work and her faith. "The whole
art of living consists in submitting to reality,"[94] she likes to say. Now
that she has refound Mario, she can finally recover her equilibrium.
Even her idea of founding a lay congregation slowly fades away. Her
letters and diary are imbued with love for her son. "He is a great being,
I have felt his soul, he is strong, kind, generous, and passionate; he
possesses a wisdom and a love that are infinitely profound."[95] Maria
calls him "pupetto" (puppet), "tesoro" (treasure), "pesciolino" (minnow),
"mio unico amore" (my only love), "capolavoro di Dio" (God's master-
piece). She treats him as an equal, trying to nourish his curious mind.
Mario will recall, "When I was a boy, I was awakened early one morning in our house in Rome by my bed shaking and a deep sound like

a rumble. I had just opened my eyes when my mother came into the room, calm and smiling, and sat down on the edge of my bed. 'Mario,' she said, 'do you see how the lamp is shaking?' I saw it. 'Can you feel how the floor is shaking?' I felt it. My mother opened her arms as though she were inviting me to a splendid surprise: 'This, Mario, is an earthquake!'"[96]

Before the International Tribunal

All of this is happening in a crucial moment for the development of the method. A few weeks earlier, Maria Montessori inaugurated her first international training course in her big new home in via Principessa Clotilde. She decided to do it in response to international pressure, worried that her method would spread in an uncontrolled manner, above all because of the Americans, who are besieging her with requests. "Without the course, they would have come here to *see*, and seeing, along with the book, is sufficient to understand enough to apply the method. So there would have been, all the same, people creating Children's Houses, but without giving anything to us, without depending on us. The course can give us the reins in hand, can make us some friends, maybe even some apostles,"[97] she explains to Donna Maraini.

She organizes the course in a hurry while she is dealing with her mother's death and rekindling her relationship with her son. She forces herself to keep her mind clear. She knows it is a fundamental moment for her work. She writes to her friend Donna Maraini, who is one of the few who have been informed of her decision to break the silence with Mario: "I feel lost...But now it is necessary to confront a situation where I need to have a clear head, strong heart! I am about to appear before an international tribunal."[98]

She needs to gain some time, so she'll be able to pick up Mario in Arezzo. She gets some help from her friend to postpone the start of her lessons as long as possible, by entertaining the students with lectures by friends and university professors. She even invites an archaeologist to present a day of lectures on the recently completed excavations of the Roman Forum.

Her course begins in February, after her return to Rome with Mario. It lasts four months and is attended by a hundred or so students. The American contingent is the largest, sixty of them who all traveled to Italy together, disembarking in Naples and then continuing on to Rome by train. The origins of the rest of the class are quite varied: one woman from the Transvaal, who complains about the chairs and prefers to sit cross-legged on the floor, two sisters from Australia, who sold their house to pay for the trip, one Indian, who had never seen snow, of which there was an unusual abundance that year in Rome.

A large majority of the students are women. In her lessons, before illustrating the teaching materials, Maria invites them to carry out a deep work of self-reflection: "Only you can prepare yourselves to observe, just as the children must learn by themselves from their experience. That is what a teacher must know, how to observe."[99] She meets with some of them in the evening, to continue their discussions. In their midst she seems even older than her age. "She always wore dresses that were long and a bit out of fashion, like my grandmother,"[100] one student recalls.

The course, in accordance with a plan that will be confirmed over the years, is divided into two parts: theoretical lessons taught in Italian, with an interpreter who translates into English; then practical exercises in a model Children's House, opened for the occasion. Starting with the next course, Maria will establish that every application for admission must also include a photograph. She believes she can only understand a person's nature by looking them in the eye. Many, over the years, will call her "clairvoyant,"[101] "psychic," or a woman with "a magical personality."[102] Maria delivers a speech with prophetic tones. "Why are you here?" she asks, looking around the room. "The cause is that little school and the revelation through which some heard, some saw, everyone believed."[103]

The course is a great success and augments the number of foreigners who travel to Rome to meet her. Even though the apartment in via Principessa Clotilde is large, there never seems to be enough room. One visitor recalls: "Her home was open to the multitudes, coming and going all day long. One woman from America waited seven hours to see her. Forgotten by the governess, she was left sitting in the waiting room, waiting patiently, without complaint, as the hours went by and the room grew darker."[104] Maria's students decide to form an impenetrable barrier, allowing them to screen the petitioners and keep them from wasting her time. "I want to meet those who come here in search of the truth," she says repeatedly. "Many come instead out of curiosity or out of a taste for novelty or the unusual. I cannot meet these thieves of time. If I saw all of those who call and responded to all those who write, I wouldn't have time for my experiments or to study, and my method has still not been completed."[105]

The First American Tensions

In the United States, thanks to Samuel McClure's publicity campaign, interest in the method is extremely high. Maria's book, translated by Anne George, arrives in the bookstores in 1912 and immediately sells out. It is enriched with a preface by Henry W. Holmes, a professor of pedagogy, who writes very positive things about the method but who also makes an observation that will often show up in academic critiques. "A system of education does not have to attain perfection to merit study, investigation and experimental use," he comments, puzzled by the fact that Maria Montessori claims to have created a scientific method but then does not accept the idea that other scientists assess it and, if necessary, improve it. Personally, he is optimistic: "Dr. Montessori is too large-minded to claim infallibility, and too thoroughly scientific in her attitude to object to careful scrutiny of her scheme and the thorough testing of its results."[106] In reality, that is just what Maria will do: insist on being the only one to assess and develop her method, thus antagonizing a large portion of American pedagogues.

A solution is found quickly for the sale of the teaching materials. Carl Byoir, a journalist with a flair for business, reads about the method in McClure's Magazine and realizes its economic potential. He goes to Rome and proposes an agreement to Maria for the exclusive right to produce and sell the material in North America in exchange for a payment of six thousand dollars. To get an idea of the value of this figure, consider that at the time the average annual income in America was eight hundred dollars. Instead of providing for a percentage on every set of materials sold, as the Humanitarian Society does, Byoir offers Maria 20 percent of the shares and the related dividends. Upon his return to the United States he creates a company, the House of Childhood, and in January 1912 he starts production. It is a very profitable enterprise because a complete set of materials costs twelve dollars to produce and sells for fifty dollars. Yet less than a year after starting production, Byoir sells his holding in the company to another businessman and abandons the enterprise. We do not know the reasons for his decision. It can't be ruled out that he came to understand Maria's difficult character and preferred to capitalize on his investment and make his exit before entering into conflict with her.

More the optimist, McClure continues to dream of getting rich by capitalizing on the method. Owing to his poor management, he has been ousted from his magazine and is in trouble with his creditors. He founds a Montessori Educational Association to manage the avalanche of requests that come in to the editorial offices, but when he announces it, he gets a telegram from Maria, annoyed that the impresario has not waited to receive her authorization: "INDIGNANT/ ANNOUNCEMENT IN JULY ISSUE PREMATURE."[107] The crisis is resolved quickly and the association begins operation. It will give rise to one of the many misunderstandings that will undermine their collaboration. Maria thinks that the association is a tool for attracting investors, while the Americans—accustomed to the tradition of committees going back to the time of the War of Independence—think of it as a way to allow for a collective leadership of the movement. The first American Montessorians apply the method with an open approach, thinking they are contributing to the development of something that is still evolving. Anne George, for example, observes that American children are different from their Italian counterparts and predicts that some adjustments will be needed.

She is comforted in this idea from the words of Maria herself, who has been saying for some time now that the method is not complete and that, more than a system of codified rules, it is based on the scientific observation of children: "That which is commonly called my method of education is in truth a first germ of positive science, which with its research methods has touched the truth where the souls of children are evolving. The Children's Houses are the first laboratories of human science; that is why their fame has traversed the world at lightning speed."[108] The principles applied in the method do not come from her but from the children, who, left free to work, reveal the workings of their minds to those who know how to look at them with attentive eyes. One of the Franciscan nuns who are students at the convent in via Giusti gave what may be the best definition of the Montessori system: "A method that is nothing other than a patient observation of childhood."[109]

Institutes, Manuals, and Other Squabbles

O ne topic of constant discussion with the American impresario is teacher training. McClure would like it to be done
in the United States, in a permanent center located in New
York City, and he announces the project in the magazine. Maria tries
to contain his enthusiasm. In the first course held in Rome in 1913,
the American students were in the majority. Why go to New York
to train teachers when they are so enthusiastic as to undertake the
voyage to Italy? She publishes a press release in *McClure's Magazine*
to clear the field of any misunderstandings: "Madame Montessori in-
tends to start, this fall, a special course for fitting teachers who wish
to open training schools for teaching the Montessori method. The
course is to be given by Madame Montessori personally in Rome. No
training school approved by Madame Montessori will be opened in
the United States this year."[110]

Her hesitation about the American training institute is based on
personal reasons. She is not willing to move to the United States
for three months while leaving her son behind in Rome. Plus, there
are economic reasons. Giving the course in Rome means taking in

all of the tuition payments there, while holding them in New York involves sharing the payments with McClure. When the candidate selected to run the institute goes to Rome to discuss the issue, she understands immediately the contours of the problem. "The Dottoressa wants money for her own school—but does not mean to pursue a center in England or in America to deflect from Rome students."[111] She writes to McClure to tell him that she is no longer interested in participating in the project. "I find Montessori very displeased, with the committee, with Miss George & us all…It's all quite impossible…and I am withdrawing from the whole movement." Despite the ominous gathering of these clouds, the relationship between Maria Montessori and Samuel McClure remains quite cordial. In June 2013 she writes to him, in her flowery French: "You have always remained very strong and chivalrous as a person beyond reproach and without fear as the gentleman and friend who remains in my trust for life."[112]

Another problem is the growing number of American books on the method. Leading the way was the writer Dorothy C. Fisher, who, upon returning home from a visit to Rome to see the Children's Houses in 1911, publishes *A Montessori Mother*, attaining great success. Other publications were soon to follow. A reader of *McClure's* publishes an article entitled "A Mother's Experiment," to recount how, after seeing the Children's Houses in Rome, she had bought the teaching material and applied the method at home with her six-year-old son. This idea of the homemade method is not bound to please Maria. But what alarms her even more is a second book by Dorothy C. Fisher, *The Montessori Manual for Teachers and Parents*, where the author explains how to put the method in practice in school and at home, suggesting with great nonchalance her own modifications and new ideas. After all, she observes, Maria had done the same thing with Séguin's material, and, she writes, surely she will find "all over the world a multitude of ingenious partners in her enterprise."[113]

Maria decides to react. She writes a manual that she has translated into English, *Dr. Maria Montessori's Own Handbook*, and printed simultaneously in the United States and England. Upon its publication, she sends an open letter to the *Times Educational Supplement* to explain the intent of the operation: "I have taken the pains of preparing myself a handbook to fulfill exactly the task which Mrs. D. Canfield Fisher's book has the pretension of fulfilling. I should be very glad if you would give me the opportunity of saying that I have not deputed—and do not propose to depute—to others the work of a practical popular explanation of my method, as I have taken great pains to do this myself."[114]

There is in her a real fear that her ideas will be badly understood and applied, but also a clear desire for control, the fruit of her imperious character, and the will to protect her economic interests. Since she has refound her son, this last aspect has become more important than before. Maria dreams of building an empire to leave one day in heredity to Mario, almost in reparation for having abandoned him at birth. "Here lies the child's future," she writes in her diary. "Make him secure in his future! Happy—full of compensations for what he suffered: and be I alone that gives him everything."[115]

Furthermore, slowly, perhaps unconsciously, owing to her success and the throngs of admirers who crowd around her, her attitude changes. In the early years, she spoke as a scientist, explaining that the mind of the child shows itself to anyone who is willing to observe it, or she complained of having to face alone such an immense task. Now she increasingly takes the position of someone who—having received a revelation—has to communicate it to the world. The risk, as her critics are starting to note, is that, as a scientist who suggests to her colleagues how to study children in the conditions of an ideal environment, she transforms into a prophetess who is the custodian of a message and who transmits it to a few initiates, selected and trained by her. This is something for which many will not forgive her. Years later, her American biographer will laconically conclude, "There are no monopolies in the commerce of ideas."[116]

The Most Interesting Woman of Europe

I n November 1913, McClure arrives in Rome to meet with her again. His affairs are in dire straits, his creditors are assailing him. His only source of profit by now are paid lectures on the Montessori method. He wants to convince Maria to grant him the rights to the images filmed in the Children's Houses in Rome, in order to attract bigger crowds. He gets a friend to lend him the money for the journey and he embarks on a ship headed for Europe. As always happens with him, one idea leads to another even bigger one, and McClure ends up inviting Maria to go to the United States. At first she refuses, not wanting to separate from her son. But McClure convinces her by organizing a program concentrated in less than one month and worthy of a celebrity: a meeting with the president of the United States, lectures in the most prestigious auditoriums, a visit to the laboratory of Thomas Edison.

"At 5:15 yesterday I finally concluded matters after a heartbreaking week," the impresario writes to his wife. "Now that I have won it is a tremendous thing. Sole rights in her films in America! Think of that. Then she comes and lectures in cooperation with me

& the films for three weeks & in the future we control her lectures and the films for her school for all time & perhaps for the whole world."[117] They sign a contract, where Maria commits herself to giving a dozen or so lectures in the United States, against an advance of six hundred dollars. Sixty percent of revenues will go to her and the rest to McClure.

The invitation arrives at just the right time. The dissemination of her method in Italy is at a dead end. In Rome, by now, Maria has more enemies than supporters. At City Council meetings, officials point out that the costs of opening a Children's House are much greater than those for an ordinary school. The minutes from a session in 1913 summarize the criticisms: "Material was purchased for 2,000 lire; another 2,000 were given to Madame Montessori, who with a few lessons trained a nucleus of teachers. [. . .] While a section of a common kindergarten serves up to seventy-five pupils, the Montessori method demands smaller classes of up to forty pupils in theory, but of twenty to twenty-five in reality! And that's not all, because this method requires double the number of rooms, special furniture, rugs, varnished tables, armchairs, etc."[118] There's also a barb for Maria, who has just concluded her first international training course: "Meanwhile, the Montessori method has spread beyond the borders of Italy. It is talked about in America and in Australia and recently Madame Montessori delivered paid lectures at fifty pounds per person, accumulating 75,000 lire in just a few days."

On November 21, 1913, Maria sails for the United States. She embarks at Naples on the ocean liner *Cincinnati*, together with McClure. Her son goes to bid her farewell at the port, and then returns to Rome with Ann Fedeli. "I saw my heroic little boy waving his hands in farewell and it comforted me at the dock," Maria writes. He jumped up and down, puffed up his cheeks and shouted: "'I'm happy!' I could hear his voice even though I couldn't see him anymore. Then the dock faded into an indistinct blot."[119] During the crossing, she keeps a diary that is mostly a dialogue with the faraway boy. "My son, what must you be doing now? It comforts me to think that you are sleeping in the little room that your mama has given you. Sleep well, my adored treasure."[120] Maria travels in first class, dividing her time between her cabin, the sitting rooms, and the lounge chairs on the deck, where she sits for hours, wrapped in a blanket, looking out at the horizon. McClure always sits right next to her, making sure nothing bothers her.

When the ship stops in Gibraltar, Maria finds two telegrams waiting for her, sent respectively by her father and her son. She bids welcome to the ocean by throwing in the water the lovely bouquet of flowers she received from her son at her departure. She senses that this journey to the United States is decisive for Mario, too. Up to that moment it had been Giuseppe Montesano who had taken care of the boy, but now it's up to her to provide for his future, to leave him something that will make up for his tragic childhood. "McClure is thinking of a Montessori-McClure company that will conquer the world and make lots of money. The boy will be the heir,"[121] she writes.

Reuniting with Mario has finally allowed her to release feelings that had been pent up for years, and the flood of emotions seems unstoppable: "Seeing you and feeling your sweet caresses, my sweetness! Beloved, God's favored one. Son, for you I am only your mother, but you are everything for me"[122] She is worried about this period of separation from him, but at the same time she is strangely calm. When the ship sails through a storm, she stays shut inside her cabin. She can hear the singing coming from third class, where the less fortunate passengers try to stave off seasickness by crowding around a violin player to listen to songs from the old country.

The American newspapers are waiting for her arrival, writing about her as the "most interesting woman of Europe."[123] The news of her presence spreads on the ocean liner, and the passengers deliver a petition to McClure for the celebrated Italian to give a lecture before arrival. The commandant invites her to visit the engine room, and the ship's doctor does the same with the infirmary and the small operating room. This long voyage is a symbolic passage, which un-derlines the great change that is coming about in the life of Maria Montessori. The woman of the past—the physician, the feminist, the teacher, the volunteer in San Lorenzo—is slowly vanishing, like the coasts of Europe on the first day of sailing in the Atlantic. In America, Maria becomes "Montessori." She leaves behind her the epic stage of her life, the one in which she struggled to study medicine, and the period of the long solitary journey in which she came to discover and define her mission. This is the beginning of the phase of success, with all of its temptations: money, power, and the desire for control.

PART FOUR

Managing Success

(1914-1934)

We have to reflect that we have only

something to jump off from, and not to

support ourselves; and that a condition

for ensuring, let's put it this way, the deal,

is to have the fewest possible enemies

and the most impressive supporters.[1]

A Triumphal Tour

aria's ship docks in New York on December 3, 1913. She is welcomed by the Italian vice consul, a delegation from the Italian-American community, and a lot of journalists. The first photographs are taken while she is still on the gangway leaving the ship. Imposing, despite her small stature, wrapped in a black fur, her expression secure, she fills the space. Next to her, McClure seems to disappear. Before going to her hotel, Maria asks to take a drive around the city. "I must see everything,"[2] she proclaims.

A press conference has been planned at the hotel. The crowd is so large that the staff checks invitations to keep out curiosity seekers. To gain entry, some students from the course in Rome carry hat boxes and pretend to be milliners with an urgent delivery for the doctor from Italy. In the suite that has been assigned to her, Maria faces all the confusion with great serenity. "But she gives, above all, the impression of poise and self-assuredness," writes one chronicler. "It is perhaps that, contrasted with our own nervousness, perhaps the mere fact that she is in a strange country and does not understand English—whatever the cause, she seems curiously detached. She is not aloof, she is interested in this odd and noisy place, but she is always apart, serene and untouched by it."[3] The concluding comment is: "Half an hour spent with the world-famous educator establishes the fact that the method is Montessori and Montessori is the method, and one may well have grave doubts, about how it will go with 'self-education' when Maria Montessori's personality is removed."

The journalists crowd around her with a thousand questions. They ask her if she is a suffragist. "Naturally, as one of the great social and political developments of the age, one must be in sympathy with the women's movement. Anything that broadens the race and the individual must be supported. But, you understand, I am not a militant."[4] Is she truly convinced that there are no bad children? "Even babies are perfectly good if they are treated properly," she answers without hesitation. "The baby, lying peacefully in his crib, exercises his senses by about his seventh day of life." The reporters take note without knowing that this foreign doctor is anticipating by half a century studies of newborns. Not all of their accounts are accurate. Some of them write that she is a countess, or that she wants to take newborn babies from their mothers. But the publicity is excellent.

On December 4, Maria is in Washington, where she visits the Montessori school that Alexander Graham Bell and his wife, Mabel, have founded in the city, hiring Anne George to direct it. Here, too, she gives a number of interviews. According to the program, at this point she is supposed to meet President Wilson, and McClure is more than a little worried because he is not certain he's going to be able to keep the promise he made in Rome. In the end, the meeting doesn't come off, officially because of an indisposition of the president, but his daughter, Margaret Wilson, accompanies Maria on a tour of the city in a White House car and organizes a meeting with high-ranking public officials.

On December 6, Maria delivers her first American lecture, at the Masonic Temple of Washington. She speaks slowly, in Italian. Anne George, standing next to her, translates into English. Behind her, the images spin from the films shot at the Children's Houses in Rome. After the lecture, a party is held in her honor, with four hundred invited guests. The high society of the national capital turns out to meet the woman who has discovered the power of the mind of the child. On December 7, the Bells organize a farewell lunch with the educators from the local schools. Then they accompany Maria to the station, where the train is waiting to take her back to New York City.

The following Monday she speaks at Carnegie Hall. The hall is full and over a thousand people are left outside. She is introduced by John Dewey of Columbia University, the dean of American educators. Maria gives a long talk, illustrating her method and expanding her vision from the school to all of humanity. "The development at which I aim includes the whole child. My larger aim is the eventual perfection of the human race."[5] In light of her success, McClure arranges for a second lecture at Carnegie Hall, to be held a week later.

Montessori Fever

On December 9, she is in Philadelphia, where she meets Helen Keller, a woman already famous in the United States, who will become even more famous, years later, thanks to the play and film *The Miracle Worker*. As a child, she lost her hearing and sight as the result of an illness. Her parents, at the suggestion of the Bells, had her assisted by an extraordinary teacher, Anne Sullivan, who found a way to communicate with Helen and helped her study all the way to her college degree. Helen Keller's story is confirmation of what Maria has been saying all along about children's natural instinct for learning. Even in the deepest darkness and the most absolute sensorial deprivation, the potent mind of the child has endless resources.

The meeting takes place before an audience of journalists. Helen is a socialist activist and, during the press conference, she speaks about the struggle for social justice. Maria prefers to steer clear of politics but without denying her past. "'I began as a sympathizer of political revolutionists of all kinds. Then I came to realize that it is the liberation of this,' putting her hands to her bosom, 'of what we have in our hearts, that is the beginning and end of revolution.'"[6] The two women communicate by way of a complicated procedure. Maria Montessori speaks in Italian, Anne George translates into English, then Anne Sullivan transforms the words into signs traced on Helen Keller's hands, and vice versa. At the meeting's end, dispensing with the complicated channel of communication, Maria embraces Helen and whispers in the ear of Anne George: "Say to her that I am too much moved to express what I feel."[7]

After stops to deliver lectures in Boston and Providence, she visits the laboratory of the inventor Thomas A. Edison in Menlo Park, New Jersey. On December 5, she is back in New York to speak a second time at a Carnegie Hall jammed with people. America, the land of liberty, seems to be enthused by the message of this Italian doctor who, in all her speeches, returns to the concept of the free development of the child. "Instead of imposing on children the results of someone else's experience from without, children should be stimulated and allowed to explore for themselves, so that their experience makes their knowledge real and a part of themselves, rather than a matter of memorized formulae."[8]

She visits Pittsburgh and Chicago, again welcomed by large audiences, thanks to McClure's excellent promotion. The newspapers talk of "Montessori fever." Despite her busy schedule, she finds time to send her students in Rome a telegram to remind them to take some flowers to her mother's grave for the first anniversary of her death. McClure is always by her side, to make sure that nothing irritates her, because by now he knows her difficult character well. "We have got safely through & once more I am able to breathe freely," he writes to Mabel Bell...The Dottoressa has been successful everywhere & excepting her neurasthenia and resulting fatigues, she has been a very good traveling associate."[9]

He arranges a weekend rest for her at the Battle Creek Sanatorium, as a guest of John Harvey Kellogg, physician and healthy-living pioneer, as well as the inventor of the process for producing Corn

Flakes, whose clinic receives not only common patients but also celebrities like McClure. To all of them he proposes sunbaths, breathing exercises, plus a rigid daily schedule of gymnastics and a vegetarian diet. Refreshed after her two days of rest, Maria arrives in New York, where on the evening of December 23 she presides over a farewell reception.

The day before her departure, she has to engage in negotiations with James Pierce, the new director of the House of Childhood, the American company that produces her teaching materials in the United States. She wants to ask him for new contract conditions. Instead of annual dividends, over which she has no control, she wants a fixed percentage on every set sold, as in her agreement with the Humanitarian Society in Milan. For a while now, she has had the idea that the company is making big profits on the material without passing on her share to her. Their discussions are long and difficult, but Maria repeats that she has complete trust in McClure, who attends the meeting and translates into French for her.

She would also like the impresario to accompany her on the voyage home, but McClure cannot leave the country because of pressure from his creditors. He entrusts Maria to the care of Mr. Bang, a young employee of the British publisher of Maria's book, who is also on his way back to Europe. The crossing from New York to Liverpool on the ocean liner *Lusitania* lasts five days, during which she almost never leaves her cabin, unable to make conversation with the young man, who does not speak French.

After transferring to London by train, she has just enough time for a drive around the city, which she has not seen since her youth, and a meeting with the press at Charing Cross station. She is very tired, but she still has to face the trip through France. She and her young companion travel by ferry and then train to Paris, where Maria leaves on her own for Italy. In his report back to McClure, the young man does not pretend that the trip was easy. "When we finally reached Paris, Doctor Montessori became very ill indeed with Neuralgia, and very nearly collapsed. However, after having spent half the night in taking baths and massages etc. she felt very much better the next day and was able to travel to Rome where...she had an excellent reception."[10]

Where Are My Trusted Friends?

aria arrives in Rome on January 5, 1914. At home, where her students have decked the rooms with fresh flowers and lighted candles, she can finally put her arms around Mario and her father again. She is tired but euphoric, still under the effect of the success attained in the United States. The first few weeks are a constant exchange of letters with the American promoter. In a telegram she writes, "PLEASE CONTINUE WRITING DAILY."[11] She tells him that she has allowed herself a brief period of rest, to get her strength back in accordance with Kellogg's principles of healthy living: massages and vegetarian diet, everything useful—she writes—for working with him to conquer the world. She doesn't know it but their collaboration is almost at an end.

The first issue that divides them is the training center in New York. McClure insists on opening it as soon as possible. Maria is hesitant. In reality, she feels the need, too. Ever since her experiments in San Lorenzo she has been dreaming of creating a development center for the method that combines a permanent study center for her and her collaborators, a model school in which to experiment with new material, and a regular training course for teachers. She is not sure, however, about leaving Italy. She sounds out McClure to find out if there are funds to finance a stay of a few years. She stipulates right from the start that she is not willing to commit herself without being paid. As a term of comparison, she explains that the British Montessorians, in order to assure her presence for regular training courses in London, have declared themselves willing to pay her a fixed sum every year. McClure cannot promise her anything because he is full of debts, but he is in a hurry. Without telling Maria, he has already registered the name of a Montessori Company, with which he hopes to manage the future business of the method, and the profits that it produces.

Maria knows that the situation in the United States is delicate. The wave of public interest is remarkable, but it could subside just as rapidly as it arose. Besides, it has to be taken into account that, by and large, the American academics are hostile, not at all disposed to accept lessons from an Italian woman who is not even a university faculty member. The most noted example is William Heard Kilpatrick, professor at Columbia University, who, in 1914, publishes a book, *The Montessori System Examined*, where he accuses the method of being part of a system of thought dating back to Itard and Séguin and therefore irredeemably outdated. "Kilpatrick was the authority, he gave the word, it was no...," one scholar would conclude many years later.[12]

Maria senses that she needs to seize the moment, and that American support and money are fundamental for the method's development. At the same time, she doesn't want to satisfy all the transatlantic requests. If the idea catches on that it's enough to attend just one of her courses in order to then train other people, it won't be long before she loses her control over the method's application in the whole country. That she is so far away and does not speak English only lends to the confusion. In a letter to Donna Maraini, she vents: "Where are my *trusted* friends, over there? Who would act on our behalf? Who *know* us? Who *would explain* the soundness of our ideas? Who are sufficiently competent to do that? A course that does not give the right to train teachers might procure all that for us. Without the course, we run the risk that, with no real defenses, all the fights and confusion will destroy the future."[13]

I Know Nothing About Business,
That I Do Know

H er relationship with McClure goes sour over the span of a few months, undermined by financial issues. They fight about practically everything: the payments for her lectures during the American tour, the reproduction costs of the films of the Children's Houses, the compensation paid by the House of Childhood. To try to resolve at least this last problem, McClure purchases a share of the company and appoints his brother Robert to manage it, but rather than improve the situation, this only makes it worse. Now it's with McClure himself that Maria gets upset, in a constant exchange of letters. She no longer calls him "dear friend" but "Mr. McClure," and starts having her lawyer write to him. She understands that the promoter is concentrated only on the financial aspect of the enterprise and she's afraid of being cheated. "I do not know anything about business, I know, however, that in spite of contracts and lawyers...that ultimately everyone can earn...on my work—while I alone remain with nothing."[14]

McClure, blocked by his creditors, is unable to come to Italy, and in March 1914 he sends his brother. He receives a telegram in which

Maria orders him not to have him come but by then Robert is already on his way. His visit is a disaster from the first day on. The emissary is given a cold welcome. After being forced to wait a long time, he receives from Maria a request to renegotiate all of their agreements. In a letter to his brother, Robert summarizes the situation like this: "If all these conditions were met, she would talk about a training school, but it must be understood that it was *she* who was organizing the class, that it was *her* enterprise, that if we had anything to do with it, it was to be as her agent, everything must be submitted to and approved by her."[15]

As if that were not enough, Maria—who in the meantime has been contacted by other Americans—withdraws her authorization of McClure to represent her. Faced with this dramatic situation, he decides to escape from the control of his creditors and sail secretly for Rome. His wife, exasperated by the psychodrama being acted out on both sides of the ocean, intimates that he should put an end to the collaboration. "How can you revive relations with her? There is no peace for you in connection with her…"[16] In the end, even McClure, the perennial optimist, has to give up. He breaks off all relations with Maria and orders his lawyer to sell her the House of Childhood. Since she does not have enough money to buy the company, the negotiations go on for a long time. They will not come to an end until 1916, when the necessary funds will be supplied by the family of Maria's new American student, Adelia Pyle.

Her correspondence with McClure describes quite well how Maria Montessori experiences those first years of the sudden explosion of her notoriety. Besieged by people who speak a language she doesn't know and who keep pulling on her from all sides, unable to trust anyone, worried by what is being done in her name, she tries to hold it all together—development and control—and she is alone at the center of a court of admirers and businessmen. Her strong, almost indomitable character, which has always got her back on her feet after every difficulty, is the same that now prevents her from entrusting herself to others. "She has command in her blood,"[17] one of her students will say years later.

For a moment she believes that McClure is the right person, but the illusion is short-lived. As always, when she is disappointed, she wastes no time in breaking off all relations. In less than four months, she goes from promises of a lifelong friendship to threatening letters, concluding with a telegram that falls like the blade of a guillotine: "DO NOT DO ANYTHING WITHOUT REGULAR CONTRACTS/FORBID PUBLICATION OF LAST YEAR'S LECTURES."[18]

Reading through these letters reveals all the contrasts that agitate Maria Montessori and all of her contradictions. She is a woman driven by strong idealism, who cannot renounce her research, but who at the same time lets herself be constantly distracted by the financial aspect of the enterprise. She goes back and forth between ideals and ambition, enthusiasm and fatigue, with her nerves always on edge. She abandons herself to the flattery of her admirers, but deep down she trusts no one. Over everything looms her ornery character, recalled even by one of her descendants. "She was a difficult woman, extremely difficult. If a person didn't suit her fancy she could be downright mean."[19] She even wonders herself about her complicated personality: "But why do I act this way—in a way that makes me enemies, makes people detest me, while everyone tries to meet me halfway, to love me, and I feel such a deep and boundless love that I could embrace all of humanity?"[20]

Away from Europe at War

I n the spring of 1914, Maria Montessori organizes a second international training school in Rome. This time it is not held in her home but at Castel Sant'Angelo. The course lasts four months, from March through June, and attracts a hundred or so enrollees, again mostly Americans. The method arouses interest everywhere, but in that moment the United States is the country that shows the most enthusiasm. Many people ask her to come back. Only she can train teachers, and this makes her presence indispensable. Her decision is made easier by the start of the First World War, which breaks out in August 1914. Italy has not yet entered the conflict but could do so at any moment. Mario is sixteen and will soon be of draft age. For Maria the idea is unbearable. Going away and taking her son with her seems like the most effective way of keeping him out of harm's way.

She accepts the invitation of the educational authorities of California, which comes by way of a former student. She entrusts her elderly father to Anna Fedeli and the omnipresent Donna Maraini; a small committee of women who commit themselves to watching over the man everyone calls Grandpa Montessori. On April 11, 1915, she and her son embark in Naples on the *Duca degli Abruzzi*. Awaiting her in New York City, eight days later, she finds two American students, Helen Parkhurst and Adelia Pyle, who will be by her side throughout her entire stay.

She stops in New York to visit the city's Children's Houses and to deliver a lecture, then she leaves for San Francisco on a transcontinental train ride. Maria recounts the ten-day trip to her father in long letters full of details: "There are barbers on the train with their own shops, manicurists, pedicurists, etc. and there are bathrooms and showers. The dining rooms have very large tables because the width of the cars is double that of European trains."[21] Outside the windows, right before her eyes, the landscape rolls by, full of "endless plains, immense as the ocean."[22]

On April 25 she arrives in San Francisco and goes directly from the station to the World's Fair, where a welcome reception has been organized. Then she takes a train for Los Angeles. She doesn't seem weary from the trip, on the contrary: "One surely marvelous thing is that I'm doing better than in Rome, in the sense that I look less ugly and less old than before, and I have the same desire and capacity to *kick up my heels* that I used to have! I run and skip and have the pleasant sensation of feeling 'rejuvenated.'"[23] The American West, so different from the east coast that had been the backdrop for the first tour, intrigues her. The organizers have arranged for first-class treatment. Maria stays in luxury hotels and has her own car and driver, always surrounded by a crowd of admirers. "She is besieged by people who want to meet her and have a chat with her, which they will then conserve like a treasure," one reporter writes. "Fortunately for everyone, she doesn't speak English. The result is that a nod and a smile is all that she can give to visitors, along with a handshake."[24]

Jealous, in Some Ways Fanatical

Oｎe detail is immediately obvious. All of those who, up to this time, worked for the method in America and who organized her first tour are absent. Mabel Bell, the president of the Montessori Educational Association, comes to find out about the trip when it has all been arranged, but she insists on trying to get in touch with Maria. By now, the leaders of the association know the foundress's complicated personality, and many discourage Bell from doing so. One of the association administrators writes to her:

It is going to be very difficult to have any business dealings with a woman of her peculiar disposition. She is undoubtedly a genius and has all the irresponsibilities of a genius, but at the same time she seems to me of a very suspicious nature. I should hate very much to have any business dealings with her, and I should be sorry if you had any with her. We do not talk Italian and all conversations with her must be made through an interpreter. She seems to me to lack the faculty of knowing who her friends are.[25]

Mabel Bell asks for help from Bailey Willis, professor of geology at Stanford, who knows French and can speak to Maria without an interpreter. The detailed report that Willis sends Bell after the meeting describes with great precision all the most evident aspects of Maria's personality: her fears of being bypassed ("She was sincerely anxious about the misuse of her name and the purity of her method"),[26] her peculiar way of conducting herself with others ("She has a way, that might be disconcerting to some people, of remaining silent, contemplating what has just been said, with an absolutely non-committal expression, for so long that you wonder whether she has understood"), her difficulty in feeling comfortable with Americans ("She feels herself a stranger, facing unknown influences, distrustful of would-be friends"), her obsession with control ("She is jealous, somewhat fanatical, independent, and intensely feminine. She demands a loyalty to her ideas, which is perhaps not consciously a demand for loyalty to her person..."). As usual, Maria's charisma makes itself felt. "For myself, I enjoyed it," Willis declares. "The fine presence, the feminine subtlety, the defensive merriment, the deep sense of purpose, the contemplative thought, the quick response to a flash of mutual suggestion, marked her as an infinitely variable personality, with whom discussion was as dangerous as it was fascinating."

Willis sends Mabel Bell the document that Maria had delivered to him, with her conditions for continuing to collaborate. In the text, Maria writes that the association must defend her method from false interpretations and guarantee the integrity of its application, hire legal counsel to study the issues related to the legal defense of her method and the Montessori name, and enlist journalists to manage the image and public relations and business leaders to take care of finances. It stipulates that the schools have to be directed by graduates of one of her training courses and use her method without contamination from other pedagogies and without modification. It reiterates that everything the association does must be approved by her. The association cannot even publish a bulletin, because any bulletin must come from the "Center." And the document specifies that the Center is "the office of Dr. Maria Montessori herself and is the place where the method continues to be developed under her direction and work."[27]

Mabel Bell is profoundly scandalized by Maria's memorandum.

It is throughout so illiberal, so at variance with my conception of all the Montessori idea stands for, that I simply do not know how to go on any further. How can any seeker after Truth say that a method must be held "without additions or modifications"? Montessori herself is reported...as having said "If it is not experimental, it is not my method." Also, in the early days she did not want it called the Montessori Method; she wanted it called the scientific method...Neither she nor any one mind, however wonderful, has the monopoly of scientific ways of doing things. Therefore she could not then have claimed any exclusive property in her principles. All she has the right to claim is the patent right to her apparatus.[28]

New Things, Houses as High as the Sky

O n this second visit to the United States, Maria has her son with her and can allow herself some time to discover the United States. The electricity, the movie theaters, the skyscrapers, the typewriters, it all impresses her and is all recounted in her letters to her father. For a few weeks, Mario tries to keep a diary intended for his grandfather, but the novelties are so numerous that he soon becomes discouraged: "New things, houses as high as the sky, fantastic illuminations, colossal exhibitions, incredible receptions," Maria writes in one letter. "How can he ever write about all this?"[29] The boy is introduced to everyone as a nephew, and he displays an ability to manage his sudden notoriety with ease: "Mario is festive, triumphant, he is the prey of the journalists and the interpreters, who, not being able to approach me, interview him. He puts on a certain air and is not stingy with information. What in the world will he have said?"[30]

Maria is always also accompanied by Adelia Pyle, who, in addition to English, speaks four foreign languages, and is thus perfect as an interpreter. Adelia had already been bowled over by Maria during her training course in Rome, but now she has decided to follow her, devoting her life to her. She considers her a veritable spiritual guide and is thinking of converting to Catholicism. In her memoirs she recounts how, one day during their sojourn in America, Maria reprimands a young girl of color who was to take care of her wardrobe and then, upset by her tears, kisses her hands to excuse herself, a stupefying gesture in Adelia's eyes, "Only a person of profound religious conviction would have done something like that."[31]

After visiting Pasadena and San Diego, Maria settles in Los Angeles, where she inaugurates a training course. She lives with Mario and Adelia in a lovely residential area. She is struck by the large spaces of the city and by the fact that everyone seems to trust one another. Doors and windows are always open, the newspaper and mail are left at the front door. Young couples go walking unaccompanied, something unthinkable in Italy. Mario profits from this open-mindedness and is always surrounded by his mother's young students. One of Maria's letters to her father recounts these days bathed in a golden light, between lessons, picnics on the grass, and young women in bloom. After a lecture and lunch in her honor, the young women, dressed in white, present themselves to her, one by one in an endless procession, to shake her hand and offer her flowers. "Everything around me is covered in roses, carnations. Ecstatic at such a kind display, I fail to notice one thing, that the young beauties, after greeting me, squeeze the hand of Mario, who is behind me!"[32]

On May 24, 1915, the news reaches her that Italy has entered the war. Maria tries to bolster her father by writing him even more letters. She tells him about every detail of her sojourn: an earthquake, the prefabricated houses transported on trucks, the electricity that transforms night into day. She also writes to him about her research, which continues even in America. One day, the neighbors' children come into her yard as they're following a pet animal and stay on, enchanted by her teaching materials, refusing to return home despite their mothers' calls. That's how the women in the neighborhood start to take an interest in her method, convincing Maria to open a small school in her house to involve their children in her educational experiments.

At the beginning of July, Maria moves to San Diego to hold a two-month course. During a break in the lessons, she makes a trip to Mexico, where she attends bullfights and cockfights and is impressed by the Native Americans, majestic figures, who, as she writes to her father, seem as one with their horses. She also tells him about the many invitations she receives to extend her stay in the United States. The one that tempts her most is an invitation to participate in the Panama-Pacific International Exposition in San Francisco to cele-brate the opening of the Panama Canal. Some of the planned events are dedicated specifically to education, and Maria could present a demonstration of her method. She knows that it would be an extraordinary showcase, thanks to the presence of visitors from all over the world. But this would mean prolonging her stay. In her letters to her father, she assesses every angle, including the finances. "In addition to that, I would pocket a nice sum of money, and it would only mean two more months. What to do?"[33] In the end, she decides to accept, after asking for his blessing.

The Glass Classroom

For this extension of her stay, she has to finance everything on her own: print thousands of flyers, pay a manager for the organization, find translators for the various languages, rent a house. She invests the income from her California training courses in the enterprise. "So I'll have my first experience in business," she explains to her father. "If everything goes well, there is hope it will turn into the official dissemination of the method, which would be a colossal thing. If it doesn't go well, I hope to cover my expenses, pocket a reasonable profit, and spend a few months of exciting work in the greatest and most magnificent exposition that the world has ever seen!"[34]

To show the visitors to the fair how things work in a Children's House, she has a classroom built with glass walls. Inside, thirty children—selected from two thousand candidates—work away, absorbed, without noticing the crowd that observes them from the outside. To direct the school, she chooses Helen Parkhurst, who, like Adelia, had attended one of the international courses in Rome.

Maria, who likes to give nicknames to the students closest to her heart, calls her Margherita, and she is very enthusiastic about her. Every now and again she goes to watch her working in the glass class- room. She sits in a corner and observes. One day, while the children are on lunch break, Maria exclaims, "We will go to lunch now, Mar- gherita." Sitting across from her in a restaurant, she looks at her and declares, "You know, when I watched you today, I thought, with that child, if Margherita would just... And you would turn and do exactly what I would have done. It's never happened before. It was marvelous, Margherita, *will* you stay on?"[35]

Margherita accepts with enthusiasm. A primary school teacher with a degree from Columbia University's Teachers College, she has a lot of experience in the field and she also shows herself to be precious for her talents as an organizer. After Maria's break with McClure, she feels the lack of a promoter to take care of the practical part of the movement in the United States. "Money was a crying need and there was really no one to advise her. And we all thought McClure had treated her very badly,"[36] Margherita recalls. Maria has a strange relationship with money. When she has enough, for example, at the end of a course, she spends it without keeping accounts. To celebrate Helen's decision to work for her, she makes her a present of a gold watch adorned with diamonds. If money is scarce, she is gripped by anxiety. Frequently, Helen and Adelia hide the bills that pile up in the house, and then turn them over to the families of the wealthiest students so they will pay them.

Maria alternates moments of great enthusiasm with moments of discouragement, where everything seems uncertain, with no security and no order. But all she needs is a hug from her son and she immedi- ately gets her smile back. "Let's put on perfume and go to Catalina,"[37] she exclaims, laughing, and drags everyone along on an outing to the island off the coast of Los Angeles, on one of those glass-bottom ferries that she enjoys so much. "Then we'd all go over to Catalina in the glass-bottom boat and have a big dinner and Adelia and I would pay," Helen recalls. Neither she nor Adelia receive any compensation for their work, but that doesn't seem to matter. They both have the devotion of the converted.

The glass classroom is a big success. Thousands of foreign visitors line up to see the children at work with the materials and then plan to import the experiment to their home countries. Maria tells her father, "In Argentina there is a little project to establish *a thousand schools!!!* The stuff of madness...they would say in Rome. You're all crazy...they would say in Naples. And it's true. Let's get our heads in order and not fly off the rails, please. If they're roses they'll bloom, but between the seed and the flower there's the finger of God."[38]

A Ball of Fire

At the end of the summer, the news arrives that her father's health has taken a turn for the worse. Maria feels the weight of being so far away, but she doesn't believe she can go home yet. She knows she's going through a delicate phase. In Italy, she no longer has a base of support. In the United States, everything seems possible but not yet achieved. It is a decisive moment, in which everything might suddenly take shape. "It seems like the saturated solution where the crystals are just about to form," she writes to her father, with an image taken from her early days of studying chemistry. "What will happen tomorrow? It seems like this thing is in the hands of God, and I am waiting with trepidation."[39]

Her prayers, every night, are for her father. She tells him that Adelia Pyle, her most devoted student, has taken a vow for his recovery. "When she heard you were ill, she took her precious pin with nine beautiful diamonds and broke it in half, she removed her diamond bracelet with its enormous black pearl, and she put all of this beautiful jewelry away to donate it to an altar; and from that day on neither she nor I have worn any jewelry. This effusion was like a tempest of love that was meant to reach you across the ocean and the desert that separates us."[40]

The tone of her letters is increasingly affectionate. She calls him, "My papa, dear little one, my little papa."[41] Sometimes she reprimands him for not eating right and not following the doctors' orders. "Obey the doctors, scrupulously, be good as though I were there. I'm already counting the days till my return." Sometimes she pines for him as though he were already dead. "I saw with my heart your venerable head on the pillow, and I would have liked to kiss it! I saw your dear hands on the sheets and I would have liked to hold them in mine, and wake you." Above all, she describes her triumphs for him and tries to console him, by recounting how the Montessori method—"your name, my papa"—is getting more and more famous in that faraway land. She signs her letters "Your little girl Maria." She will not see him again. On November 25, 1915, Alessandro Montessori dies in Rome, at age eighty-three, and is buried next to his wife.

Maria leaves from New York a month later, on December 20, together with Mario and Adelia. She has to decide whom to leave in control of the movement in the United States, and her choice falls on Helen Parkhurst. She creates a new American Montessori Association, with herself as president, Helen Parkhurst as legal representative, and the mother of Adelia Pyle as treasurer. This decision throws the association presided over by Mabel Bell into confusion, and a few months later it transforms into a local association concentrated in the area around Washington, DC, under the direction of Mabel Bell and Anne George, and without any relationship to the foundress of the method.

Maria is so enthusiastic about Helen Parkhurst that she gives her a mandate to establish the long-awaited training center in New York, a school that offers regular courses and issues diplomas to teachers, under Maria's remote supervision. This is an important decision, a sign of her great esteem for her American student, and provokes some jealousy among the first circle of her disciples. It is clear to everyone that Helen occupies a special place in her heart.

Their last farewell is very solemn and gives rise to a very curious incident. Helen confesses to being upset by a strange dream she had the night before. She recounts that she had seen a great ball of fire that came down from on high and struck her. Without hesitation, Maria comments, "Margherita, I was that ball of fire."[42] Then, suddenly serious, she puts her hands on her shoulders and says, "Margherita, I will never leave you, but you will leave me." Finally, she looks at a holy card that she keeps in her purse and exclaims in a loud voice, "Saint Anthony, why did you do this to me?" Parkhurst is flabbergasted by this rare display of emotion, so extraordinary for her teacher. Only several years later will she understand the significance of her words.

La Escuela Montessori

In December 1915 Maria Montessori doesn't have much reason to return to Rome. Her father is dead. The city government has forgotten her. The Franciscan nuns have withdrawn their protection. Apart from her old friend Donna Maraini, there is very little by now that binds her to her hometown. The big house in via Principessa Clotilde, which was supposed to be the center of the movement, was restored to its owners when funding to pay the rent dried up. Moreover, returning to Italy still means running the risk of her son being drafted and sent to the front to fight. Maria decides to accept the invitation of Anna Maria Maccheroni to spend Christmas in Barcelona, where her student has moved recently at her request. The outbreak of the war has forced the British Montessorians to cancel the first international course that was to be held in London, and Maria decides to hold it in Spain, a neutral country. As usual, she has no precise plans. This is one of the many transitional moments of her life, in which she waits to see where her destiny will take her. She has done this ever since she was very young: profoundly fatalist and always self-assured. "She faced life differently than most! She saw, I might say, that there is an unknown side of life,"[43] one student says of her.

She steps off the ocean liner in the Spanish port of Algeciras, accompanied by Adelia and Mario. There to welcome her is Anna Maria Maccheroni, whom Helen Parkhurst compares jokingly to Saint John the Baptist, because she always goes ahead to prepare the way of the Lord. After a three-day stop in Madrid, they arrive in Barcelona. Here they attend Christmas Mass and go to a concert. In the concert hall, when the poignant notes of the "Cant del Ocells," a traditional Catalan composition, rise to the rafters, Maria weeps at the thought of her father dying in her absence. Embarrassed, she withdraws precipitously, but soon discovers that the Catalan authorities are as embarrassed as she. At the end of the concert, they crowd around her offering consolation. One of them will write, "She had cried with us, she was completely ours."[44]

Catalonia has been awaiting her for years. The local authorities discovered the method way back in the days of San Lorenzo, attentive as always to pedagogical experiments because of the Catalan revival movement. As often happens, the first initiative is born of an individual, in this case a religious, Father Antonio Casulleras Calvet, a missionary of the congregation of Saint Vincent de Paul, who in 1909 returns from Guatemala with the project of creating nursery schools attached to local churches. When he hears about what Maria Montessori is doing in Rome, he is struck by the similarity of the two projects and asks the Catalan government to look into it.

The municipality appoints a teacher, Juan Palau Vera, to go to Rome. He remains very impressed by the Children's Houses in San Lorenzo and comes back to Barcelona with Maria's book and a set of materials. In March 1914, supported by the Consell d'Investigació Pedagògica, and especially by its secretary, Eladi Homs, he opens the first Children's House inside the Casa Provincial de Maternitat i Expòsits, a large public hospital complex in the city run by nuns, which, since the 1800s, has been a home for street orphans. Left on their own in a large empty room with the material brought from Rome in the center, the children run, shout, and throw everything into disorder. But in the span of a few weeks, the normalization described by Maria sets in, and it is as though the children have been transformed. Soon the first explosions of writing begin to erupt.

Encouraged by this initial success, the Catalan government sends some teachers to Rome to attend the 1914 international training course and issues a formal invitation to Maria to send one of her trusted students to Barcelona. In the spring of 1915, before embarking on her second American voyage, Maria asks Anna Maria Maccheroni to go to Spain.

"I arrived in Barcelona by sea from Genoa," Maccheroni recalls. "They had me visit the Maternitat, where they took in abandoned children. I remember the beautiful building, the wide corridors with their polished floors, the sparkling glass of the electric lightbulbs, the wardrobes full of the children's white bed linens and their little cribs, also white. A baby in each one. There my admiration ended."[45] One look is enough for her to understand that this environment with its immense and cold rooms, full of orphans rescued from the streets, is not the kind of place she needs to create the model school that her mistress is expecting from her. She asks the government to provide her with a structure just for her. She starts with five children and, in the span of a few months, she has a hundred. The Escuela Montessori, attended by the children of the city's upper class, is an immediate success. In the meantime, other Montessori schools are opened by the former students of the training course in Rome.

The Divine Friend of Children

Right from the start, the Catalan experience is a thoroughly blended mixture of method and religion. Anna Maria Maccheroni, who is a fervent Catholic, accepts the proposal of a local priest to apply her teacher's ideas to the teaching of catechism. The results attract the attention of the local Catholic hierarchy, who invite her to a big liturgical congress held in Monserrat, to illustrate the method and involve the confessional schools. Maria Montessori approves, happy to see that someone appreciates the religious aspect of her work, a facet that she, for reasons of political convenience, cannot make explicit in other places.

Years later, speaking of her collaboration with the missionaries of Saint Vincent de Paul, she will say:

> Even though those priests did not know me or know that I was Catholic, and even though in my book I made no direct profession of religious faith, it seemed to them that my method was Catholic in its very substance. The humility and patience

of the teacher, the higher value given to facts over words, the sensory environment as the beginning of psychic life, the silence and calm attained with small children, the freedom to improve oneself left up to the soul of the child, the meticulous care in preventing and correcting all that is wrong or even simple error or tenuous imperfection, the correction of error incorporated in the learning material itself, and the respect for the inner lives of the children, professed with the cult of charity, were all principles of pedagogy that seemed directly emanated from and inspired by Catholicism.[46]

In a short time, the Montessori schools in Barcelona develop a complete Catholic teaching methodology. Specific material is prepared, with a liturgical calendar and an illustrated missal, texts that explain the key moments of the Mass and the mysteries of the breviary, with colored tags and movable schemas that recount the passion and death of Jesus, the "Divine Friend of children."[47] It is all completed by a small chapel, where everything, from the altar to the sacred vessels and furnishings, are child-size. In the school gardens, the children plant grain and grapes, which they harvest themselves and take as offerings for the sacrament of the Eucharist. "Who could reproach the sentiment that animates us? Truly every facet of that little school lived on faith,"[48] Anna Maria Maccheroni recounts. As usual, everything is tested by the reactions of the pupils. "The child must be able to penetrate the supernatural life in his own way," says Maria Montessori. "Even before God, the child must be a child."[49]

This religious fervor is also evident at the international course held in Barcelona in February 1916. Maria hopes to attract some of the applicants to the canceled course in London, and she sends publicity materials about the new course to the British Montessorians. Faced with the explicitly Catholic formulation of the course description—"Fundamentals of scientific pedagogy, teaching in the Children's Houses and in elementary schools up to ten years of age, Catholic religious education"[50]—the British teachers are put off and in the end only five enroll. The course is attended by 185 teacher trainees, for the most part from Catalonia.

Handmaiden in the World

A fter the course in Barcelona, Maria is supposed to deliver a series of lectures in various cities of Catalonia, but at the last minute she cancels them and leaves for a vacation in Majorca with Mario and Adelia, who by now is like a second child for her. In Spain, Adelia decides to become Catholic and she has herself baptized with the name of Mary, in a solemn ceremony held at Montserrat.

Relations with the Catalan Montessorians are not always easy. Here, too, there are arguments and conflicts. True to her imperious character, Maria is annoyed by the decisions of the local administrators. Moreover, she finds it intolerable that in the local teachers colleges her method is taught together with other pedagogies. The government tries to persuade her to establish herself in Barcelona on a permanent basis, offering her a chaired professorship in pedagogy and a seat on the City Council, but she keeps all her options open. In a very explicit letter to an administrator, she emphasizes that everything she does for Catalonia comes more from sentiment than a financial calculus. A course of a few months in London, she explains, brings in sums equivalent to years of work in Barcelona. During one particularly sharp conflict, she reaches the point of resigning from all of her positions and asking that her name be withdrawn from the Catalonian schools, but once again the perseverance of her local admirers wins out. Elsewhere, no one hears about the break, which is very quickly resolved.

The application of her method to Catholic education, as experimented in Catalonia, offers her the chance to attempt to revive her contacts with the pope. Her grave personal crisis, caused by the separation from her son, has been resolved now for some time, and she no longer entertains the idea of starting a lay congregation, but Maria still hopes that the pope will support her method and push Catholic schools to take the road of renewal. For some years now, the Church has been headed by Benedict XV, a pope who has attenuated the Vatican's opposition to modernism, and this makes her confident. She turns to Father Tacchi Venturi, the powerful general secretary of the Society of Jesus, and recounts for him her spiritual evolution:

Perhaps Father Rinaldi has mentioned to you an earlier attempt to form a religious association in 1910. It seemed that there were some difficulties regarding the method that stopped it but I believe instead that it was immaturity that made it die aborning. It is remarkable, however, that *all* those who belonged to it—either died repeating their vows (Signora Ballerini)—or remained absolutely faithful to them, bringing in other proselytes even when there was no way to welcome them. But awaiting the "promise" as the Jews awaited the Messiah.[51]

She tells him that the Handmaidens of the Sacred Heart, the sisters of the Catholic order that as a young woman she thought of joining, still consider her one of them, and they call her "Handmaiden in the World." She knows well that her official image provokes profound distrust in the pope, and she is upset about that: "I don't know by what decree of Providence, our work was to be for years made only of aspirations and love—remaining hidden—as a sentiment remains hidden in the soul, when a person cannot manifest it. And precisely those in which our hopes were placed disowned us and persecuted us! And it was precisely the work that God placed in our hands that kept us from reaching our goal!"

She sends Father Tacchi Venturi some articles that she is writing on religious pedagogy. She reiterates that her faith is strong and that the Catholic hierarchies need not fear her image as a progressive scientist nor the positivist tone of her writings.

If some word, some expression may make one believe the contrary, it is a personal error of mine, an error of exposition owing to the scientific language in which I was educated and trained. (I studied in the most acute era of materialism; my mind was shaped by the doctrines of Darwin. I studied physiology with the famous materialist Moleschott.) That scientific language is like my mother tongue, and some involuntary accents of it are still with me. But who would want to send away a good servant just because she whistles when she says an *s*?[52]

The Advanced Method

In 1916, Maria publishes a new book entitled *L'autoeducazione nelle scuole elementari*, published in English in 1917 in two volumes with the title *The Advanced Montessori Method*, and later in numerous other languages. It adds another important piece to the method, which, however, has still not reached its conclusion. Maria's pedagogy is a work in continuous progress, like a great cathedral, and embraces ever vaster horizons. In these pages, Maria talks about children's rights, something that was still unexplored at the time, and explains that she aspires to a renewed humanity, based on a new principle: the child as a rights holder, rather than as the property of adults. Her dream is that the child will become the engine of history. "What is this work?" she asks, speaking of her method. "It is the first social and human work that we have allowed the child to accomplish in the world. We have seen the works of men and women; well, this is the work of the child."[53]

Her method for elementary schools also remains faithful to the principle of the pupil's activity and practical experience. At the beginning, to introduce numbers, she uses coins, then she moves to figures on sandpaper, as she did with letters. In the end, she works out a system that uses beads arranged in groups of ten on metal wires. This allows the child to visualize the decimal system and then, through assembly, elevation to the second (square) and third power (cube). The decimal system becomes something that can be handled, compared, even spread out on the floor, in long colored rows. As Maria has been explaining all along, learning, for a child, does not mean listening to an adult, but making experiences. The material is what makes it possible to organize knowledge. "The hand touches the evident, and the mind discovers the secret,"[54] she will say one day, with another of her lightning-bolt phrases.

She has a very ritualized way of presenting the learning material. She puts it in front of the child, waiting for him to approach it. She explains in a few words how it works. Then she observes. If some piece of the material does not attract attention, she takes it back to improve it. The brain of the child and its extraordinary power remain her principal objects of study. She talks of the "absorbent mind" to indicate how a child's intellect works, that they learn by living—absorbing reality—starting when, as soon as they are born, they grab onto the vocabulary and syntax of their mother tongue simply by listening to their parents talk as they bend over the crib. "The psychic form of the child is different from that of the adult," she says. "The child inhabits his environment in a relationship different from ours. Adults admire the environment, they can remember it, but the child absorbs it into himself."[55] Yet again, this is an intuition that will be confirmed by the neurosciences decades later, when they study the cerebral plasticity of the child's brain.

Thanks again to observation, she understands that there are privileged moments for learning. This is what she will call the theory of "sensitive periods," phases of growth, which manifest a particular disposition to grasping certain concepts. If they are allowed to pass without taking advantage of them, learning happens anyway, but with more difficulty and with less depth. "A child learns to adjust himself and make acquisitions in his sensitive periods. These are like a beam that lights interiorly or a battery that furnishes energy."[56] She identifies several sensitive periods: sensitivity to movement, to language, to the environment, to a sense of religion.

One of the first such periods to manifest itself, toward the second year of life, is sensitivity to order. At this age, she explains, the child needs order as much as he needs air to breathe, and if it is denied him, he suffers and expresses his frustration by engaging in what adults call a tantrum. This might seem a paradoxical observation, seeing as the current conviction at the time is that children are disorderly by nature. But it is a need so delicate, she admonishes, so easily crushed by the outside environment, that it often goes unobserved. "When an object is out of place, it is a child who perceives it and sets about putting it where it belongs. A child of this age notices a lack of order in the least details which escape the notice of adults and even older children."[57] She recalls a small pupil in the glass classroom in San Francisco, who, every afternoon before going home, put all the chairs back in their place against the wall, exactly where they were placed at the beginning of the lessons. "One day, as he was putting a big chair back in place, he stopped with a dubious look and turned back to place the chair so it was slightly crooked; which, in fact, had been its original position." Yet again, her extraordinary capacity for observation helps her to grasp things that others do not see.

Freedom with Material

$\int$ he will continue to work for a long time on the central elements of the advanced method—math and geometry—and her experiments will lay the groundwork for two books, published in Spanish in 1934: *Psicoartimetica* and *Psicogeometria*. She would like to conclude the trilogy with a final volume—*Psicogrammatica*—but she won't manage to complete it. As her titles indicate, she proposes with these books to use the materials as an aid to mental order: "The material is not meant to teach arithmetical operations, even less so to facilitate or simplify them. The aim is to entertain the mind of the child with exercises that induce him to reason and to search for the proof of the facts presented in an operative and attractive way."[58] She speaks increasingly about education as an aid to personality development. What she wants to demonstrate is not how to teach concepts but how to raise well-balanced individuals, secure in themselves and in harmony with others.

Every time she recalls her beginnings and considers the pedagogies that preceded hers, she is convinced that she has achieved something new and revolutionary. "Pestalozzi gave children freedom without material. Froebel the material without freedom. I gave them freedom with material,"[59] she sums up, citing two great pedagogues from the past. She concentrates very much on the theme of freedom, knowing full well that many accuse her of encouraging anarchy. For her, freedom and the chance to do anything are two very distinct concepts. "My goodness, get on your feet right now,"[60] she shouts one day at the directress of a Children's House, while the children are climbing on top of her. Her ideal is for the child to work in freedom because the idea of what he must and must not do is inside of him, like a fruit born of his sensibility, following that profound transformation that she calls "normalization."

Freedom, she admonishes, must be cultivated with care and patience, day after day, so that it emerges from the pupil's personality. It makes no sense to do what traditional schools do, namely, keep the children submissive and passive for years and then start talking about freedom and self-determination as though they were abstract terms. Once again, she is thinking of a worldview and not only of education: "Sure, it will be hard to obtain freedom in the great social groups as long as children are forced to spend years of their education in situations of constant submission, as happens now in most countries. Their character will be constrained to manifest itself like the behavior of a freed slave in ancient Rome; the character of a free man is something totally different."[61] It is a subtle message, which is not always understood. Maria ends up being attacked by everyone: by the traditionalists, who accuse her of letting the children work with too much freedom, and by the anarchists, who accuse her of channeling freedom into a system that is too rigid.

While she is in Italy in 1916, she takes a copy of her book to the grave of her mother, who was the first to believe in her. She also sends one to the minister of public instruction. She hasn't taught in her home country for a long time, and even her last official post, the one at the Teachers College, is by now uncertain. Periodically, deans and ministers ask her to go back to teaching, on penalty of losing her position. Each time she manages, through the Honorable Bertolini, Donna Maraini's brother-in-law, to buy time, justifying her absences on account of illness or because she's been called to do pedagogical work at the Ministry of Public Instruction, or because she is on indefinite leave of absence. After a long series of delays, her position will be declared lapsed by the authorities at the Teachers College. Her last tie with Italy, her qualification as a university teacher, left inactive for a long time, will be officially declared lapsed by the ministry many years later, in 1929.

For a while, she seems to have established a base in Barcelona, while the war is raging in the rest of Europe. In February 1917, before a Spanish notary, she signs a power of attorney for Anna Fedeli, so that her student can represent her for all financial and property questions in Italy. In October 1918 she accepts the directorship of the local teacher-training center and becomes a member of the Municipal Consell Pedagògico. She returns to Italy often to see her friend Donna Maraini. Now that her children are older, the noblewoman has decided to live openly her homosexuality, which in the past she had been forced to hide. She has taken into her house a young lover and her small children. Her hospitality is legendary. Every day her goddaughter, the oldest child of a Montessori teacher of humble origins, comes to play in the enormous gardens of her villa. A little girl with violet eyes and ruffled hair by the name of Elsa Morante, she will one day become one of Italy's greatest writers.

When Maria returns to Italy, she tries to visit the few Montessori schools that have survived her absence. Even though the government is no longer interested in her method, some of her students still work to keep the flame alive, often while honoring the strong social commitment of San Lorenzo. One teacher opens a Children's House in Naples, where she accepts pupils from the most disadvantaged social classes. From the outset, the children give her puzzled looks because she doesn't shout at them and doesn't distribute slaps in the face like all the other adults they know. "But aren't you going to hit us?" they ask suspiciously. When she has them sit down to their first shared meal, setting the table with care, they refuse to dirty those clean knives and forks and insist on eating with their fingers. Everything for them is new and almost enchanted. "On one of the first days, one little boy showed a lively interest in the lessons on how to ask for things and how to ask for permission. Surprised by the prodigious results obtained by these words, he starts to expect miracles from the things themselves, and says 'please, please' to a closed cupboard door."[62]

The White Cross

D uring the years of the Great War, a wealthy American expatriate in Paris, Mary Cromwell, decides to use the Montessori method with the children of refugees from the lands invaded by the Germans. She informs Maria, who invites her to visit a Children's House in Milan and authorizes her to produce the teaching materials in a workshop in Paris, which employs disabled war veterans. Within just a few months, Mary Cromwell starts working with the children, who are profoundly traumatized by what they have seen: "Their games were always these, put one object on top of another, even the heaviest, and pile them up, as if those children were tormented by the desire to rebuild. Their acts reflected the scenes lived in their destroyed villages."[63]

In the face of the horrors of the war, Maria puts aside her desire for control and thinks up a system for multiplying the Montessori classes for the civilian victims of the conflict. "The idea is to start training small teams of six teachers: one is the chief, one is the secretary, four are the teachers who will teach the children," she writes.

They have special and stable discipline and wear a uniform. Let's suppose there is a team of six Americans who go to France. They go into the simple shelters of the refugee children and they make four classes with a cheery environment, colorful, pleasant. Then they set up a sort of Children's House, with practical living exercises, etc. Each class then welcomes ten Belgian and French women, single women or war widows, and they have them stay there to observe, alienated and silent. Little by little, some of them start to help out, and so it goes; six months later, each of these ten women starts up a class of forty children, and so after six months we will have provided for 1,600 children. The four Americans become supervisors, inspectors, each one overseeing ten classes. Then we start over again and after six more months there are four hundred teachers, forty supervisors, and four inspectors general, who provide for 16,000 children.[64]

There starts to take shape in her mind the idea of an international association to take care of the youngest civilian victims of the war. She believes that psychic wounds need to be treated with the same or greater care than that given to physical wounds, because a child traumatized by war becomes an adult who carries inside him the germs of a future conflict. "What we need to do is institute a White Cross for children, parallel to the Red Cross for soldiers wounded in war," she explains in a letter. "The doctors for nervous disorders and the teachers, specially trained, are to the White Cross what the surgeons and nurses are to the Red Cross, and they would go to provide their services to children."[65]

As always, she knocks on all doors. She asks for help from socialists, physicians, and religious. She knows the best arguments to use for each group. She explains to Augusto Osimo, secretary of the Humanitarian Society of Milan, that they need to listen to the people's cry for help. She tells Giulio Cesare Ferrari, an influential psychiatrist and academic, that in the new association, specialists in nervous disorders would finally be given the prestige they deserve. She suggests to the Jesuit priest Tacchi Venturi that the White Cross could be her opportunity to come out into the open as a Catholic. She knows that the official support of the pope would be fundamental for the success of the enterprise, and to obtain it she is willing to create the association inside the Church. "Let's put this method into the hands of your master. Let's make it so the Lord bears it like a gift of the Eucharist."[66] The pope does not grant his approval and does not go beyond sending his private blessing. The White Cross project is forgotten.

The Teachers College

During the war years she goes frequently to Milan. Augusto Osimo, secretary of the Humanitarian Society, has become a friend by now. The society workshops are the main producer of her teaching materials in Italy, even though all the work is done by artisans and in a relatively disorganized fashion. The secretariat is inundated with letters complaining about stalled orders, shipping errors, and delays. There are a lot of protests because the cost of the materials goes up every year, with the paradoxical consequence that customers place orders at the catalogue price, but by the time they take delivery, the price has been raised.

The Milanese Children's Houses are not under the control of Maria Montessori, who finds the quality of the teaching to be wanting. The teachers themselves admit in their reports that the children's sensorial preparation is not working, normalization is not being achieved, that there is no sign of the explosions of writing that were seen in San Lorenzo. It is the proof that what Maria has been saying all along is right: the material by itself is not sufficient. There has to be a capable teacher, a voice that, as she likes to repeat, knows how to bring out the soul of the child. Working with children, she admonishes, is first and foremost a spiritual undertaking. "I had this intuition; and I believe that it was not the teaching material but this voice of mine calling out to them that awakened the children and pushed them to use the material and to educate themselves."[67]

During this time, Augusto Osimo is her biggest supporter in Italy. Maria also discusses with him her idea for a permanent training center, the recurring dream that has never become reality. "Milan gave me an extraordinary impression of greatness, of nobility, and there, not in Rome, will be the center that I so much desire,"[68] she writes to him. As early as 1911, she authorized him to hold at the Humanitarian Society a brief training course, directed by Teresa Bontempi, inspector of the schools in Switzerland who had attended the course at Villa Montesca. Maria had even chaired the exam commission, but she was not satisfied with the results. In the future, she wants to organize the courses personally and hold them in what Osimo hopes to transform into a permanent Teachers College.

The first course is held between Maria's two American sojourns, in December 1914, organized in a great hurry to take advantage of her presence in Italy. The official course name is Preparation Course for Children's Education According to the Montessori Method. It lasts seven months and is conceived as a true and proper teachers college, where Maria teaches Scientific Pedagogy while the other professors teach subjects such as Hygiene, Pediatric Physiology, Pedagogical Anthropology, Natural History, Physical Education, and Drawing. In addition to the theory courses, there are many hours of internships. Maria starts the lessons but she soon withdraws, taken by other commitments, and asks Anna Maria Maccheroni to take her place. This choice is also destined not to last. She soon decides to send Anna Maria to Spain and replaces her with Anna Fedeli, only to withdraw her as well, to take her with her to the United States. At this point, she sends a new replacement, Lina Olivero. When Osimo, confused by this turnover of the teachers of the method, who by the way cost the Humanitarian Society three times as much as the other teachers in the course, dares to protest, Maria responds that she has an international mission to lead.

The Teachers College remains in operation, with ups and downs, during the war, but without Maria, who again sends Anna Fedeli to Milan with the task of representing her. When Anna comes down with tuberculosis, the situation gets even more complicated. As Osimo's wife describes in a letter: "Signorina Maccheroni is the only one, among the living, whom Montessori believes able to train Montessorian teachers."[69] But during this period, Anna Maria Maccheroni is working in Barcelona. In 1918, the Spanish flu epidemic provokes the cancelation of the course when the Milanese authorities close all schools in the city to limit the spread of the disease.

The Montessori Babes

For the duration of the war, Maria Montessori prefers that her son remain in neutral Spain or, still better, across the Atlantic. For this reason, she accepts a series of invitations to hold training courses in the United States, in a sojourn that attracts less press coverage than her previous tours but lasts longer, from the end of 1916 to the end of 1917. While he is with her in California, Mario falls in love with one of his mother's students. Maria gives her blessing to the marriage, which is arranged in just a few weeks. Family memories even suggest that the young woman was actually chosen by Maria in order to keep her son away from Europe. What is certain is that on December 5, 1917, in San Diego, Mario, who is only nineteen, marries Helen Christy, who is twenty. The young woman's family disapproves of the rushed wedding with a foreigner, and a Catholic to boot. Immediately following the ceremony, the newlyweds leave for a honeymoon in South America, which Maria has established must last until the end of the war. She finances it all herself. By now the income guaranteed by the sales of teaching materials and training courses allows her a life of ease.

In the autumn of 1918, Mario and his wife arrive in Cadiz, on a ship from Panama, and they establish themselves in a large villa in Sarria, in the suburbs of Barcelona. This move confirms Spain's status as a base for the Montessori family. Mario's first children are born here: Marilena in 1919 and Mario Jr. in 1921. When her first grandchild is born, it is Maria who assists her daughter-in-law during the birth, because the midwife arrives late. Years later, she will write some important things on this topic, suggesting that the newborn baby be placed on the mother's belly and that the birth should take place in a calm and dimly lighted environment, yet again anticipating by decades the tenets of natural childbirth. "Why do we pay so little attention to birth, the biggest crisis that life can face?" she writes.

Up to the moment of birth, the baby's growth happens inside a shock-free refuge with a constant temperature; here, he is absolutely at rest, swimming in a liquid element that welcomes and supports him but never changes. Here, not even the least light penetrates nor the least sound. From this dwelling, the baby is brutally projected into the outside air. From darkness and silence, he finds himself in the hard world of humanity. Hard contact with solid objects: the cold hands of adults take him into their care, often without the slightest delicacy. Not to mention the trauma of birth itself, the pressure on the bones, the struggle to get out of the maternal womb. He arrives like a wounded pilgrim from a distant land, weak and exhausted. And in these conditions, what help does he receive? What succor? Everyone takes care of the mother. The doctor checks to see if he's healthy, that he's alive, as though to say, "Fine, you're alive, now take care of yourself."[70]

The birth of her first grandchild consoles her at least in part for the defection of Helen Parkhurst. As Maria had predicted, her student leaves her to create her own pedagogical system, which she calls the Dalton Plan, from the name of the locality where she opens her first school. After this falling out, in 1918, the training center in New York closes as well. Maria loses interest in the United States, where she no longer has an official representative, and the United States loses interest in her. Everything on the other side of the ocean seems to conspire against her method. The first Montessorians have been excluded, the media have moved on to other novelties, the academics are hostile. Attention for Maria Montessori and her ideas fades with a rapidity comparable only to the speed with which it was born. It will not be until the 1950s and the enthusiasm of a Catholic teacher named Nancy McCormick Rambusch that the method makes a comeback in the country.

Helen Parkhurst, always very severe toward her old teacher, will declare herself convinced that the main cause of this failure is Maria's ornery character: "She could explode like a volcano."[71] Maria's first American biographer also points her finger at her personality as well as her rigidity in the application of the method, sustaining that everything about her seemed made to elicit suspicion among the Americans: "[A] woman, a foreigner, and a Catholic. She was at the least an outsider, at the most an anomaly."[72]

Her grandchildren—the Montessori babes, as Maria calls them—compensate her for these failures. Sources of joy and at the same time objects of study, as they grow up they quickly become conscious of the exceptional nature of that imperious woman, their father's emotional center, their mother's bugaboo. Helen will never have an easy relationship with her mother-in-law. For a long time, she will try to resist Maria's pressure that she convert to Catholicism, finally giving in just to obtain a bit of peace.

Everybody ends up giving in with her. One granddaughter recalls, "We never considered Maria Montessori as our 'grandmother.' For us she was the center of the universe: the being that observed, decided, demanded, explained, commanded."[73] At home, everyone walks on tiptoe so as not to disturb her when she's working, and

Maria is always working. At times, she can seem old-fashioned, with her dark dresses and her heavy build, but her mind is sharp as an arrow: "Intellectually, she was a visionary, an inventor like Marconi, Bell, or Edison. Emotionally, she was a woman from a good family of the Victorian age."

Her grandchildren grow up according to the purest Montessori method, free from all physical or mental constriction, observed carefully by this woman who for years has been trying to penetrate the mystery of childhood. "Let [the children] run outside when it's raining, let them remove their shoes when they find a puddle of water; and when the grass of the meadows is damp with dew, let them run on it and trample it with their bare feet; let them rest peacefully when a tree invites them to sleep in its shade; let them shout and laugh when the sun wakes them in the morning..."[74] The Montessori babes soon become bright and cosmopolitan children, accustomed to a large, nomadic family made up of an imperious, queenly grandmother, an Italian father, an American mother, and a sort of aunt, Adelia. Their home is frequented by a host of the most diverse visitors—government functionaries, Hindu holy men, theosophists, Catholic nuns—and, in the entryway, suitcases and trunks are always ready for a new journey.

A Socialist Friend

Every time she leaves home, Maria Montessori takes her son with
her. Ironically, the only country where she can't have him enter
is Italy. Like a lot of other Italians who find themselves abroad
during the war, Mario risks criminal prosecution for not having come
home to fight. She does everything she can to resolve the situation.
She asks for help from Augusto Osimo, who, thanks to his militancy
in the Socialist Party, knows a lot of politicians, first and foremost
among them the member of Parliament Filippo Turati. Faced with
the risk to her son, Maria, usually so fatalistic in adversity, appears
to be very anxious. She tells her friend about her humiliating visits
to the Italian consulate in Barcelona, where she tries in vain to convince the functionaries that Mario was unable to respond to the call
to arms because he suffers from epileptic attacks caused by a fall from
a horse. She wants this to be recognized in official fashion and Mario
to be exempted, but the deputy Italian consul in Barcelona, who is
also a member of the military, seems to be quite indisposed, as does
the Spanish doctor, who insists—to her great indignation—on keeping the young man under observation to assess his epileptic crises.

Maria asks Osimo to intervene with the Italian authorities, and she does not hesitate to propose that he also resort to requesting favors and offering bribes. She herself goes to Rome to meet with friends who still have some political influence. In the end, she manages to make contact with Turati. The archives of the Humanitarian Society conserve some letters in which the founder of the Socialist Party assures Maria that he has taken the case to heart and contacted a high official in the army. He tells her he is sure that Mario will soon be able to see his pending criminal charges erased and obtain an exemption. There are no other details in the archives, but thanks in part to a general amnesty approved by the government in 1919, Mario can soon come back to Italy.

During her stays in Italy, Maria rekindles her discussions with Osimo about a training course to be held at the Teachers College of the Humanitarian Society. In the autumn of 1920, she returns to Milan to give some lectures. She dreams of a permanent center, not only to train teachers, but also to carry on her experimentation. Her method is still not complete, she says again. For the teaching of history, she puts together an ingenious time line, where the pupils can mark down the main political and military events. For the middle schools, she works on a teaching program that is more complex but without losing its Montessori identity, that is, its practicality and the involvement of the students in every activity: "The little ones think with their hands, the middle schoolers think with their feet."[75]

Maria has great ambitions for the Milan training center. She foresees regular courses, with her presence in Milan for four months a year: the first two months to teach the method, the other two devoted to experimentation. She reaches an economic agreement with Osimo: a fixed salary of 29,000 lire, the equivalent of a high-level government administrator, and 50 percent of the students' tuition payments, but only those of foreign students. The financial issue is increasingly important because Mario and his children are her dependents. Maria explains this frankly in a letter to Osimo: "The others in my family are doing relatively well, but without work. And so on my strong shoulders there is more than a little weight."[76]

In May 1921, Osimo is diagnosed with a tumor. Since the two of them have not signed a contract, Maria asks him to formalize their agreement on the production of the teaching materials and the percentages due her. Osimo has the Humanitarian Society send her a contract, but she sends it back to Milan, asking for some changes in the remuneration for each set of materials sold. There will be no more time to talk about it, because Osimo will die in 1923.

In 1925 the Humanitarian Society interrupts its production of the material. At that point, Maria relies exclusively on the company of Ernesto Bassoli and Sons in Mantua, which, after various changes in name and ownership, will give rise in the 1950s to the Gonzagarredi company, still in business today. One of the artisans recalls the first meetings with Maria: "She didn't know how to draw; she was very precise, however, in explaining how she wanted each chair and object. She explained patiently how the solid joints had to be made (of light wood, with easy-to-grip knobs, well polished...) while the carpenters took notes. Later, when it was time to build everything in her absence, they frequently argued with one another, each one claiming to have understood better than the others."[77]

Development Around the World

U p to now, the great if ephemeral explosion of American interest in the method has monopolized Maria Montessori's attention. But in reality the method is also spreading in the rest of the world. It is not easy to follow its development, tied, often by chance, to encounters, visits, individual initiatives. One of the first countries to send school administrators on a visit to Rome is Argentina, strongly tied to Italy because of the massive Italian emigration there. New Zealand also moves early, already in 1912, thanks to the Rome visit of a woman, Miss Newman, a professor at the Auckland Teachers' College, then on a tour of Europe. Australia follows soon after, sending four teachers to the training course in 1913.

It is mostly women who are the driving force of the phenomenon. Russia gets interested in the method thanks to a teacher named Julia Fausek, who opens the first Children's House in Saint Petersburg in 1913, and the next year goes to Rome to see the foundress's work in person. After the Russian Revolution, she manages to keep her Children's House open and to create some others. In 1925, she even obtains funding from the Soviet government for a second trip to visit various Montessori schools in Europe. But soon afterward the dicta-torship forces her to close her classes. Julia Fausek dies in 1942 during the German siege of Leningrad.

In distant countries, Maria relies on the local Montessorians and lets them work autonomously. Sometimes, as in Russia, she lets them hold courses where her students train other students, and she limits her role to signing the final diplomas, in return for payment of some compensation. The situation is quite different in countries where it is possible for her to exercise more direct control. Holland is one such country. Already in 1914, Maria is invited to deliver some lectures in Amsterdam. Three years later, she gives her permission for the creation of a Dutch Montessori Association, strongly supported by the public administration. For a short period, she thinks of opening her permanent training center in Holland: "[O]ur reception here has been sufficiently impressive. University people here being ready to recognize the scientific value of the work. The University of Amster-dam have expressed their wish that the university itself shall be the headquarters of the work that is to be done."[78]

In France, things are more difficult. The first dissemination of the method comes about thanks to the theosophists and continues thanks to the Catholics, and this makes the method suspect in the eyes of the authorities, who consider it too confessional. The first to introduce the Children's Houses in France is a theosophist teacher named Pujol-Ségalas, who attends a training course of Maria's in Rome in 1910 and then a year later opens a private school. Another theosophist, Jeanne Barrière, the daughter of the French ambassa-dor in Rome, does the same. The academics, on the other hand, are not very interested in the method, since Séguin by now is seen as representing an outdated past that has largely been forgotten. In the first postwar years the initiatives are rekindled, thanks above all to Jean-Jacques Bernard, son of the playwright Tristan Bernard, and to his wife Georgette, who will be for a long time close friends of Maria.

In managing the method in the various countries, Maria insists on certain points, particularly the prohibition on blending it with other pedagogies and her personal control over the training of teachers. She knows too well that if the use of her material is not accompanied by the adults' work on themselves and by a different philosophy of life, which sees the child in a new way, its impact will remain limited. She is impatient with those who want simply to import an educational method that is more effective, fast, and successful, without understanding that what she wants to promote is a new vision of humanity.

The child—father of the man, as she likes to repeat, citing the poet William Wordsworth—is always at the center of her reflection, studied and observed as a superior being. If we so often regret that children grow up—she will say in a lecture—it means that there is something about growing up that is wrong. During a training course, she invites the students to sit and work with the learning materials of the associated children's class, noting that adults are clumsy and ridiculous compared to the children. "There is no doubt that our faces are less beautiful and less expressive than they might be. The whole of our personality resembles that of heavy animals who carry their bodies from place to place, who have no other mission than to transport their bodies."[79]

British Pragmatism

E ngland also expresses interest in the method early on, thanks to an Anglican pastor, Bertram Hawker, who, while traveling to Australia in 1912, stops in Rome and is invited by the British ambassador to visit the Children's House for the children of diplomats. Hawker is so impressed that he cancels his voyage to Australia and stays on in Rome to get to know Maria Montessori and study her method more intensely. Upon returning home, he opens a Montessori class in his own home. That same year, Maria's book on the method is translated into English, and the British government appoints a functionary, Edward Holmes, to come to Rome and then make a public report.

As in other countries, there are internal conflicts and splits within the national Montessori Society on the usual issues: training and contamination with other methods. There is no lack of critical voices among British pedagogues, because many of those who are concerned with primary school find the method too rigid on the exclusive use of Montessori materials. Others recall the legacy of Séguin, very much alive in the country's schools for "phrenasthenic" children, and they point out how the principle of physiological education and part of the teaching material are not Maria's but those of the French pedagogue.

British pragmatism resolves things each time, however, and the movement has a relatively smooth history. A London company, Philip & Tacey Ltd., obtains the exclusive rights to build and sell the material. The first training course is held in London in the autumn of 1919 and is a great success. The newspapers cover the event with enthusiasm. The *Times Educational Supplement* publishes accounts of the lectures in installments. Maria Montessori leaves England in January 1920, assigning Anna Maria Maccheroni to stay in London to supervise the development of the movement. Thanks to Maccheroni's presence and the organization of the British Montessorians, who raise sufficient funds, the groundwork is laid for an agreement calling for Maria to hold regular training courses in London.

On the occasion of the first London course, an English journalist, Sheila Radice, publishes a book, *The New Children: Talks with Dr. Maria Montessori*, which makes a great contribution to publicizing Maria's ideas. In the book, Radice describes how important it is to see Maria in action in the classroom. "I've never been able to convince anyone with words," she has the foundress say about the method. "Maybe we need to invent a new form of language to describe this phenomenon. Fortunately, there are the children, who do what they do, and if people don't believe me, all they have to do is visit the schools."[80] Responding to the journalist's questions, Maria tries to be very concrete, but on occasion her spiritual side comes to the fore: "We wait for the successive births of the child's soul. We give him all the possible materials, so that nothing is lacking for the soul that proceeds by attempts, and in the end we see the perfect ability that is achieved, careful not to interrupt the child, so that he can conclude his efforts."[81] To those who say that her approach is too extreme and a break with all that is known about children, she responds with an evangelical image: "If the ways of the Lord do not follow human logic, it is not the fault of the Lord but of the limitations of human logic."[82]

Many English Catholics are attracted by the method. Their headquarters is the convent of the Assumption Sisters in Kensington Square in London, where Maria and Anna Maria Maccheroni are often guests. Maria also holds lectures there for Catholic schoolteachers, sometimes on very specific themes, such as original sin, about which the traditionalists attack her often, suggesting that her ideas on children's natural inclination to knowledge are a denial of Catholic doctrine.

As was the case even during the time of the convent in via Giusti, the Catholic hierarchies look on Maria with suspicion. A sister from the London convent invites Maria to meet the Mother Superior of her order in Paris, to clarify her doctrinal position. Maria is supposed to make a stop in the French capital on her way back to Barcelona, but at the last minute she cancels the meeting, perhaps tired of justifying herself to those who, instead of welcoming her as a prodigal daughter, multiply the difficulties. "It all seems so distant and difficult," she writes to the sister. "It seems that God commands patience. But my heart is still full of faith in ultimate success."[83]

During one of her stays in London, Maria is received at court by King George V and Queen Mary. The only record of the meeting is a photograph conserved in the family archive. In gala dress, with her long white gown and a tiara placed on her head, Maria looks at the camera almost as though she were an empress preparing to visit one of her peers. "She was like a queen," one English student commented. "She made royal entrances."[84]

Between Socialism and Psychoanalysis

The first contacts in Germany and Austria also date back to the time of San Lorenzo. The book on the method is translated into German as early as 1913, and in the same year Maria Montessori signs an agreement with a company in Berlin, Johannes Müller, for the production of her materials. During the course of the First World War, some private experiments are conducted, like that of Ida Hohenemser, a distant cousin of Donna Maraini, who, in 1914, opens a Children's House for workers' children in her apartment near Jena. But it is during the Weimar Republic that things take shape in a more systematic fashion, thanks to Clara Grunwald, a Jewish socialist schoolteacher, who lives her profession as a vocation. Clara persuades the Berlin authorities that the method can be a tool for rebuilding the country after the disaster of the war. In 1919, with a teacher who had attended one of Maria's courses in Rome, she inaugurates a public Children's House in a working-class neighborhood. As a socialist, she considers Maria's ideas not only a great pedagogical discovery but also an instrument of liberation for the children of the proletariat. In 1921 she participates in a training course in London, and from then on she devotes all her energies to the dissemination of the method in Germany.

Clara founds the Deutsche Montessori-Gesellschaft (Dmg), of which she becomes the president, and she immediately encounters an obstacle on the issue of training. She has a lot of enthusiasm and the support of local authorities, but without teachers she can't move forward as fast as she would like. In 1923, she finally manages to organize a first course, with Maria's participation. She plans another for 1925, but this time she does not get authorization. She decides to do it anyway, creating a certain irritation on Maria's part, who, however, is present for the 1926 course. Maria's doubts about the conduct of the movement in Germany continue to grow. She finds the Dmg directed by Clara to be overly socialist and she complains that all the students enrolled in the training course appear to be atheists. It ends up in a fight, with Maria refusing to sign their diplomas and Clara threatening legal action. In the end they come to an agreement, but there is open conflict between the two women.

Typical of her decisive character, Maria takes immediate measures. As Sheila Radice had rightly noted, Maria has a personality that is, to say the least, authoritarian. "The unity of intent and principle that characterized her life and her profession made it difficult to conceive the diversity of opinions, even on basic things, that exists in the world outside of her method."[85] She creates a new association, Vereins Montessori-Pädagogik Deutschland (Vmpd), with some seceding members of the Dmg, herself as honorary president, and a lawyer in Berlin, Herbert Axter, as director. Her choice of members of the Honor Committee appears to indicate an alignment with moderate views: Konrad Adenauer, then mayor of Cologne; Paul Löbe, president of the Reichstag; Thomas Mann, the famous writer. In 1929 a long dispute begins, in which the new association accuses the Dmg of heterodoxy. The quarrel involves all the Montessori schools in the country, whose teachers are called upon to take a position. Clara writes to a friend: "On a personal level, I am bitterly disappointed in her. Her conduct is in deplorable contradiction with her pedagogy. Despite that, her method is right and worthy of being represented. And I will do it!"[86]

The rise of Nazism makes everything more difficult, because the new regime suspends all forms of public funding for the Montessori schools, accused of being havens for Jews and socialists. Clara is not able to work anymore but she continues to teach privately, and becomes part of an underground network that helps persecuted students to emigrate. When her friends offer to help her emigrate while there is still time, she answers that she will go when she has brought to safety the last Jewish child in Germany. In April 1943, the deportation order arrives for her as well. Thanks to her advanced age, she has the right to be registered with the symbol "T" for Theresienstadt. Her students, however, are registered as "O," Ost, that is, for the camps in the East. At the time, news of the Shoah is fragmentary, but everyone knows that Theresienstadt is a less severe camp. Clara asks that her destination be changed, so she can be sent together with her students, directed to Auschwitz. So the children will not be afraid, she tells them that they are going for a train ride. The date of her death is unknown.

The story of the movement in Austria is very similar. Here, too, the central figure is a young Jewish socialist schoolteacher, Lili Roubiczek, who attended the same London training course as Clara. When World War I ends, conditions in Vienna are dramatic and a large part of the population is suffering from hunger. In 1922, Lili opens the first Children's House in one of the capital's poorest neighborhoods. She soon finds herself leading a group of young women working with enthusiasm for the idea of changing the schools and, from there, the condition of the proletariat. They work for free and sleep at the school, living on—one of them recalls—potatoes and cabbage. Lili's spirit of invention is endless. She creates Montessori spaces in department stores, where children can go while their parents shop. She organizes regular meetings with physicians and psychologists to compare their respective knowledge and experience. Maria appreciates her very much and leaves her ample freedom. "I think she was the only one of her students who could experiment and broaden the system," one collaborator recalls. "Lili accompanied her often on her travels, as a catalyst and interpreter. Her dedication to Dr. Montessori at that time was limitless."[87]

When Maria goes on an inspection visit to Vienna, she is very satisfied by what she sees. She allows Lili to hold some training courses. Her only doubt, as in Germany, regards the strong social-ism and atheism of the teachers. What will divide Lili and Maria, however, will be psychoanalysis. Lili is very much attracted by it. In 1931, she begins her training as an analyst, to the great displeasure of Maria, who is contrary to any mixing of her method with other schools of thought. In 1933 Lili has a last exchange with Clara Grun-wald: "Many thanks for your benevolent opinion on my essay that appeared in *Zeitschrift für Psychoanalytische Pädagogik*. The Dotto-ressa did not like it, she was very angry because of my 'mixing' of her pedagogy with psychoanalysis. She wrote me a terribly irate letter and she forbade me from any further 'mixing.' Apparently she prefers to limit herself rather than give up something of her discovery."[88] The Nazi annexation of 1938, which makes the Montessori schools illegal in Austria as well, intervenes to forestall a final break. Lili is forced to emigrate to Palestine and then to the United States, where she continues her involvement with education and psychoanalysis.

Coming Home

I n 1922, Italy too decides to reconsider the situation. The minister of public instruction, Antonino Anile, who knows Maria personally, asks her to carry out an inspection in the Montessori schools. She accepts and writes letters full of enthusiasm to her Italian friends, in which she even imagines a general reform of preschool education in the country according to her method. The Fascist march on Rome, which ushers in the Mussolini government in October, does not interrupt the ongoing process. The new minister of public instruction, Giovanni Gentile, confirms that the method must be given a new start in Italy.

The first direct contact with Mussolini is established by Mario, who, over the years, has become increasingly active in the management of the movement. In the winter of 1923, Mario writes a letter to Mussolini that underlines the contrast between the development of the method abroad and its abandonment in Italy. Mussolini commissions reports from the Italian consulates on the activities of Montessori schools in their respective countries and he is struck by the flattering results of the survey. He realizes that at the time Maria

Montessori is the most celebrated Italian in the world. Having heard that she is currently in Rome, he asks to meet with her. As a young man, Mussolini had been an elementary-school teacher and as a socialist activist he had worked with the Humanitarian Society, so he is familiar with the approach used in the first applications of the method in Italy. The newspapers report the request on Maria's part for a strong man who will help the method take hold in Italy and the response of the head of the government is "I'll do it!"[89]

Mussolini announces that he wants to transform Italian schools according to the Montessori method, but it is obvious from the beginning that few are willing to follow him. "The Montessori method is established and those who don't understand it are ignorant,"[90] he retorts, unperturbed by the resistance of his education officials. He is attracted by the idea of having classes of industrious and disciplined children, as well as by their precocious acquisition of writing and reading, crucial in a country that is still struggling with illiteracy. Maria, for her part, hopes that the moment has finally come for her to return home. She moves from Barcelona to Rome with the family—Mario, Helen, the grandchildren, and the faithful Adelia—and rents a villa in Parioli, one of the capital's most elegant neighborhoods.

She is happy to be back in the city where she grew up, and to show it to her grandchildren: "She took us around in the baby carriage, telling us the stories and legends of every monument, church, or fountain,"[91] one of them recalls. Mario is also happy to rediscover his home, which he left when he was a boy. "He recounted with pleasure that brief Italian 'belle époque,' when, as a dazzling young man, he drove a shiny Lancia Lambda with all the gay accompaniment one can imagine,"[92] one friend remembers. Other private images from that period come down to us from the notes of Elise Herbatschek, an Austrian student who frequently comes to Rome: Maria taking her along to an audience with the pope, delighted to lend her something to wear; Maria reciting poetry aloud; Maria going on holiday with her son and her students. Elise especially remembers a road trip to the Alps, in an Isotta Fraschini luxury car, with long rest stops in the fields for picnics. While Mario and the students amuse themselves, Maria looks on from afar. She has a way all her own of withdrawing into observation, as she does in the classroom with the children. "She sat there in silence. If you approached her, she spoke to you."[93] Elise also writes about a vacation at the seaside in Ostia. As always, Maria remains off on her own, on a beach chair, wrapped in her dark clothes, and she watches them amused as they run on the beach. "In her presence, we all felt like children,"[94] Elise comments. A fervent socialist, she is not enthusiastic about the collaboration with fascism, but she limits herself to commenting: "Mussolini was helping her a lot, and that was enough."

A Hard Year

I n 1924, the Opera Montessori, an agency with public and private funding, is created in Rome to promote the growth of the method. Mussolini donates ten thousand lire from his personal savings. The project includes annual training courses and a journal. The summer of 1924 is a dramatic moment, marked by the assassination of the socialist Member of Parliament, Giacomo Matteotti, and by the so-called Aventine secession of the Italian Communist Party from the Parliament, followed by the special laws, which in the span of a few months install the dictatorship. Maria remains faithful to her policy of not getting involved in politics. Her signature is not among those on the Manifesto of Fascist Intellectuals published by Giovanni Gentile in the Italian newspapers on April 21, 1925, nor on the Manifesto of Anti-Fascist Intellectuals published in response by Benedetto Croce in the daily *Il Mondo* on May 1, 1925, and signed by Giuseppe Montesano. Maria no longer has any contact with her erstwhile lover, nor does Mario, who on the day he left school to go live with Maria broke off all relations with his father.

For Maria, 1925 is a hard year for another, exclusively private, reason. Adelia Pyle abandons her to follow Padre Pio, an Italian Capuchin friar, described by the *vox populi* as the first stigmatized saint since the time of Saint Francis. Adelia hears about Padre Pio after moving to Italy. She knows that he lives in San Giovanni Rotondo, on the Gargano peninsula in Puglia, and that every day he receives hundreds of pilgrims who hike up to his hermitage to see him say Mass and have him hear their confessions. She asks Maria for permission to go down there together with a friend. She sets out on the long journey, by train from Rome to Foggia, then the rest of the way to San Giovanni Rotondo by bus. The minute she finds herself in front of Padre Pio she is overcome with emotion: "I fell to my knees and said, 'Father.' He placed his wounded hand on my head and said, 'My child, stop traveling around. Stay here.'"[95]

Adelia returns home out of loyalty to her teacher, but the memory of Padre Pio stays with her. "There is a saint living in this world and it pains me not to be near him," she tells Maria one day. "I want to go back there, and I would be happy if you came with me!"[96] Maria agrees, curious to see with her own eyes this figure that everyone is talking about. They leave together for San Giovanni Rotondo. They attend Mass said by Padre Pio along with the other pilgrims. Maria takes some pictures as they are about to reboard the bus. Adelia suddenly stops in her tracks and says, "I can't. I feel paralyzed as though someone has nailed my feet to the ground."[97] Maria takes the bus for Rome alone, while her student remains in San Giovanni Rotondo, from where she will never move again. She will become a Franciscan tertiary, open a house for pilgrims, and live at Padre Pio's side until her death in 1968, just a few months before that of her spiritual father.

Maria is deeply hurt by Adelia's desertion. From that moment on, no one in her family has permission to say her name, not even her grandchildren, who have grown up thinking of Adelia as their aunt, and not Maria's American daughter-in-law, who loved speaking her mother tongue with Adelia. The name of Adelia becomes a forbidden name, just like the name Giuseppe.

Within the family, as always, what Maria says goes. Her grandchildren remember her as the center of everything, an imperious personality nonetheless capable of sudden playfulness and great tenderness. She is a captivating presence, with a contagious laugh, who loves good food, crime novels, and the movies. If she likes a movie, she is capable of remaining in the theater an entire afternoon, watching it three times in a row.

Curious about everything, she loves sharing her discoveries with her grandchildren. "When in her reading she discovered interesting ideas and arguments she would tell us about them, commenting and explaining."[98] She loves playing solitaire, concluding the game quickly, while talking constantly with the family, enveloped by the smoke from her ever-present cigarette. If she plays cards together with everybody, however, they'd better let her win. They all know her difficult personality, which can lead to sudden angry explosions. Mario always makes excuses for her, explaining to his children that their grandmother is a genius, and thus different from other people. Maria's relations with her daughter-in-law are particularly stormy, and that is no help to Mario's perennially troubled marriage.

Bombastic Pronouncements,
Covert Impediments

On the Italian front, collaboration with the Fascist regime is complicated. Maria spends a large part of her time abroad, holding training courses and lectures, and this does not help her keep an eye on the Opera Montessori, undermined by internal rivalries, and the development of Montessori schools, impeded by ministerial functionaries. On February 21, 1926, the first national training course opens in Italy. This occasion, too, is marked by dissidence and polemics, which seem to presage what will be the tone of the decade of collaboration with the regime: bombastic pronouncements from on high, covert impediments from below, and in the end nothing to show for it.

When Maria is offered an honorary membership in the Fascist Party, she is quite perturbed because she does not like being associated with any political movement. When asked about this topic, she repeats that the only party that interests her is the children's party. Beyond that, she is quite aware that, despite Mussolini's proclamations, the Italian school system is not doing anything to welcome her method. She begins to lose hope. In 1927 she decides to move the family back to Barcelona. It is her way of expressing her dissent, but it is also a decision that leaves the field open to her enemies.

Her disappointment also extends to the Catholic Church. For some time, she hoped that her return to Italy could put her in a good light with the Catholic hierarchy. She cultivated relationships with influential religious, multiplying her declarations of Catholic orthodoxy. "Whatever errors are recognized," she writes to one of them, "I am ready to correct them, because I believe that the whole truth is in the truths of the Church."[99] She publishes her most openly religious books: *The Child in the Church*, *The Life of Christ*, and *The Holy Mass Explained to Children*. But all of this does not procure for her the support that she expects. As always, she is walking the tricky dividing line between her personal faith and her great intellectual freedom, ending up being suspect to everybody. "The religious people condemned her for her positivism; the positivists condemned her for her use of a religious language,"[100] she will say to Mario one day.

In 1929 Pope Pius XI issues an encyclical in which he criticizes scholastic innovators, accusing them of pedagogic naturalism, and reasserts that children are to be corrected in their disorders and passions, if necessary, also with severity. Maria feels targeted, and she responds in the journal of the Opera with an article in which she comments on the unrelenting desire of adults to punish and control children. From this moment on, there are no more attempts on her part to win over the Catholic hierarchy. Family memories even speak of an openly anticlerical period in which Maria vents in private, accusing the Church of keeping the faithful in ignorance. What's certain is that we know of no public declarations of hers against the Church, and that her faith survives even this umpteenth disappointment, becoming, if possible, even more discreet.

Things don't go any better with the Italian academics, who make war on her. Her biggest enemy is Giuseppe Lombardo Radice, a powerful advisor to Minister Gentile, who opposes her in every way. He accuses her of failing to acknowledge how much she owes for her teaching materials to her French masters, and—in a clear provocation—speaks of an "Itard-Séguin-Frères method of the Charité-Bourneville-Montessori."[101] He criticizes the fanatical bent that the method often takes on in the hands of her students, suggesting that the idea of the practical living exercises was taken from the approach of the Agazzi sisters. The list of his accusations could go on and on. In a note written curiously in the third person, Maria comments: "It must be observed that L.R. and M. are not 'adversaries.' Adversaries are those who fight against each other. Here, instead, the fight is only by one side: it is the attack without response, the attack that still fails to awaken the defense."[102] She concludes: "The attacker is a person who occupies a well-paid post, a socially secure position, an important academic chair, and who wields excessive power; the person attacked has no post, never had anything from her country and chose exile, even though her work shines throughout the world as one of the most illustrious Italian works of our times."

Her relationship with Mussolini nevertheless remains cordial, as demonstrated by the letters conserved in the national archives in Rome. Maria addresses the dictator with great confidence. In 1928, she writes: "I have only a few years left of effective energy; and only your protection can make it so that my remaining energies succeed in completing the design, which surely Divine Providence has outlined, to help the men in the children of the whole world; and he placed it, Excellency, before you so that it might have the radiant center of His race, of which you are the Savior."[103]

This leaves the field open to the opposition of the bureaucrats. The work of Maria's enemies is facilitated by the succession of eight different ministers of public instruction in ten years. Every initiative is conducted in chaos and disorganization. Even the creation of a permanent teacher-training center—her never-abandoned dream— turns out to be a failure. The institute, called the Regia Scuola Magistrale di Metodo Montessori (Royal Teachers College of the

Montessori Method), is inaugurated in January 1928 and situated temporarily in a school, pending the construction of a permanent site. The structure will never be built. Maria will soon be forced to recognize the obvious: the institute is not supported by the Ministry of Public Instruction and struggles to get off the ground, amid the resistance of bureaucrats, internal power struggles, and lack of funding.

Montessorism Without Montessori

To make things worse, in 1930 the appointment of a new president of the Opera Montessori falls to Emilio Bodrero, a Fascist zealot who has no sympathy for the foundress. The conflict does not take long to erupt. Maria reprimands Bodrero for collaborating abroad with Montessori associations that she does not recognize. For his part, he takes every chance he gets to speak badly to Mussolini of this woman who, with her cosmopolitan life and her libertarian view of children, corresponds so little to Fascist ideals.

In 1932 Maria accepts an invitation to go to Geneva to participate in the meetings of the International Bureau of Education. She gives a lecture entitled "Education and Peace," in which she describes humanity as a child lost in a forest at night. She repeats that the only cure is to start from education. Asked by Mussolini for an opinion on the lecture, Bodrero comments with a long critical report in which he emphasizes how Maria's words in defense of peace among peoples contrast with the virile and bellicose vision proposed by fascism.

In July 1932, Maria's enemies score an important victory. Giuliana Sorge, her student and directress of the Royal School of the

Montessori Method, is accused by some colleagues of having pronounced a phrase critical of Mussolini and is suspended from her post. Sorge hurriedly sends a long letter to the Duce to confirm her adherence to fascism. Mussolini intervenes to reinstate her as a public school teacher but she is transferred to a traditional school in Milan. Maria needs to choose a new director. She proposes another trusted collaborator, Adele Costa Gnocchi, and takes the opportunity to request the renewal of the entire teaching staff, whom she considers inadequate. The minister of public instruction stalls for time, commissioning an internal inquest, and then lets Maria's request and the candidacy of Costa Gnocchi drop, naming in her place a male professor who has no relationship with the movement.

A director of the Royal School the Montessori Method who does not have a diploma in Montessorian training, a president of the Opera who detests the foundress. It is clear that Maria's enemies are doing all they can to sabotage her Italian experiment. The Italian State Archive conserves a memorandum from 1932, in which some functionaries, worried about the foundress's lack of Fascist faith, write: "Since any solution proposed by Montessori cannot guarantee the loyalty of the school, it is necessary that we have the courage to transform the Montessori School into a 'Montessori-type' school, thus eliminating the doctor herself. In other words, Montessorism without Montessori."[104]

As far as she is concerned, Maria has already made a number of concessions to the regime. For example, she has accepted the offering of a course in Fascist culture at the Royal School of the Montessori Method. And in a 1931 letter to Bodrero, with a copy to Mussolini, she had written of "connecting the principles of the Montessori method to the directives of the Fascist regime, especially to its directives in the field of education and organization of the Balilla youth corps."[105] After explaining all of the advantages of the method, from force of character to perfect discipline, she concludes, "In sum, my method can collaborate with fascism so that it will realize the possibilities to construct great spiritual energies; create a real mental hygiene that, when applied to our race, can enhance its enormous powers that—I am certain—outstrip the powers of all the other races." Realizing the uselessness of all her efforts, she returns to Italy less and less willingly. She would like to resign from the Opera Montessori, but Mario persuades her to wait and to write again to Mussolini, asking for his intervention.

The Break with Fascism

■

S olicited by Maria to intervene, Mussolini asks Emilio Bodrero to report to him in writing. In his report, Bodrero admits that Maria is right when she complains that, after Giuliana Sorge's dismissal from the Royal School of the Montessori Method, her requests for the directorship and the teaching faculty were not approved. As to the other reason for his conflict with the foundress—Bodrero's relationships in various countries with what Maria calls "unauthorized Montessori associations"—he justifies himself by saying that they are powerful, and that in many cases the break between the foundress and the association managers did not come about over questions of method but because of personal conflicts.

When Maria reads the report, she feels slandered and immediately resigns. "Mr. President of the Opera Montessori, I have taken cognizance of the letter written by you to S. E. Chiavolini and copied to the Head of Government. It contains insinuations and false statements against me, such as to render incompatible my adherence to a way of working plainly damaging to the Opera Montessori and to me personally. With this letter, I declare, therefore, my withdrawal from the Montessori agency which you direct."[106] The letter is dated January 15, 1933. After ten years of collaboration with the regime, Maria resigns, with one of her sudden changes of course, described so well by the journalist Sheila Radice: "Dr. Montessori lives intuitively. I have heard her say that, just as children follow, unconsciously, the path that will lead them to speaking, to writing, to reading, so she herself acts, not knowing whither her actions tend."[107]

From that moment, the secret police put her under surveillance, but—apart from malign observations regarding her millionaire fortune—the police fail to find any evidence of antifascism. In 1934 Maria is again in Italy to attend an international Montessori convention held in Rome. As she is giving her speech, she is booed by some members of the Guf, the Fascist university student group, present in the audience. One observer comments on the incident with obvious satisfaction: "Montessori shortly thereafter hurriedly ended her speech and her son, announcing the next lecture of the convention (first in English, then in French, then in German, and finally, as an afterthought, in Italian), added these strange words: *if they don't disturb us.*"[108] This same Fascist intellectual writes a series of malicious articles in which he writes above all about the economic aspect of the movement and defines the method as an "abundant gold mine."[109]

In 1936 the Opera Montessori and the Royal School of the Montessori Method are closed, as are the schools which apply the method. The collaboration with fascism concludes in failure. Maria is, as always, fatalistic, and comments on the situation to her son like this: "God used the only method he had to make us understand that we have worked enough here and that he needs us elsewhere."[110]

The break with fascism coincides with a financially difficult moment for the family. In January 1933, Filippo Del Giudice, the lawyer charged with managing the family's wealth, flees abroad, leaving behind an enormous financial disaster and all of his clients ruined. He was a close friend of Mario's, to the point of having served as the godfather at the baptism of one of his children. In addition to the

Montessoris' money, he also looked after the holdings of many professionals in Rome and some Catholic religious orders. His story will have some curious twists and turns, because Del Giudice will land in London, where he will become an important movie producer, but the lost money will never be repaid.

The financial failure of her business lawyer is only the first of a series of setbacks in the 1930s that will destroy Maria's financial holdings. The Spanish Civil War in 1936 and then the Nazi property seizures in Holland during the Second World War will end up swallowing the rest of her wealth, bringing her back, in a certain sense, to the purity of her origins. The last phase of her life begins, the one in which she finds herself alone again, a wanderer and dependent on the economic aid of her admirers, just as she was at the beginning of her adventure. Organizationally, she gradually gives up more and more of the leadership of the movement to her son, while she prefers to concentrate on the development of the method, which she manages to take to ever higher levels, turning it into a proper philosophy of humanity.

PART FIVE

Cosmic Education

(1934-1952)

If I hadn't had the certainty that man
could be improved, I wouldn't have had the
strength to fight for fifty years, starting over
again and again the work that others had
destroyed. I wouldn't have the strength, at
my age, to go on traveling the world,
preaching this truth.[1]

The AMI and Mario's Rise

I n the years following the First World War, Maria Montessori is not the only one working to change the schools. After the horrors of the conflict, there is increasing debate and frequent appeals are made to the idea of a "new education." In 1921 an international congress on this theme is held in Calais, France, during which the New Education Fellowship (NEF) is founded. Maria is among the first to be invited to the congress but she declines the offer. At first, she delegates Mary Cromwell, who lives in France, to represent her, and then Anna Maria Maccheroni, and finally an English Montessori official, who delivers a lecture on the method. A complete set of teaching materials is displayed in the exhibition hall. The congress participants volunteer to play the role of children in a reenactment of a Children's House. One of them comments, enthusiastically, "We are all Montessorians."[2]

In reality, Maria is not interested in having her movement be absorbed into a larger framework. Her independent character, like her decision to create a system with patented materials and in-house training, help her to remain distinct from the other innovators.

Unlike her, all those who participate in the work of the new association are more or less forgotten today, while the name Montessori has passed the test of time. For a few years, Maria follows the work of the NEF as an observer, but in 1929, during an NEF congress in Denmark, she founds the Association Montessori Internationale (AMI).

The AMI's first headquarters is in Rome, then in 1932, as the break with fascism is developing, it moves to Berlin, then to Barcelona, and finally to Amsterdam, where it remains today. Maria is the president, but she relies more and more on her son, named director general, to handle the practical aspects of the movement, such as the production of materials, the coordination of national groups, and the organization of training courses. She devotes herself primarily to research. "She was always at work on some new idea. If she was left alone for a few minutes she would be found intent on testing some new teaching material," one student says. Another recalls that, while she was with her at a movie theater, Maria whispered to her that she had had a new idea for visualizing the Pythagorean theorem with the children.

In a movement that is almost entirely female, Mario is one of the few men at the top. The Romanian Montessorian Ilie Sulea Firu, speaking about the 1931 international course in Rome, recalls "A sea of women students from all over Europe and only three men, Lazar Popp, Romanian like myself, Arturo Piga, the envoy of the University of Chile, and myself; we were like three goats in a herd of sheep. Maria Montessori always spoke as though there were only women present. So Mario, her son, came over to sit with us."[3]

Mario, who was once an abandoned and traumatized boy with a difficult family history, has become a cheerful and exuberant man who has a lot of success with women. "He had a great need to be loved, perhaps dating back to his childhood,"[4] one of Maria's students recalls. "Perhaps because of an unsatisfied childhood need." Things must not have been easy for Mario. As a young man, he dreamed of becoming a professional athlete. He especially loved boxing, but very soon the Montessori movement occupied all of the space. Introduced as "the nephew and secretary of the Dottoressa,"[5] for years he had a subordinate role. People spoke or wrote to him when they were unable to get to his mother. Or when they had to get around the difficult character of the foundress, who could fly off the handle for nothing. There are lots of anecdotes illustrating this facet of Maria's personality. One day, during one of her lectures, she gets the impression that the interpreter is not reporting her words exactly and she starts beating her feet on the floor, shouting, "No! No!" Another time, when a room-service waiter interrupts her while she is working in her hotel room, she goes into a huff, knocking the tray full of food on the floor. In these cases Mario is the only one who can calm her down.

There are those who have wanted to see him as the prime mover of Maria's work. "Because of one child, she helped all children,"[6] said one religious who supported her in the dramatic years of her separation from Mario. To be sure, it can't be ruled out that her personal experience had an influence on her pedagogical reflections. It has been noted by many that considering a child's development as the realization of his innate capacities rather than as the effect of adult intervention may have been reassuring for a woman who had missed the first fifteen years of life of her only son.

One of his daughters describes Mario as a character from a novel. "He loved the wind, storms, and the sea. He loved the struggle of the elements. He loved horseback riding, rowing, and swimming. Always impeccably dressed, he loved well-tailored clothes. He loved to make extravagant gifts: never just one rose, at least sixty! He loved food, loved to cook, loved to drink and smoke. He loved beautiful women, music, and song."[7] One student of Maria's talks about his playful exuberance during the practical demonstrations of training courses. "Seeing Mario work with the children was something really strange, he seemed like anything but a Montessorian!"[8] She remembers him as he handled the sandpaper numbers, completely ignoring the Montessorian three-period lesson, hiding them behind his back, then mixing them all up to invite the children to see what happens. "He played with them. When he did it, nothing was said, if I had done it she would have excommunicated me!"

Mario has a hearty laugh and a great sense of humor, exactly like Maria. Speaking about a course held in Rome, he comments wryly:

> Giovanni Gentile, the minister of education, read a noble and cultivated speech before an audience that included the entire diplomatic corps. When it was Maria Montessori's turn, she delivered a splendid lecture, turning page after page of a pile of papers that she had urgently asked an assistant to bring her. When she had finished, the famous philosopher congratulated her warmly and stretched out his hand to take the pages left on the lectern. We all noted the amazed expression that came over his face: the pages were all blank! Later on, my mother said, jokingly, "Everyone reads their speeches. I wanted to cut a nice figure, too, and do as they had done!"[9]

The two of them are always together, as alike as two drops of water, cheerful, profoundly complicit. "Mario and I hold each other tight," Maria writes in a letter to Donna Maraini, and perhaps no other expression better describes their life together, ever since that long-ago day in February 1913 when she went to Arezzo to take him back, against everything and everyone.

Among the Peoples

I n the 1930s, Maria Montessori lives the life of a nomad. "How I long to stay put! A conclusion to this work! But it may never be given to me. Maybe my life's work will be a 'flight' among the peoples of the world!,"[10] she writes to Donna Maraini. She travels constantly to give training courses, moving around the countries of Europe with the regularity of a metronome. Every time she attracts crowds of students, often quite colorful. In 1934, after attending a course in Nice, one student commented:

> The sweetest things about the course were the various episodes: a seminarian from Paris who sleeps in a garage because he has no money; two girls whose grandmother had left them a small annuity bond for when they would marry, and they sold it to pay for the course, and they have no one in the world to help them! And on and on, for lots of people come from far away and who eat only once a day! But there was also an amusing English group, that is, an entire family. There are ten of them, their father has enrolled them all, including

two teachers because he's going to open his own Montessori school on a big estate of his.[11]

Tirelessly, she uses her lessons to illustrate her ideas, which are always centered on the child and his needs. She repeats that every activity must be born of the child's will and from the child's curiosity, never imposed from outside, not even with tender and seductive means. This is the only way the child will truly learn, without ever getting enough of it: "Work without interest—forced labor—is extremely tiring, and so is inactivity."[12] She also explains that children do not do things for a utilitarian motive but for the pleasure of doing them. She likes to recall the anecdote about the directress of a Montessori school, who is curiously observing a little boy bent over a page of a story about a Greek myth. She is convinced that he must be absorbed in some sort of complex thought, until the boy raises his head with a big smile on his face and says, "I found 26 adjectives on just one page."[13]

By now, her vision is clear and it leads her to sustain the necessity of radically rethinking the relationships between the generations. For millennia, adults have been enacting a struggle against children, in a systematic oppression that they have given the name of education. It is time to move on to something new: "What is necessary is to transform the adult soul. To modify adults and their relationships with children. And having done that, we will have made the children's happiness, we will have learned from them something that they cannot teach us unless we leave them free to teach it to us, the way of the kingdom of heaven. Peace, the resurgence of our hearts, the resolution of the problems that bring sadness to our souls, the solutions that elevate it to greater heights, the triumph of the spiritual life over the material life."[14]

Whenever she can she stops off in Spain to see her grandchildren, who are growing up in Barcelona with their mother, since Mario is always traveling with Maria. The Montessori babes have become four, with the birth of a baby boy, Rolando, in 1925, and a baby girl, Renilde, in 1929. After her break with fascism, Maria makes the Catalan city her base again, and for several years the local movement reflourishes, with an international Montessori course, a Montessori review, a Montessori museum. In October 1935, Maria opens an experimental class in her home to test out her methods for middle-school children. A sitting room is transformed into a laboratory where ideas and materials are tried out on a daily basis. She has the help of a new student who has come from Italy, Maria Antonietta Paolini, whom Maria calls Pao.

In the summer of 1936, the outbreak of the civil war brings the Spanish parenthesis to an end. Mario is in England preparing a congress to be held in Oxford, and he reports the family news like this:

Tanks driven by the loyalist militia were running through the streets, arresting people who were supporters of Franco. Being Catholic and Italian only increased the danger. A tank stopped in front of the door to our house. The armed *milicianos* inside it looked very attentively at our house. As my oldest boy told me later, their mother drew back from the window and called the children together. "One day," she said to them calmly, "we all have to die. Some sooner, some later. Now let's pray to God and let's ask Him to lead us where we have to go." Then they heard the sound of the tank driving away. My son went downstairs to the ground floor and cautiously looked outside the front door. The men had gone away, but they had left a note: a script in red with these words: "Respect this house, it belongs to a friend of children." It was signed with the Communist emblem: the hammer and sickle.[15]

The British Montessorians arrange passage for Maria on a navy ship. The grandchildren remain in Spain with their mother. They manage to embark a year later on an Italian ship, while Helen, by now divorced from Mario, stays in Spain. The children go to Genoa and leave from there for London. They are accompanied by Pao, who once again leaves everything to follow Maria, continuing her life as a "happy gypsy."[16] After the Second World War, she will be the leader of the Montessori Center in Perugia and will live the rest of her life in the memory of her teacher. In her final years, she would show her visitors Maria's letters, conserved as relics in a little wooden box: "This is my great treasure. When I am in a bad mood or there is something getting me down, what do I do? I open it and I say: let's see what she says to me today. I have a constant conversation with her, I talk to her and I feel her hand in mine."[17]

Children of the Earth

After the congress in Oxford, Maria Montessori accepts an invitation from a Dutch student, Ada Pierson, for what at the outset appears to be a temporary arrangement. The daughter of a very wealthy man, Ada Pierson makes available to Maria a huge villa in Baarn, then a house in Laren. Maria moves to Holland with her family and with Pao, who recalls: "We were refugees but the Dottoressa, despite the precariousness of the situation and her age, didn't lose her enthusiasm and the courage to start over from the beginning."[18] She latches on yet again to the idea of a permanent center and asks her student to create a model school. In the evening, she asks for an account of her day. "She wouldn't ask me, 'What did you do today?,' she asked me, 'What did you see today?' It's a marvelous philosophy, I always felt it to be a religion, and with her we talked about our mission."[19]

In Laren, Maria keeps developing her method, turning her attention to the adolescent age group, the group she calls *Erdkinder*, a German term that can be translated as Children of the Earth. She has groups of adolescents work in her house and in some experimental classes. She seeks out the real adolescents, beyond the projections of adults. She says once again that it is difficult to study them in school or in the family, where the environment doesn't let them emerge, but, on the contrary, deforms them; the family by crushing them with prohibitions and misunderstandings, the school by preparing them only for work and humiliating them with rules. "At fourteen, at sixteen, the kids are still subject to the small-minded blackmail of the 'bad grade' with which their teachers weigh their work," she says. "It's a method analogous to the one with which inanimate objects are weighed, with the mechanical mechanism of a scale. The work is 'measured' as though it were lifeless matter, and not evaluated as a product of living."[20]

With this approach, she explains, what comes out of schools are not balanced adults but "psychic dwarves."[21] For teenagers, work in class should be shared between teachers and students. Her proposal is for a single secondary school, where all fields of knowledge are brought together, and studied full time, possibly with internships, because adolescence is the age of community living. Everything—sciences and humanities—must be part of a grandiose vision of creation, because adolescents love epic enterprises. The schools have to concern themselves with the development of their personalities, more than preparation for a profession. And it must be remembered that adolescence is a new birth: "Kids from twelve to fifteen are to be considered as 'newborns' of the adult epoch; they are entering, by their very nature, into the social life of men and women. A delicate age, full of surprises."[22] She dreams of rural schools, where teenagers can grow in contact with nature, work in a sort of big, self-managed collective farm, under the supervision of their teachers, and sell the products of the land, always accompanying manual labor with intellectual labor.

In extending her method to the age of adolescence, she is following the growth of her grandchildren. When they were born, she turned her attention to the first months of life, at a time when nobody

talked about neonatal life. Now that they are growing, her attention
turns to the passage from childhood to adulthood. She spends a lot
of time observing them. She reads with them: Dante, her great passion; the Bible; the *Iliad*; the memoirs of famous explorers. When the
kids exchange comments in Dutch, she protests, "Don't go speaking
Turkish around me!"[23]

Even though she is almost seventy by now, she has not lost her
energy or her curiosity. A letter to Donna Maraini recounts her discovery of the long Laren winter. Under the power of her expressive
pen, the great unknown North unfolds slowly as in a fairy tale.

Eighteen degrees below zero! I find myself here in this small,
isolated place. In this same little house of glass and wooden
beams, in this moment all surrounded by snow that is burying
everything little by little. This intense cold that I had never
felt so acutely, is interesting; and the consequences it produces
are all new to me. For example, I had put a basket of little
round potatoes in a grotto exposed to the cold, and my ears
start to hear the sound of stones pelting the ground. It was the
two Marios, father and son, who were throwing on the ground
those potatoes that had turned into little rocks. Then they
brought me an onion, which looked fresh, but only a knife
pounded by a hammer could cut it. What strange events! Did
you know about such petrification? This morning we came
across a true stalactite: the water dripping out of the faucets
had formed little columns of limpid ice. When we washed
ourselves, the water wouldn't go down the drain because the
drainpipes were blocked by ice. You can't imagine the festivity
and joy that these things bring to young people. The schools,
even the high schools, take a half day off to give the kids a
chance to go skating on the big river in Amsterdam, the Am-
stel (you remember the one that ran past your hotel?). People
drive their automobiles on the waters of the Zuiderzee, the sea,

that is, and they go out to the islands that have now formed
a single continent. Anyone who can has flooded their yards
and tennis courts so they can go ice skating. Everyone is out
spinning and dancing on the ice. They no longer wear hats
but soft woolen hoods; leather berets that cover their ears.
Mariuchino [Mario Jr.] still goes by bicycle from our village,
Laren, to the nearby village of Baarn, where the high school
is, and he goes happily on his way in defiance of the snow.
Even big Mario keeps up his daily car trips between Utrecht
and Amsterdam. What silence, despite so much movement.
And even I, the old lady, have kept holding my lessons in
Laren and Amsterdam. Yesterday was my last lesson before
the Christmas vacation. A woolen hood, a fur coat, blankets,
and hot water bottles in the automobile. On the road, I went
by countless sleds of young people, and I saw the dances in the
artificially frozen fields. Now I am on holiday. In our school
in Laren all the radiators blew up and the children have all
been left working around coal stoves; but nobody is missing
at school.[24]

The Great Vision

W ith the passage of time, the breadth of her vision continues to expand. It's not just a matter of the schools but society as well, and then the world. If her attempts at collaboration with the Catalan and Italian authorities have failed, it means that she needs to look beyond any single government, to open up her gaze to the entire planet. In 1934, at the moment when she is breaking with the Mussolini regime, she writes to a student:

> This work was before me for twenty-five years without my seeing its expansion, that is, its social goal for all of humanity. Do I seem mysterious to you? Or visionary? Surely not. You are one of those who understands. Do you remember when we parted in France? You believed that you had done what you needed to do and you split off from the group. Well, it was in Combloux, the great passage from the "school" to "society": the great vision. After that, everything broke open in Rome, like shards of an eggshell out of which came a life destined to fly high, to escape into space. That's how it is.[25]

She is always open to new relationships with all kinds of very different people, from Clarence Gasque, Zoroastrian and militant vegetarian, to Inayat Khan, Indian musician and mystic, founder of the international Sufi movement. These are the years in which she starts to evoke the concept of cosmic education—to educate people to a grand holistic vision, where every person is bound to all others and to the entire planet—which she will develop in the last phase of her life: "There exists a plan to which the entire universe is subject. All things, animate and inanimate, are subordinate to this plan."[26] Her mystical side had not disappeared, on the contrary, after giving up on trying to get the support of the Catholic hierarchy, she finds new ways of expression, more personal and more free, and the end point is always the same: a vision of great respect for the child. "Those who do not believe in God, beginning and end of everything, and those who would, therefore, consider humans themselves as the supreme being," she writes, "inexorably fall into a domineering attitude toward children and inevitably begin, under an apparent preoccupation, a struggle with the child to make him into their own idea of what is a model and an ideal."[27]

As the world is racing toward the Second World War, she gives numerous lectures on the theme of peace. As always, she does not start from ideological positions. Peace, for her, is not an abstraction but a hands-on experience. She has seen it in action in her classes, where the children, placed in the right conditions, do not display any of those aspects of aggression and possessiveness that are so often attributed to them. She does not speak of educating to peace but of educating in peace, so that the children are new creatures, capable of nonviolent dynamics. Putting someone in a position to experiment unhurriedly, to take the measure of their own capacities, to feel personally responsible for the class, all of this creates peace. On the contrary, authoritarianism and competition—the ingredients of school as traditionally conceived—create violence. Like everything that she has been teaching for years about work and school, peace, too, needs time, patience, and faith. Personally, she has no doubt: "If we help children, the next generation will be better human beings."[28]

Her dream is that an epoch, the epoch of the adult, has finally come to a close, and that a new epoch has begun, the epoch of the child, who is a citizen of the universe, indifferent to distinctions of race, religion, or politics. Even faith, understood as dogma bound to a church, looks to her more and more like something obsolete.

The answer to all these contradictions [religious and linguistic divisions] lies in an adequate education; no other political or social means will be able to obtain any results. Reawakening the spirit calls for something sacred and profound and the new children of a civil world must be infused with a profound sentiment and enthusiasm for the holy cause of humanity. Then there will be no need to teach religion, something which in reality is not possible, because the reverent respect for truth, internal and external, will develop naturally and freely.[29]

To create peace we need to facilitate an education of vast expanse, she repeats to anyone willing to listen, a school that dilates the mind. Not the traditional school, committed to putting into the minds of children ideas and notions tied to a "world that is by now slouching toward its end."[30]

In the 1930s Maria Montessori stops being only an educator, albeit an ingenious one way in advance of her times, to become a philosopher. She directs her gaze increasingly to all of humanity. She is not concerned with politics, faithful to the position she has always held, but she does see its errors, for example the punitive peace treaties signed at the end of the First World War, which are sending the world plunging toward a new disaster. In a lecture held in Brussels in 1936, she says: "A vanquished people is today a malady for humanity. The impoverishment of one does not make the wealth of the other, but the decline of all. We are all part of a single organism, a Single

Nation which was the unconscious spiritual and even religious aspiration of the human soul."[31] When she speaks of the future, her intuitions are surprising, even to the point of prefiguring virtual reality ("The short and long waves, means of mysterious invisible communications but nevertheless capable of transporting the thoughts of all of humanity, in absolutely immaterial ways, to whom do they belong?"),[32] alternative sources of energy ("Solar energy in the end will be transformed into a sort of bread more substantial than our own"), and globalization ("Earthly obstacles no longer separate one country from another and people can roam the world without making roads").

Even when she talks about school she always knows how to move beyond the limited space of the classroom to see things on a grand scale, in a broader scope. She says that adults are blind and that children are seers. This prophetic tone is not well received by academics, who accuse her of being insufficiently scientific, but it inspires her disciples, who gather around her in almost religious devotion. "The difficulty of writing soberly of Montessori and her work lies in the fact that only those who have not understood her are able to do it," says one British Montessorian. "As soon as the first glimmers of truth begin to shine in, the whole world seems different, students and scholars fall into a state of trance for which enthusiasm is a decidedly inadequate word. It would be more appropriate to call it religious fervor. It becomes, in short, a dream of salvation."[33]

India

The last great adventure of her life is tied to the Theosophical Society. Founded in 1875 by Helena Petrovna Blavatsky, a Russian aristocrat who traveled far and wide in Asia collecting the teachings of various "masters of ancient wisdom," theosophy preaches universal brotherhood, religious syncretism, and a vision of humanity as a center of enormous and still-unexplored latent powers. As a young woman at the time of the 1899 feminist congress in London, Maria enrolled in the Theosophical Society, in the European section, because the Italian section did not yet exist. Her son claims that she even contributed to the arrival of theosophy in Italy, and to the first Italian translations of theosophical texts, although proof of these claims is unavailable. What is certain is that the theosophists, always very attentive to the theme of education, are among the first passionate supporters of the method. They invite Maria many times to come to India, where the society has its headquarters, but each time she is forced to turn down the invitation because of other commitments.

Nevertheless, she feels that there is great potential in India and she is frustrated at not being able to visit the country. In 1927, Elise

Herbatschek, her Austrian student, accepts the invitation of a friend who has moved to India and wants to open a Children's House there. Her decision creates a diplomatic incident with Maria, who wants Elise to stay at work in Vienna and so does not approve her departure. For two years, despite sending Maria regular monthly reports, Elise receives no response. However, when she meets Maria at the founding congress of the AMI, in Denmark, she receives a warm welcome: "No words can describe my relief and my joy when the Dottoressa took me into her arms. She had forgiven me."[34] Maria asks her to tell her everything about India. After the congress, she takes Elise along on a trip through Denmark. "We went through all the castles with a carload of children, Montessori's little grandchildren sitting on the hood of the car."

In 1939, George S. Arundel, president of the Theosophical Society, goes to meet Maria. "It was our desire to meet her, but we had no idea that she, who understood children so well, was herself, in her amicable sensibility so much like a child," his wife recalls. "When we went to visit her, we realized that we could simply have knocked on the door and gone in. She was there, we met, and in the great affection and understanding between us was there not perhaps the memory of past incarnations?"[35] The next year Arundel returns to Holland with an official invitation for Maria.

The intention is to organize a sojourn of six months, to hold a course at the Theosophical Society and a series of lectures. The initiative is supported by India's most prestigious figures, from Tagore to Gandhi. The latter had met Maria in London a few years earlier and had agreed to deliver an opening address at the start of her training course. "I was hoping to find you and your children here in London. And for me it is an unspeakable joy to see how these children are guided to the virtues of silence, in what fragrant peace they respond, coming forward, to the pleasant call of their teacher."[36]

On September 1, 1939, Germany invades Poland, initiating the Second World War. The plans for Maria's journey to India are at an advanced stage, but for a brief moment it is feared that it will have to be called off. Arundel has confidence, however, in Maria's strong personality, and he writes in the society's review: "We have every reason to believe that Madame Montessori, fighter that she is, will be coming despite all the difficulties. She has already expressed her desire to leave and the British government of India has posed no obstacles."[37] The training course, which is scheduled to be held before Christmas, already has a hundred or so registered students.

Maria leaves from Amsterdam on October 25. Mario is with her, as always, having left the children in Holland with Ada Pierson. Maria's student is only a few years older than the older children, Marilena and Mario Jr., who are twenty and eighteen respectively, and she plays the mother to the two younger ones, Rolando and Renilde, who are fourteen and thirteen. Probably it is already planned that she will marry Mario. "Maria Montessori thought well of Ada," one descendant recalls. "I think she had understood during the years that she lived with Mario that my grandfather needed a woman who was stable, reasonable, and intelligent. Ada devoted her life to my grandfather, the reason for which she did not have children of her own. She was the person who reunited the family, because with the life they had led, Maria's grandchildren were not very close-knit and relations with their parents were particularly difficult."[38]

The journey lasts nearly a week, by train from Amsterdam to Naples, then by plane, with various stops along the way. Once in India, Maria and her son make a stop in Bombay and from there they fly to Madras on a small mail plane of the Tata line, piloted by the founder in person. Waiting for them there is a welcoming committee, with dozens of children lined up like an honor guard. They are then accompanied by a driver, who takes them on a tour of Madras in the Arundel family's Chevrolet.

The Great Spirit

M aria recounts her new adventure to Donna Maraini, in one of her long, colorful letters.

I have made this "tremendous" effort to come to India! To the South of India. I have traveled in an airplane, flying over seas and deserts: across Egypt, Syria, and Mesopotamia. I crossed all of India from north to south in an Indian airplane the size of a fly, a two-seater, smaller than an automobile. Gliding over places where the tigers reign and there are scattered savage-like populations. From the cold of Holland, I passed rapidly, in four or five days, to a torrid zone, where everything is dry, scorched by the sun, and the woods of palm and banana trees are inhabited by cobras. The seashore, I mean to say the sea next to the shore, where one could go bathing, is full of sharks. Among peoples who speak languages descendant from Sanskrit; who have customs inconceivably different from our own, and who nevertheless are not at all savages, on the contrary, they have a mental and spiritually pure form, un-corrupted by politics, not excited by fighting and armaments. With "sentiment," with primitive "emotions": open to under-standing the Child, and the humane philosophy that derives from that. Three hundred students, among them a hundred or so men already employed for some time, many doctors from the university, heads of institutes and heads of families and women, just a few of whom were teachers in search of methods for immediate use in their schools, but most of them Indian women avid for liberation, cultivated, and interested in the destiny of their country. We did the course, in a sort of large cabin, whose walls were straw mats held up by canes, whose roof is dried leaves. I'll send you some photographs.[39]

The society's headquarters is in Adyar, in the middle of a large, shady park. In the morning, Maria often finds a monkey sitting on the doorstep. In the evening, she takes long walks on the beach. One student recalls, "At times, she stood contemplating the beauties of nature as a yogi does."[40] Maria loves the Indians' natural spirituality and she has the sense that this country has a lot to give her: "I am just emerging from a sort of enchanted state, a union with these In-dian students, like a great cloud of affection. I have done everything I could for them and they lived for us."[41]

In India, she is able to express more freely her spiritual side. In a lecture entitled "The Child, the Eternal Messiah," she declares:

I feel, as I am here before you, that this is one of the most important moments of my life. For many decades, the child has revealed to me something that is hidden in the depths of his soul. But what a lack of understanding, how many misunderstandings, have I found in so many countries, be-cause the people thought that I was talking about a peda-gogical method, while I was talking about a revelation that had come to me from the soul. But here, among you, I feel understood down to the depths, because to enter into the soul, into the spirit, one must have a spirit and a soul that are awakened.[42]

She does not forget that in Europe, where she has left her grand-children, war is raging. On Christmas Day, 1939, she gives a speech that has the usual evangelical tone, but it is particularly heartfelt:

It is not music or joy that are in our hearts. We are thinking of other things, of the murder of the innocents, of the suf-fering and the tears of the mothers, of the innocent blood shed by the mad, barbarous fury. It is the flight into Egypt: children are leaving their country in search of refuge. Yet are not these events strictly tied to the birth of the child, of our Savior? It is the child that everyone is searching for and that no one has yet discovered: only the humble have seen him. Even the most powerful man in the world, in order to find him, must rely on a star. And that is how it is happening today, too. The child is born and we must search for him: there is a savior among us. Our century has been called the century of the child, while the adult has been overwhelmed and swallowed up by his own little diabolical machinations. Our hope is in the child. If we understand that the fallen adult must look to the child for salvation, human society will be reconstructed and redeemed.[43]

Her Indian students consider her a Great Soul, they bow down to her when they come to her lessons, and they take their leave, kissing her hand when they go. "She was thought to be a sort of prophet," Mario recalls. "Certain Hindus and theosophists considered her the reincarnation of some great religious teacher of the past. Every-where we were treated with the respect and the generous hospitality accorded to a guru. She was considered a teacher inspired by God, come to reveal the mental and spiritual potential of childhood and to show, through them, the way to redeem humanity—and I her devoted apostle. Wherever we went, Doctoressa Montessori was considered a blessing that was coming into their home."[44]

Enemies and Foreigners

S he writes numerous letters to her grandchildren. Having left them in a continent at war has reopened for her the old wound of having abandoned her infant son. When, in the spring of 1940, news arrives of a possible Nazi invasion of Holland, she has a long discussion with Mario about what to do. The grandchildren are Italian citizens, with their mother in Spain and no legal relatives in Holland. She makes a plan to have them leave for India, even though it is complicated. Just as the plan is starting to come together, in May 1940, the Nazis invade Holland and communication is interrupted.

At the start of her stay in India, she thinks she will have Pao come join her, and she writes to her, in her customary Mother Superior tone: "Are you weak or are you strong? Are you ill or healthy? Are you still that one who ran to answer a call or are you another? Are you worldly or do you feel the missionary spirit? Are you still free and is there no bond binding yourself and all your heart? Make your examination, and then put this question inside yourself: would you come to India? And if yes, when?"[45] Her student responds with enthusiasm and starts the bureaucratic process for the journey, but the spread of the conflict brings everything to a halt.

On June 10, 1940, Italy declares war on Britain. For the British authorities governing India, Italians become foreign enemies. Mario is interned in the camp in Ahmednagar, near Madras, and Maria is confined in the headquarters of the Theosophical Society. The head of the Montessori movement in Great Britain writes an open letter to the *Times* to protest. Less than two months later, on August 31, the viceroy of India sends a telegram to Maria: "We have long thought what to give you for your seventieth birthday. We thought that the best present we could give you was to send you back your son."[46] Even if the secret of her youth is no longer what it used to be, this is the first time that Mario is indicated as her son in an official document.

In 1942, the English authorities transfer them for reasons of security to Kodaikanal, a mountain locality in the state of Tamil Nadu, where traditionally Westerners take refuge during the monsoon season. The house is comfortable and has everything they need—few stairs, a fireplace, a big garden—but Maria suffers in this forced exile. To pass the time she devotes herself to her customary activity—observing children—and opens a class for her neighbors' children. Lena Wikramaratne, an Indian student who accompanies her, takes care of the day-to-day operations: "Night after night Dottoressa Montessori guided me, but above all she wanted to see the spontaneous activity of the little ones, see what happened. This kept the Dottoressa occupied, as she was rather depressed by being forced to live on that mountain."[47] She also manages to organize some training courses, which will produce the book *To Educate the Human Potential.* The Theosophical Society provides her with the assistance of a young American who speaks Italian, and thanks to this collaboration two more books are written: *The Absorbent Mind* and *The Discovery of the Child.*

Mario is, as always, by her side. He adores going on outings in the mountains with the students, returning each time loaded with leaves and flowers. It is during this stay that Maria and Mario put together most of the material for teaching natural history, which will later become a classic of the Montessori method. They work together in the evenings. They have no teaching materials nor books, but they have a lot of time, and this allows them to examine thoroughly lots of elements.

In March 1944, the British government notifies them that their compulsory residence in Kodaikanal is finished. Maria and her son leave for Ceylon, accompanied by Lena Wikramaratne. "She told me that she had always wanted to see the land of Sindbad the sailor; she had read about the island when she was little."[48] She travels a lot throughout India and holds courses in Karachi, Srinagar, Ahmedabad, and Poona. The Indian privileged classes have embraced the Montessori method with great enthusiasm. The vice president of the Indian Montessori Society is Saraladevi Sarabhai, heir to a wealthy family of industrialists. To instruct his children, he calls the British Montessorian Edwin M. Standing, a teacher of Quaker origins converted to Catholicism and rebaptized by Maria with the name Benedetto.

The British authorities propose that Maria speak about her method on government radio, so that her words can be broadcast all around the world. Mario recounts: "I was happy about this opportunity, but she said: 'Think of all the children who in this moment are dying from the bombs dropped from the airplanes of the Allies, in Italy, in Holland, where our children are, and in Germany too. What will people think when they hear my voice speaking about children on behalf of the Allies?' She also said that in these conditions her work would become a means of propaganda in service to the war."[49]

The Completion of the Idea

D uring her long Indian sojourn, Maria Montessori trains a thousand teachers. "She was at home in India," one student recalls. "The Indian girls were so lovely and they understood her and loved her and she needed that at the time. She felt she had been rejected in Europe and America, but in India, every word of hers was soaked up."[50]

In the memories of the Indian students, Mario has a larger and larger role. "He was a volcano, dynamic, full of temperament. He helped her in every way; without him, she would have been able to do very little."[51] It is Mario, who speaks English fluently, who conducts all the activities with the children and the practical in-class exercises with the training course students. Maria limits herself to delivering lectures, translated by Mario. She is happy to see her son taking the helm, even though it bothers her that they have less time together: "I can't manage to have him with me even for a fraction of a second. He gives himself body and soul to these Indian students, for discussions and repetitions without end."[52]

The forced inactivity weighs on her as well. After an entire life always on the run, her Indian sojourn strikes her as too calm. "I am doing well," she writes to an Italian student, "but my vivacity and faith are waning. Maybe because everything is going fine and I don't have anxiety; I miss the stimulus of the struggle!"[53] Mario shares her impatience, and suffers being so far away from his children, but—as she has taught him ever since he was a boy—he tries to see an opportunity in everything that happens: "If we had been free, we wouldn't have accomplished anything of what we accomplished, we wouldn't have had the time. And the conditions would have been lacking. It was as though Divine Providence had wanted that limitation of our freedom so that we could concentrate on completing the missionary work that Dottoressa Montessori was destined to carry on."[54]

Not all of the Indian sojourn is easy for Maria, who is by now on in years. The heat is oppressive, the insects torment her, the local cuisine does not agree with her. "She called us rabbits because we were vegetarians. She would say, 'You rabbits, are you happy?'"[55] one student remembers. She has a car take her to Madras on frequent trips to buy Western food.

Apart from Mario, she has no one to talk to in her mother tongue, and every now and again Mario says to the students, "Please, go keep my mother company, she's lonely."[56] She spends hours observing the Indian children, whom she finds delightful. She loves the naturalness with which their mothers take them everywhere, propped up on a hip or wrapped in strips of cloth tied around the back. It is in these years that she works systematically on her pedagogy for the age from birth to three years. She holds specific courses on newborns, to explain how the first months of life are fundamental for mental development and must be taken into consideration by pedagogy. "The idea of starting education at birth is revolutionary. If we want a new humanity, we must start building right from infancy."

As usual, she is looking beyond school. "This is not a pedagogical method, but a method of living and culture which I believe is very necessary in this time. The important part of the Montessori method for the world is putting the value of childhood in the right light as the age that constructs humanity, taking it to perfection. Up to now, childhood has been thought to be constituted by weak beings who must be helped and loved; in reality, it is a great force that can be a great help to us adults."[57]

In September 1945, with the Japanese surrender, the Second World War comes to an end. After the long silence, correspondence between India and Europe can start up again. Maria receives news from Holland, where her grandchildren are all safe and sound: Marilena has gotten married, Mario Jr. has taken part in the Resistance, Renilde is in high school, Rolando in a boarding school. She does not return home immediately and stays with her son for another year in Asia, to visit Kashmir and hold some new courses, indefatigable as always. "I've got a good head and lousy legs,"[58] she writes in a letter.

She is satisfied with what she has accomplished in India. In her first letters to Donna Maraini she talks about the work that has allowed her to bring her idea to completion: "I believe it has reached its compete development. Beautiful in its interpretation of the child, with his 'absorbent mind,' with his 'preparation for adaptation,' and finally, the comprehensive plan for 'Cosmic Education,' which is a crowning and a bringing to completion."

She makes Donna laugh by telling her how she has been transformed into an Indian: "I have totally forgotten my black dresses! I wear white where it is hot, and every color possible where the climate is not tropical. I would really look funny if I came dressed this way to Europe! It has been years since I have worn either hats or gloves. I always go out without a hat, with my white hair, like our women of the people. I have green, red, yellow, and pink dresses, floral patterns, veils and scarves, sandals and dainty shoes with raised tips. Do you find this news interesting? Can you picture your old Maria in your imagination?"

The Method Is a Small Thing

I n the summer of 1946, Maria is ready to return to Europe. She is staying in a hotel in Karachi, waiting for a seat to open up on a flight. Finally, she and her son manage to board a small aircraft with thirty seats, together with a group of Westerners liberated from Japanese concentration camps. After a stop of just a few hours in Rome, they land in Amsterdam. The airport that she used to know is no longer there; all that's left is a bomb-cratered runway and some temporary barracks. While Mario takes care of the luggage, Maria remains immobile in the midst of that desolation, sitting on a piece of wood. All of Europe is in ruins, and the Montessori movement will have to be rebuilt as well.

Although she is almost eighty years old, Maria gets right to work. In September she is already on a flight to England to hold a training course. Upon landing, she asks to take a drive around the city to see the damage from the bombing. Then, in the house prepared for her by an English student, she notes the tableware service put together from the surviving pieces of various houses. Grabbing a dish towel, she says, "Your silver needs polishing." The student recalls, "She was always thinking about her work... She was always willing to help you figure out how to handle a problem with the children. She would give a suggestion, and if that didn't work, she'd think of something else, and finally, if nothing seemed to work, she'd say: 'The only thing you can do now is pray.'"[59]

Her religious faith is intact. Her letters to her students continue to be full of the evangelical images that have enriched her whole life. "We depend on the child, all of our personality comes from him. What's more, this would be, for those able to understand it, a Christian realization, because the supernature of the child, guide to the Kingdom of Heaven, and first citizen of that realm, was left only in the letter of the Gospel, without penetrating the spirit, the conscience of Christians."[60]

She keeps a correspondence with Luigia Tincani, an Italian religious and foundress of an order of teaching missionaries very active in Asia, who has been interested in the method since the 1930s and is now working for its revival in Italy. With her, Maria can talk openly: "The materialist trend that has gained so much strength in these last few years must be resisted not only with material force, but above all with spiritual force, and, as I said earlier, there is no religion that comes as close to a scientific approach as the Catholic religion. It saddens me greatly that my work in India is mostly in the hands of Hindus, Theosophists, and Muslims; unfortunately, the Catholics there have little interest in it."[61] She has overcome her disappointment with the Catholic hierarchies, and, in one letter, she defines herself with irony as a missionary who has spent her life roaming the world and speaking to the wind. Thanks to her friend, in May 1947 she obtains a private audience with Pope Pius XII.

She continues to think that her method has many points of contact with Catholicism—"The psychological observations that I have been able to make correspond in an impressive fashion to the care that the Catholic Church gives, by accompanying the human being during his whole life, from birth to death"[62]—but she keeps her personal faith separate from her pedagogical work. She has done that all her life, creating a nonconfessional method that adapts to every culture and every religion. To one Dutch disciple who has just converted to Catholicism, she writes a very evenhanded message that may be considered her final statement on the subject: "Remember that the method is not necessarily Catholic; it is a new approach to education and it is for everyone. The method is a small thing. As I have said in the past, it must be considered as similar to 'a bar of soap,' a small addition to civilization; everyone—atheists, Jews, Christians—can use this bar of soap to wash themselves."[63]

My Country Is a Star

Elderly, dressed in clothes from a bygone era, Maria crisscrosses ruined and impoverished Europe trying to rebuild the Montessori movement with the help of her son. From London, where training courses have started back up, she writes to Donna Maraini:

> Here, there are shop windows with a few hats, etc., but they can't be purchased without coupons. And we have not yet been here long enough to have any! And I have certain straw hats, left in Amsterdam before the war and that my grandchildren saved. Stuff from seven years ago! I am humiliated. In India I didn't have any hats and my clothes were made of veils and gold, almost all of them white. Mario's clothes are old, too, and now they are all a little tight! And in India he also had his best clothes of white silk, or cotton, and Indian dress for Muslims. What a romance! What is most inconvenient for me is providing for myself, while in India I was accustomed to having a lot of servants and a personal maid, who did nothing but wash and iron and run to answer my every call. When I

left her in Madras, thinking that I might not have anyone to help me in Europe, she cried and said, "Poor Mother!"[64]

When the course ends, she goes to Scotland with Mario to be proclaimed an honorary member of the Educational Institute of Scotland. It is on this occasion that—to the question which country is her homeland—she responds with a phrase that will become famous: "My country is a star which turns around the sun and is called the Earth."[65] The family's home base is now Holland, but Maria is constantly on the road, a tireless traveler. "I remember that one time she left Amsterdam in the morning on a plane, arrived in London around ten o'clock, sent for me so that I could have lunch with her and I watched her leave again after lunch at two o'clock,"[66] one student recalls.

In Italy, a committee is set up, chaired by the ever-present Donna Maraini, to revive the movement. Things are set in motion to have Maria awarded a pension from the university, a project, however, that will not be approved. In April 1947, Maria arrives in Italy, invited by the government for a two-month stay. She is received by the Constitutional Assembly, which is giving the country a new political identity after the dictatorship. To the journalists who ask her about her collaboration with fascism, she says, "They closed my schools because they were based on an international idea and because I refused to teach war. So I went to Spain. For me there is always freedom. I do as I believe." She answers all of their questions, does not embellish the situation, and does not deny her past. "I do not want to be described as a fiery anti-fascist. Politics does not interest me. Besides, political ideas are all wrong. We have to create a new world, with a new cut and new material, not the crazy quilt of rags and silk that is seen today."[67]

She repeats that she does not want to be associated with any political party or regime. She has always declared, with a form of recklessness that borders on opportunism: "I want anybody's help, without regard to his political or religious convictions."[68] She knows that her insight goes well beyond any ideology, and she never tires of repeating it when, for example, she recalls her beginnings in San Lorenzo:

People of all religions and political parties, of all social classes, were vitally interested. But the most singular thing was knowing why people who had feelings and ideas so diverse, or even opposed and contrasting, such as for example monarchists and communists, Catholics, Jews, and Buddhists, were so intensely interested in these childhood manifestations, and what they found in them that was so important with respect to their own convictions. Well, the reason was this, that each of them found there a piece that was missing for the accomplishment of his ideals, and saw in those manifestations the help necessary for the triumph of his own principles. That is, every part of the adult world, with every party, with every religious faith, with all ideals, even though faiths and ideals were without any affinity among them, recognized in the child the necessary element for their own triumph.[69]

In her lectures, she does not hesitate to exclaim, "I am saying revolutionary things!"[70] She is not afraid to scandalize and shock with her anticonformist theories: "I have been working with children for many years and they have taught me to rebel against mistaken or obsolete ideas in which many parents still believe." She says she is convinced that many adults who say they love children actually have contempt for them without realizing it, considering them weak and incomplete. Adults, despite all of their psychological theories, still have understood almost nothing of the mystery of the child, a mystery, she says, that is full of miracles.

The reason for this fundamental misunderstanding is that adults and children are different, almost creatures from separate planets.

An example she loves to talk about is work. The common way of thinking is that adults work and children play, something that she forcefully denies. Children work all the time, they work hard, but they work differently:

> The misunderstanding arises because children do not work with a conscious purpose like those who work to produce. From the age of around two, children want to do what adults do; it is not, however, the result of the activity that interests them, but the activity itself. They do not want to learn to wash and dress themselves in order to be clean and well dressed. Their interest is in learning and in repeating over and over again the movements necessary to putting on their clothes and washing their faces. Haven't you ever watched a child, with his face red from the effort to reach the objective of putting on his socks and shoes, and then deliberately take them off in order to start all over from the beginning?[71]

The Epoch of Surprises

I n July 1947 Mario marries Ada. The family archives conserve a
fragment of a movie of the party held following the ceremony, in a
garden full of friends and relatives. A little boy, completely naked, is
running around among the guests. A few minutes later, he reappears
wearing a pair of shorts, and sticks his hands in the wedding cake.
The newlyweds pay no attention to the disaster and drive off in a
convertible accompanied by applause. Maria, sitting alone off to the
side, smiles. "I am glad that Mario has a big loving family, with father,
mother, sisters and brothers, uncles and aunts, etc., etc., because I
thought so often that I would leave him abandoned in the world,
without family, with children by now independent. I seem to have
placed him in a safe nest. And I can die consoled,"[72] she writes to her
friend Donna Maraini.

In August, she leaves with him again for India, where there is still
a lot of work to do, and the response is extraordinary: "they are enrolling children in the Montessori school from birth, the way they do
at Oxford."[73] She arrives in India while the country is going through
its bloody separation from Pakistan. Even this tragedy, which causes

endless destruction and millions of victims, is filtered through her gaze as an educator. She writes to an Italian student: "You see how Gandhi is in difficulty despite the pacifying power of his admirable and extraordinary life. It's that he addresses himself to adults. If he had directed his message to children he would have transformed the Indians, who are now slaughtering each other."[74] Yet again, she maintains a total political neutrality and collaborates with both the Indian and Pakistani authorities.

In July 1949 she returns to Europe. She lands in Amsterdam and then leaves on a long European tour. She is in France to receive the Légion d'Honneur, in Holland to be inducted into the Orange-Nassau Order and be awarded an honorary doctorate, in Switzerland to receive an award from the Pestalozzi Foundation, then in Austria, England, Scotland, and Ireland. She returns to Italy several times. In May 1950 she is in Florence to attend a meeting of UNESCO and in Perugia to deliver some lectures. She writes to a Dutch collaborator: "This is the epoch of surprises for me. I was greeted with applause on entering the general meeting of UNESCO. And here in Italy they conferred on me the title of Ordinary Professor at the University of Perugia. How will I manage to sustain all these things? If I only had the time to be able to earn them! There is such a lot of work to do, isn't there?"[75] During her stay in Italy she makes a special request of her son. "She said to me: 'I'd like to make a tour of the places where I lived.' I remember that I got a car and she said to me, 'Let's go up to the Marches.' It was the first visit she made there incognito, because at the time they recognized her and they wanted to honor her. But she said: 'No, alone, let's go alone!' And we came here to Ancona, and we went to Chiaravalle. She went all around and said: 'Now I'm happy, now, even if I die I've seen my hometown.'"[76]

She is nominated three years in a row for the Nobel Peace Prize, but each time the Stockholm Academy prefers someone else: in 1949 John Boyd Orr, director general of the Food and Agriculture Organization; in 1950 Ralph Bunche, United Nations mediator in

Pakistan; in 1951 Léon Jouhaux, vice president of the World Federation of Trade Unions. All men, as noted by Grazia Honegger Fresco, one of the foremost experts on Maria Montessori in Italy, who "did not 'produce' peace, but 'repaired the damage of war.'"[77] It is very likely that her collaboration with fascism weighed against her candidacy.

I Don't Think, I See

Increasingly, she finds it unacceptable that her work is pigeonholed within the confines of education. She feels that she has done much more, by creating a point of contact between pedagogy, psychology, sociology, the cognitive sciences, and even theology. While everyone crowds around her to talk about teaching materials, she is elsewhere, as though she had left through an attic door. "If not only the name but also the concept of 'method' were abolished and replaced by some other designation, if we were to talk of 'an aid for the human personality to win its independence, of a means to liberate it from the age-old prejudices on education,' then everything would become clear. It is the human personality and not a method of education that must be considered; it is the defense of the child, the scientific recognition of his nature, the social proclamation of his rights that must replace the piecemeal conceptions of education."[78]

Rather than school, she now talks about humanity. Rather than pupils, children. Observing them has been her life's work, and a constant challenge. What does it mean to be a child? That's the question she has always been asking herself. How can adults put themselves in their place? That is a most difficult thing, because the distance between the mind of an adult and the mind of a child is astronomical. "We are containers, impressions pour into us, and we remember them and transmit them to our minds, but they remain distinct from our minds," she explains. "The child, instead, undergoes a transformation, the impressions not only penetrate the mind, but they shape it. They are incarnated in the child."[79] That's why adults rarely understand children. They insist on judging them with their own measuring stick, and they can't help but get it wrong. What adult, she wonders, can understand the child's way of being in the world? That state of grace in which "he is always enthusiastic, is always happy,"[80] for example. Or the child's way of being with objects, to the point of "becoming" the thing that he loves. Or his infinite slowness, for us incomprehensible, which is the way the world seeps into him and he seeps into the world.

From childhood, her thoughts move to the adult person, further enlarging her message. Her observations on the working child—the need for meaning, freedom within the rules—can also inspire the theory of factory work, and help unions and industrialists conceive of less alienating ways of organizing human activity. As early as the 1920s, she was writing to her Italian socialist correspondents about the great interest of the British trade unions who had invited her to speak to factory workers, and she pronounced herself convinced that, as with education, so with justice and labor, the answer would come from well-conducted experiments in the field, not from ideologies.

Her study of children's attention can also tell us a lot about the attention of adults. She has always believed in slowness, in striving to fully understand. As a young woman, she was already writing, concerning the Jesuits and their techniques of concentration: "Meditate and be still with your thought, intensifying it, polarizing it on the object of mediation. To read a book in one night is to consume ourselves aridly; to mediate half an hour in the morning is to allow a free expansion of ourselves, which mostly remains suffocated by an avalanche of uncoordinated sensations. We do not know the art of expanding ourselves, and we do not know how to regulate our activities."[81]

She receives invitations from all parts of the world, carefully screened by Mario, who invariably responds, "It all depends on Mammolina's health."[82] When she is tired, she complains of feeling like a circus elephant, carried from one country to another. When she is in a good mood, she enjoys discussing with him the details of each new trip. She gives him more and more room. During their visits to Montessori schools, it is often Mario who takes center stage. She prefers to stay off to the side, observing. What attracts her attention is always the single child, perhaps the most insignificant, the one who is performing an apparently useless exercise. Who is, in other words, as she says, meditating.

She knows well the solitude of the child, this most potent creature exiled in a world made for adults. And she knows well what it means to meditate, that is, to work with great intensity. She knows that there is a deep nexus that binds solitude, concentration, and creativity. To concentrate one's own energies one must be composed and self-possessed: "The individual has intimate needs, for which, while he abandons himself to some mysterious work, he requires complete solitude, separation from everything and everyone. No one can help us achieve this intimate isolation which makes accessible our most concealed, most profound world, as mysterious as it is rich and full."[83] She does this, in her study in Holland, every time that her travels leave her a little time. She writes, takes notes, gazes out her window, intent on observing some image that captures her attention. "I don't think, I see,"[84] she confided one day to one of her students.

The House by the Sea

In 1950 Donna Maraini dies, and Maria goes to Italy to commemorate her in a public ceremony. In her speech, she retraces the two great interests of her life, medicine and pedagogy, and tries to understand how they can still be renewed:

> There are two social classes whose needs are neglected and nearly forgotten: children and the sick. In the former lies the hope of the world; nevertheless, their needs are not understood by adults in the right way. They are our forgotten citizens. A sick person is a being that feels more than others do. But he has almost lost his dignity; his human personality almost doesn't exist anymore, only his illness exists. People do not see "the person" in him, do not understand the humiliated person who feels alone, abandoned by life, relegated to solitude, condemned to inactivity, dependent on others for everything.[85]

As she bids farewell to her lifelong friend, she looks ahead, to the possible development of her thought. Their long friendship of more than half a century was based on the conviction that they were working for humanity. Already, as a young woman, in a letter written to mollify Donna Maraini's husband, irritated by all the time his wife was devoting to the method, she explained: "Perhaps I will seem presumptuous in putting it this way, but the work that we call mine is not mine: what counts is not my work, but the most sublime work of nature, 'the human spirit that unveils itself.' This is what attracts your wife's heart and makes her my companion in all manner of contemplation of this discovery."[86]

As her time is coming to an end, she reviews the work accomplished, almost as though she felt that much of it had not been grasped by the world. One of her granddaughters recalls that in her last years, she often sighed, shaking her head: "They haven't understood anything."[87] She realizes that she will go down in history for having elaborated a pedagogical method and teaching materials, while she knows that the true revolution is her having seen the true child, not an inferior being but absolute potentiality of the future. Maybe even—as she often says in her mystical parlance—savior of the world. This is, above all else, what matters to her, especially now that the end is approaching, and she returns more and more frequently with her memory to the first results obtained in San Lorenzo, to that inspired moment when it all began.

"Distressingly, the profound significance of these marvelous manifestations was not fully appreciated and they were not sufficiently considered as the results of the children's own strengths, bestowed on them by the Creator. In these prodigious manifestations of the soul of the child too much was seen as the product of an educational method,"[88] she observes bitterly. Everyone focuses on the material, without seeing beyond it, for example, to the transformed mentality of the child. "What slipped down to the common schools was a freer way of studying and of giving individual and objective tasks. The 'miracle' was officially forgotten."[89] But that is what interests her. And the more years go by the more it seems the only important thing. "We need a world full of miracles,"[90] she keeps on saying.

She prepares her last will and testament, which speaks only of Mario: "He is the sole heir, and only competent depository; and therefore, the right and legitimate continuer of the work that I have undertaken and that I hope he will be able happily to continue and complete to the benefit of humanity, which we have loved together, finding in the common ideal and in common action the highest comfort of our lives. So be it: may his children be his collaborators; and may the world render him justice, according to his merits, which I know to be great and sublime." Beneath her signature, she adds, "And so my friends and those who work because of my work may feel the debt they owe to my son!"[91] In the only document in which she officially calls him her son, she reiterates the promise that she has made to herself ever since the days when she took him back with herself as a boy: to build a great enterprise that compensates him for his long abandonment. The work for which she gave him up at birth has become an international enterprise that justifies and maintains the adult man that Mario has become. The circle has been closed.

Traveling is now very complicated, and Maria spends more and more time in Holland, particularly in Noordwijk aan Zee, a seaside village famous for its long sandy beaches and its fields of tulips. In the 1950s, before mass tourism, the village is a quiet succession of villas built by the rich families of Amsterdam's upper class. Among them, the villa of the Pierson family, a large, spacious house full of verandas and windows, with a well-shaded garden. Above the front door the inscription: HET HUIS AAN ZEE (the House by the Sea).

It is a place imbued with beauty. Beaches that seem endless, wooden palisades painted white, limitless skies where the clouds stream by. Maria especially loves to go there in May, when the flowers are in bloom. Every so often, she asks her son to take her in the car to admire the fields of tulips which stretch as far as the eye can see into the hinterland, covering the countryside with colors. From her room on the second floor she can look out on the sea, which is just outside the big windows, beyond the dunes hemmed by tall grass blowing in the wind.

She agrees to get some bed rest during the day because that's what the doctor has ordered, but inactivity weighs on her. In a letter to an Italian friend, she writes that she would like to be young so she could work more. She has trouble walking, and her vision is weak. She sits in her room waiting for the mail or the Italian newspapers, with the news of the world. One day, while she is brushing her hair with the help of one of her granddaughters, she brusquely puts the brush down and says to her: "You know, I've done."[92] "You, done?" the young woman responds, incredulously. "Yes, I'm telling you that I've done."

On May 6, 1952, Mario and his wife Ada are receiving some collaborators in the living room on the ground floor. Mario brings a tray of food up to Maria's room and sits down on the bed next to her. He tells her that the day before, he received an invitation to go talk about the method in Ghana. "There are no children that need help more than the children of the African countries," Maria responds with enthusiasm. "We have never been there, but do you remember the pictures that the white nuns of Nigeria sent us? Do you remember that little girl, with her face surrounded by the smooth locks of her hair, busy building the pink tower? We definitely have to go. We have to, you and I, organize a course like the ones we did in India and we have to train our assistants *in loco*."[93] Her son reminds her of the heat, the infectious diseases. "So, you don't want me to come! One day, I'm going to go and I'll leave you behind," she reprimands him with affection. Mario gives up and goes to get the map of Africa. When he comes back he finds her lifeless in the bed.

"I would hope to be able to take my leave without having to say good-bye to anyone, quietly and unseen,"[94] she had written a few days before in a letter. She had given her dispositions for her funeral long before, asking to be buried where she died, because every country was her country. She is buried in the Catholic cemetery of Noordwijk aan Zee. On her tomb—surrounded by fragments of seashells forming a light-colored marine gravel—her name, dates of birth and death, and a phrase in Italian: "I pray the dear children, who can do anything, to join me in making peace in mankind and in the world."

Author's Note

When she was young, Montessori was mad, and when she was old she became clever,"[1] an Italian academic commented in 1950 after attending a dinner in her honor. I would say that the phrase also sums up the sense of this book. I wanted to understand if Maria Montessori was a madwoman, as some say, or a clever businesswoman, as others believe, or a great spirit, as her followers are fond of calling her, or much more than all that. I wanted to discover the real person beyond the global trademark, which still bears her name.

To do that, I had available to me an imposing bibliography, which, however, was devoted above all to her ideas, while, with regard to the person, it tended to repeat over and over the same information. To reconstruct her life, I had: a solid but dated American biography (Kramer, 1973); a couple of eyewitness accounts (Maccheroni, 1956, and Standing, 1957); a lot of Montessorian monographs, first and foremost that of Grazia Honegger Fresco, very well informed but also careful not to damage the image of the foundress; and a large mass of texts and articles by specialists.

I started off from this material, to put all of the known information in order, beginning with her studies and the years of her youth (precious sources for this period: Matellicani, 2007, and Babini and Lama, 2010). I did research in archives, where I had some hope of finding material: the AMI Archive in Amsterdam, the Humanitarian Society Archive in Milan, the National Archive in Rome, the McClure Manuscript Collection in Bloomington, Indiana, the Bank of Italy Historical Archive in Rome, the Historical Archive of the Leonardo da Vinci Institute in Rome, the Archive of the General House of the Franciscan Missionaries of Mary in Rome, the Archive of the National Association for the Interests of Southern Italy in Rome, the Library of Catalonia in Barcelona. I read many unpublished documents, which I was not given permission to cite but which I have used to reconstruct the narrative.

The AMI Archive in Amsterdam opened its doors to me, even though I am not a Montessorian. I knew that I would be given permission to use only a limited number of unpublished citations and so I have used—for primary sources such as the notebook of Alessandro Montessori, Maria Montessori's university notebook, Maria Montessori's notes on her childhood, the Montessori-Maraini correspondence, which I read in its entirety—excerpts already cited in books, particularly by Honegger Fresco, 2017 and 2018, Alatri, 2015, and *Maria Montessori e le sue reti di relazioni*, 2018.

I emerged from five years of research with the book I had promised myself to write: the story of a life. I am not an expert in pedagogy and I leave to others the task of explaining Maria Montessori's thought in all its complexity. I have recounted everything that is known of her biography as of the current state of the documents, without preconceptions and without allowances. I have shown the positive sides of the person—her force of character, her absolute emancipation for her time, her nearly psychic visionary capacity—and the negative sides. Maria Montessori was a genius, and rarely are geniuses easy to deal with. She was authoritarian, convinced that she had a mission entrusted to her by God, and very opportunistic, seeking support wherever she might find it. And she was also a woman who founded an enterprise, something which many have not forgiven her.

As soon as the name Maria Montessori is mentioned, most of the adults present rush to say that her ideas cannot be applied in schools for the masses, that they work only with the children of the rich, who attend private schools. The fact is that much of the hostility elicited by Maria Montessori stems from the radicality of her message. This woman born in the 1800s says things that are still disturbing today, even though many of her ideas—fortunately—have become part of the common wisdom. Maria Montessori asks adults to give up their position of strength and superiority with respect to children, in which they have placed themselves, consciously or not, since the beginning of time.

She does not speak only of education; she speaks about human relationships. You don't have to be a teacher to be troubled on reading her books. Personally, I know that I now look at children differently. I especially remember one day, while I was on the train that was taking me to Rome to consult an archive. Next to me was a very small child, who was opening and closing a jar of baby food as his mother was trying to feed him, constantly taking it out of his hands. It seemed to me a demonstration of what Maria Montessori said as long ago as 1907. Children do not play, they work, often harder than we adults do, but we still do not hesitate to interrupt them.

On this point, her theory still challenges us today. Maria Montessori asks uncomfortable questions. One of the many: when we meet children, why do we touch them without asking permission, even if it is just to caress their hair, while we would never allow ourselves to do that with their parents? Right, why? If I have encouraged some among my readers to change their gaze—and so also their behavior toward children and childhood—this book will have served its purpose.

Notes

PART ONE

1 Maria Montessori, Lecture VII of the Rome Course, 1931, in *Il Quaderno Montessori*, Spring 1999, p. 55.
2 Maria Montessori, Notes on Her Childhood, AMI Archive (also the following citation).
3 Edwin M. Standing, *Maria Montessori: Her Life and Work* (New York: Plume, 1998), pp. 21–22.
4 Notebook of Alessandro Montessori, AMI Archive.
5 Rita Kramer, *Maria Montessori: A Biography* (New York: Da Capo Press, 1988), p. 28.
6 Standing, *Maria Montessori*, p. 21.
7 Ibid.
8 *L'Italie*, French newspaper in Rome, August 18, 1896, AMI Archive.
9 Anna Maria Maccheroni, *Come conobbi Maria Montessori* (Rome: Edizioni Vita dell'infanzia, 1956), p. 27.
10 Ibid., p. 26
11 Maria Montessori, Notes on Her Childhood, AMI Archive (also the following citation).
12 Kramer, *Maria Montessori*, p. 308.
13 Maria Montessori, Notes on Her Childhood, AMI Archive (also the following citation).
14 Paola Giovetti, *Maria Montessori: una biografia* (Rome: Mediterranee, 2009), p. 14.
15 Notebook of Alessandro Montessori, AMI Archive.
16 Grazia Honegger Fresco, *Maria Montessori, una storia attuale* (Turin: Il leone verde, 2018), p. 26.
17 Annalucia Forti Messina, *Il sapere e la clinica* (Milan: FrancoAngeli, 1998), p. 208.
18 Maccheroni, *Come conobbi Maria Montessori*, p. 28.
19 Phyllis Povell, *Montessori Comes to America: The Leadership of Maria Montessori and Nancy McCormick* (Lanham, MD: University Press of America, 2010), p. 35.
20 *Illustrazione popolare*, March 5, 1899, AMI Archive.
21 Kramer, *Maria Montessori*, p. 218.
22 Maria Montessori, university notebook, May 5, 1891, AMI Archive.
23 Maccheroni, *Come conobbi Maria Montessori*, p. 29.
24 Kramer, *Maria Montessori*, p. 42.

25 Ibid., pp. 41.

26 Ibid. pp. 42–43.

27 Maria Montessori, university notebook, May 5, 1891, AMI Archive.

28 Kramer, *Maria Montessori*, p. 45.

29 Maria Montessori, university notebook, May 5, 1891, AMI Archive.

30 Ibid.

31 Ibid.

32 Ibid., August 23, 1891, AMI Archive, unpublished, by kind concession of Carolina Montessori (all citations in the paragraph).

33 Ibid.

34 Ibid.

35 Ibid.

36 Maccheroni, *Come conobbi Maria Montessori*, p. 29n.

37 M. L. Heid, *Uomini che non scompaiono* (Florence: Sansoni, 1944), p. 68.

38 Kramer, *Maria Montessori*, p. 46.

39 Honegger Fresco, *Maria Montessori*, p. 37.

40 Kramer, *Maria Montessori*, p. 49 (all citations in the paragraph).

41 *L'Italie*, French newspaper in Rome, August 18, 1896, AMI Archive.

42 Ibid. (all citations in the paragraph)

43 Kramer, *Maria Montessori*, p. 54.

44 Povell, *Montessori Comes to America*, pp. 37–38.

45 Kramer, *Maria Montessori*, p. 56.

46 Anna Matellicani, *La "Sapienza" di Maria Montessori: dagli studi universitari alla docenza 1890–1919* (Rome: Aracne, 2007), p. 149.

47 Kramer, *Maria Montessori*, p. 56.

48 Giovanna Alatri, *Il mondo al femminile di Maria Montessori, Regine, dame e altre donne* (Rome: Fefè, 2015), p. 22.

49 Sheila Radice, *The New Children: Talks with Dr. Maria Montessori* (London: Hadder and Stoughton, 1920), p. 35.

50 Heid, *Uomini che non scompaiono*, p. 32.

51 Interview of Giovanni Bollea by Lia De Pra, AMI Archive.

52 Maccheroni, *Come conobbi Maria Montessori*, p. 31.

53 André Michelet, *Les outils de l'enfance* (Neuchâtel, Switzerland: Delachaux et Niestlé, 1972), vol. 1, p. 69.

54 Yves Pelicier and Guy Thuillier, *Un pionnier de la psychiatrie de l'enfant: Edouard Séguin* (Comité d'Histoire de la Sécurité Sociale, 1996), p. 46.

55 Robert J. Fynne, *Montessori and Her Inspirers* (London: Longmans, Green, 1924), p. 157.

56 Édouard Séguin, *Idiocy and Its Treatment by the Physiological Method* (New York: Teachers College, Columbia University, 1907), p. 181.

57 Civil Status Archive of the City of Rome, Act no. 1304, part B, in Valeria P. Babini and Luisa Lama, *Una "donna nuova"* (Milan: FrancoAngeli, 2000), p. 108.

58 Marta Gandiglio, "Sulle tracce di Maria Montessori," thesis, University of Rome, 1997–1998, AMI Archive.

59 Paola Boni Fellini, *I segreti della fama* (Rome: Centro editoriale dell'Osservatore, 1955), p. 27.

60 Carolina Montessori (ed.), *Maria Montessori Sails to America: A Private Diary, 1913* (Laren, Holland: Montessori-Pierson Publishing, 2013), pp. vi–viii.

61 "*Caro Olgogigi*": *Lettere ad Olga e Luigi Lodi* (Milan: FrancoAngeli, 1999), p. 16.

62 "L'idea Montessori," August 1929, p. 1, in Alatri, *Il mondo al femminile*, p. 20.

63 Carolina Montessori (ed.), *Maria Montessori Sails to America*, p. 54.

64 Maria Montessori to Donna Maraini, July 30, 1911, AMI Archive.

65 Carlo De Sanctis, *Giuseppe Ferruccio Montesano* (Bari: Grafiche Cressati, 1962).

66 https://www.anarcopedia.org/index.php/Luigi_Lucheni.

67 Kramer, *Maria Montessori*, p. 77.

68 *La conferenza Montessori*, in *Il Don Chisciotte di Roma*, January 23, 1899, AMI Archive.

69 Fellini, *I segreti della fama*, p. 22.

70 "*Caro Olgogigi*," p. 315.

71 *Il Don Chisciotte di Roma*, January 21, 1899, AMI Archive.

72 Kramer, *Maria Montessori*, pp. 80–81 (all citations in the pararaph).

73 Ibid., p. 82.

74 *Il Caffaro di Genova*, May 1899, AMI Archive

75 *Corriere della Sera*, July 18, 1899, AMI Archive.

76 *La Gazzetta dell'Emilia*, July 7, 1899, AMI Archive.

77 *L'Italia al femminile*, no. 6 (February 19, 1899), AMI Archive.

78 Letizia Comba (ed.), *Donne educatrici: Maria Montessori e Ada Gobetti* (Turin: Rosenberg & Sellier, 1996), p. 37.

79 *Scena Illustrata* (Florence, October 15, 1899), AMI Archive.

80 *Idiocy and Its Treatment by the Physiological Method by Édouard Séguin*, 1866, p. 91, in Robert J. Fynne, *Montessori and Her Inspirers* (London: Longmans, Green, 1924), p. 172.

81 Fynne, *Montessori and Her Inspirers*, p. 153.

82 Michelet, *Les outils de l'enfance*, vol. 1, p. 57.

83 Fynne, *Montessori and Her Inspirers*, p. 208.

84 Michelet, *Les outils de l'enfance*, vol. 1, p. 57.

85 Suzanne Stewart-Steinberg, *L'effetto Pinocchio* (Rome: Elliot, 2011), p. 394.

86 Fellini, *I segreti della fama*, p. 26.

87 Maria Montessori to Sante De Sanctis, undated, in Renato Foschi, Erica Moretti, and Paola Trabalzini (eds.), *Il destino di Maria Montessori* (Rome: Fefè, 2019), p. 158.

88 Kramer, *Maria Montessori*, p. 88.

89 Fellini, *I segreti della fama*, p. 100.

90 Ibid. p.22.

91 Kramer, *Maria Montessori*, p. 95.

92 Giovetti, *Maria Montessori*, p. 42.

93 *L'antropologia pedagogica: Conferenza tenuta agli studenti di filosofia nell'Università di Roma, di Maria Montessori* (Milan: Valardi, 1903), p. 15.

94 Kramer, *Maria Montessori*, p. 91.

95 Matteo Fiorani and Giovanni Bollea, "Per una storia della neuropsichiatria infantile in Italia," in *Medicina & Storia* 11 (2011), pp. 21–22 (also the following citation).

96 Carolina Montessori (ed.), *Maria Montessori Sails to America*, pp. viii–ix.

97 Ibid., pp. ix–x.

98 Fellini, *I segreti della fama*, p. 26.

99 Montessori, Notes on Her Childhood, AMI Archive.

100 Gandiglio, "Sulle tracce di Maria Montessori."

101 Fellini, *I segreti della fama*, p. 26.

102 Gandiglio, "Sulle tracce di Maria Montessori."

PART TWO

1 Maria Montessori to Donna Maraini, undated, AMI Archive.

2 Maria Montessori, Notes on Her Childhood, AMI Archive.

3 Rita Kramer, *Maria Montessori: A Biography* (New York: Da Capo Press, 1988), p. 93.

4 Fulvio De Giorgi (ed.), *Maria Montessori: Il peccato originale* (Brescia: Scholè, 2019), p. 133.

5 Maria Montessori to Padre Pietro Tacchi Venturi, San Diego, September 23, 1917, in "Maria Montessori e le sue reti di relazioni," in *Annali di storia dell'educazione e delle istituzioni scolastiche*, no. 25 (Brescia: Marcelliana, 2018), p. 31.

6 Ibid.

7 Paola Giovetti, *Maria Montessori: una biografia* (Rome: Mediterranee, 2009), p. 44.

8 Anna Matellicani, *La "Sapienza" di Maria Montessori: dagli studi universitari alla docenza 1890–1919*, p. 91.

9 Grazia Honegger Fresco (ed.), *Montessori: perché no?* (Turin: Il leone verde, 2017), p. 70 (all citations in the paragraph).

10 Matellicani, *La "Sapienza,"* p. 93.

11 Ibid., p. 91

12 Honegger Fresco (ed.), *Montessori: perché no?*, p. 69 (also the following citation).

13 Valeria Babini and Luisa Lama, *Una donna nuova* (Milan: FrancoAngeli, 2010), p. 147.

14 "Maria Montessori e le sue reti di relazioni," in *Annali di storia dell'educazione e delle istituzioni scolastiche*, no. 25 (Brescia: Marcelliana, 2018), p. 28.

15 Giuseppe Zago (ed.), *Sguardi storici sull'educazione dell'infanzia* (Fano: Aras, 2015), p. 285.

16 Maria Montessori to Rossana, undated, in Giovanna Alatri, *Il mondo al femminile di Maria Montessori, Regine, dame e altre donne* (Rome: Fefè, 2015), p. 43 (all citations in the paragraph).

17 Maria Montessori to Donna Cristina, AMI Archive.

18 Maria Montessori, "Caratteri fisici delle giovani donne del Lazio," extract from *Atti della Società Romana di Antropolo gia* 12, no. 1 (1905), p. 43.

19 Maria Montessori, Notes on Her Childhood, AMI Archive.

20 Paola Boni Fellini, *I segreti della fama* (Rome: Centro editoriale dell'Osservatore, 1955), p. 26.

21 Kramer, *Maria Montessori*, p. 98.

22 Anna Maria Maccheroni, *Come conobbi Maria Montessori* (Rome: Edizioni Vita dell'infanzia, 1956), p. 94.

23 Ibid. pp. 16–18 (also following citation).

24 Germana Recchia, *Maria Montessori: nei dintorni dell'uomo nuovo* (Laboratorio Montessori, 2013), p. 78.

25 Maria Montessori, "Ancora sui minorenni delinquenti," in *La vita* (August 6, 1906), p. 3 (also the following citation).

26 Ibid. (all citations in the paragraph).

27 *L'Alleanza*, no. 30 (October 26), AMI Archive.

28 Maria Montessori, "Proclama alle donne italiane," in *La vita*, February 26, 1906, AMI Archive.

29 Alatri, *Il mondo al femminile*, p. 62.

30 Valeria Babini and Luisa Lama, *Una donna nuova*, p. 193 (also the following citation).

31 Ibid., p. 16.

32 Ibid., p. 144.

33 *Acts of the First National Congress of Italian Women* (Società editrice Laziale, 1912), pp. 272–281.

34 Fulvio De Giorgi, "Maria Montessori modernista," in *Annali di storia dell'educazione e delle istituzioni scolastiche*, no. 16 (2009), pp. 199–216 (also following citation).

35 *La Civiltà Cattolica*, no. 2 (1908), pp. 513–532.

36 Giuseppina Le Maire, "Come vivono i poveri di Roma: Il quartiere di San Lorenzo," in *Nuova Antologia*, no. 39 (1904), p. 525.

37 Letizia Comba (ed.), *Donne educatrici: Maria Montessori e Ada Gobetti* (Turin: Rosenberg & Sellier, 1996), p. 75.

38 Maria Montessori, *La scoperta del bambino* (Milan: Garzanti, 2018), p. 38.

39 Ibid., p. 37.

40 "How It All Happened: Dr. Montessori Speaks," in *Ami Communications* (1970), AMI Archive.

41 Kramer, *Maria Montessori*, p. 112.

42 Maria Montessori, *La scoperta del bambino*, p. 157.

43 Maccheroni, *Come conobbi Maria Montessori*, p. 73.

44 Grazia Honegger Fresco, *Maria Montessori, una storia attuale* (Turin: Il leone verde, 2018), p. 245.

45 Maccheroni, *Come conobbi Maria Montessori*, p. 83.

46 Anna Maria Maccheroni, "Il bambino cerca di vivere," in *Vita dell'Infanzia* 1 (nos. 5–7), 1952, pp. 21–22 (also following citation).

47 Maria Montessori, *Autoeducazione nelle scuole elementari* (Rome: Loescher, 1916), p. 162.

48 Maccheroni, *Come conobbi Maria Montessori*, p. 72.

49 Maria Montessori, *Il segreto dell'infanzia* (Milan: Garzanti, 2017), p. 152.

50 Ibid., p. 158.

51 Kramer, *Maria Montessori*, p. 265.

52 *Building the Brain's "Air Traffic Control" System: How Early Experiences Shape the Development of Executive Function*, Working Paper no. 11 (Cambridge, MA: Center on the Developing Child, Harvard University, 2011), p. 2.

53 Kramer, *Maria Montessori*, p. 217.

54 Ibid., p. 139.

55 Sheila Radice, *The New Children: Talks with Dr. Maria Montessori* (London: Hadder and Stoughton, 1920), p. 165 (also the following citation).

56 Marziola Pignatari (ed.), *Maria Montessori cittadina del mondo* (Rome: Comitato italiano dell'Omep, 1967), p. 156.

57 Ibid., p. 116.

58 Kramer, *Maria Montessori*, p. 126.

59 Maria Montessori, *La scoperta del bambino*, p. 54.

60 Ibid., p. 377.

61 Ibid., p. 371.

62 Ibid., p. 375.

63 Ibid., pp. 218–221.

64 Pignatari (ed.), *Maria Montessori cittadina del mondo*, p. 129.

65 Speech by Maria Montessori, in *Conferencia: Journal de l'Université des Annales*, February 1937.

66 Maria Montessori, *La scoperta del bambino*, p. 245.

67 Mario Montessori, "Maria Montessori mia madre," in Sélection du Reader's Digest, September 1965, p. 74 (also the following citation).
68 Maria Montessori, La scoperta del bambino, p. 257.
69 Ibid., p. 258.
70 Maria Montessori, Il metodo della pedagogia scientifica applicato all'educazione infantile nelle case dei bambini (Rome: Opera Nazionale Montessori, 2000), p. 508.
71 Pignatari (ed.), Maria Montessori cittadina del mondo, p. 156.

PART THREE

1 Maria Montessori to Donna Maraini, August 22, 1910, AMI Archive.
2 Ibid.
2 Maria Luciana Buseghin, Cara Marietta: Lettere di Alice Hallgarten Franchetti 1901–1911 (Città di Castello: Tela Umbra, 2002), p. 486.
3 Ibid., p. 517.
4 Anna Maria Maccheroni, Come conobbi Maria Montessori (Rome: Edizioni Vita dell'infanzia, 1956), p. 49.
5 Maria Montessori to Donna Maraini, October 23, 1909, AMI Archive.
6 Giovanna Alatri, Il mondo al femminile di Maria Montessori, Regine, dame e altre donne (Rome: Fefè, 2015), p. 127.
7 Ibid., p. 128.
8 Maria Montessori, Lecture in course at Rome, 1913, AMI Archive.
9 Maccheroni, Come conobbi Maria Montessori, p. 52.
10 Maria Montessori to Donna Maraini, September 4,1909, AMI Archive.
11 Grazia Honegger Fresco, Radici nel futuro: la vita di Adele Costa Gnocchi (1883–1967) (Molfetta: La meridiana, 2001), p. 26.
12 Buseghin, Cara Marietta, p. 407.
13 Ibid., p. 447.
14 Ibid., p. 42.
15 Ibid., p. 74.
16 Maria Montessori to Donna Maraini, August 22, 1910, AMI Archive.
17 Maccheroni, Come conobbi Maria Montessori, p. 20.
18 Maria Montessori to Donna Maraini, undated, AMI Archive.
19 Gerald L. Gutek and Patricia A. Gutek, Bringing Montessori to America (Tuscaloosa: University of Alabama Press, 2016), p. 199.
20 Maccheroni, Come conobbi Maria Montessori, p. 81.
21 Maria Montessori to Donna Maraini, undated, probably November 1911, AMI Archive.
22 Maccheroni, Come conobbi Maria Montessori, p. 23.
23 Maria Montessori to Donna Maraini, November 16, 1909, AMI Archive (all citations in the paragraph).
24 Maria Montessori to Donna Maraini, November 4, 1909, AMI Archive.
25 Elisabetta Ballerini to Donna Maraini, December 12, 1909, in Alatri, Il mondo al femminile, p. 94.
26 Maria Montessori to Donna Maraini, November 14, 1909, AMI Archive.
27 Maria Montessori to Donna Maraini, November 4, AMI Archive.
28 Maria Montessori to Donna Maraini, November 16, 1909, AMI Archive.

29   Fulvio De Giorgi (ed.), *Maria Montessori: Dio e il bambino e altri scritti inediti* (Brescia: La Scuola, 2013), p. 352.

30   Maria Montessori to Padre Tacchi Venturi, September 23, 1917, in "Maria Montessori e le sue reti di relazioni," in *Annali di storia dell'educazione e delle istituzioni scolastiche*, no. 25 (Brescia: Marcelliana, 2018), p. 37.

31   Maccheroni, *Come conobbi Maria Montessori*, p. 188.

32   Maria Montessori to Donna Maraini, November 16, 1909, AMI Archive.

33   Raniero Regni, *Infanzia e società in Maria Montessori: Il bambino padre dell'uomo* (Rome: Armando, 2007), p. 87.

34   Maccheroni, *Come conobbi Maria Montessori*, p. 21.

35   Marziola Pignatari (ed.), *Maria Montessori cittadina del mondo* (Rome: Comitato italiano dell'Omep, 1967), p. 257.

36   André Michelet, *Les outils de l'enfance* (Neuchâtel, Switzerland: Delchaux et Miestlé), 1972, p. 100.

37   Maria Montessori to Giuliana Sorge, 1950, in Grazia Honegger Fresco, *Maria Montessori, una storia attuale* (Turin: Il leone verde, 2010), p. 253.

38   Maccheroni, *Come conobbi Maria Montessori*, p. 78.

39   Ibid., p. 87.

40   Maria Montessori, *Il segreto dell'infanzia*, p. 163.

41   Henry Gidel, *Marie Curie* (Paris: Flammarion, 2008), p. 225.

42   *"Caro Olgogigi": Lettere ad Olga e Luigi Lodi* (Milan: FrancoAngeli, 1999), p. 430.

43   Ibid.

44   Maria Montessori to Donna Maraini, August 22, 1910, AMI Archive.

45   Rita Kramer, *Maria Montessori: A Biography* (New York: Da Capo Press, 1988), p. 146.

46   Pignatari (ed.), *Maria Montessori cittadina del mondo*, p. 153.

47   Maria Montessori, *Il segreto dell'infanzia* (Milan: Garzanti, 2017), p. 187.

48   "Il materiale Montessori in cataloghi editi a New York, Londra, Bucarest, Berlino, Gonzaga tra gli anni Dieci e Trenta," in *Il Quaderno Montessori* (Castellanza: Associazione Centro Nascita Montessori, 1993), p. 157.

49   Maria Montessori to Donna Maraini, September 9, 1910, AMI Archive.

50   Ibid.

51   Giuseppe Zago (ed.), *Sguardi storici sull'educazione dell'infanzia* (Fano: Aras, 2015), p. 291.

52   Maria Montessori, *Formazione dell'uomo* (Milan: Garzanti, 1949), p. 42.

53   Raniero Regni and Leonardo Fogassi, *Maria Montessori e le neuroscienze: Cervello, mente, educazione* (Rome: Fefè, 2019), p. 60.

54   Maria Montessori to Donna Maraini, August 1911, AMI Archive.

55   *"Caro Olgogigi,"* p. 553.

56   Anna Fedeli to Donna Maraini, August 8, 1911, AMI Archive.

57   Central State Archive, Ministry of Public Instruction, Personnel files of university teachers, II versamento, I series, 1900–1940, b 101.

58   Renato Foschi, *Maria Montessori* (Rome: Ediesse, 2012), p. 84.

59   Maccheroni, *Come conobbi Maria Montessori*, p. 185

60   Maria Montessori, *Il segreto dell'infanzia*, p. 192 (also the following citation).

61   Maccheroni, *Come conobbi Maria Montessori*, p. 70 (also the following citation).

62   Maria Montessori to Donna Maraini, September 3, 1912, AMI Archive.

63   Maria Montessori, *Il nuovo metodo di educazione*, in *Opera Montessori*, January–February 1932, p. 23, AMI Archive.

64 De Giorgi (ed.), *Maria Montessori: Dio e il bambino*, p. 81.

65 Renato Foschi, *Maria Montessori*, p. 68.

66 *La cura dell'anima in Maria Montessori: L'educazione morale, spirituale e religiosa dell'infanzia* (Rome: Fefè, 2011), p. 60.

67 Maria Montessori to Donna Maraini, November 16, 1909, unpublished, by kind concession of Carolina Montessori, AMI Archive.

68 Honegger Fresco, *Maria Montessori, una storia attuale*, p. 187.

69 Lorenzo Bedeschi, *L'antimodernismo in Italia: Accusatori, polemisti, fanatici* (Milan: San Paolo, 2000), p. 228.

70 Maria Montessori to Marie de la Rédemption, undated, in Alatri, *Il mondo al femminile*, p. 205.

71 Kramer, *Maria Montessori*, p. 179.

72 Maccheroni, *Come conobbi Maria Montessori*, p. 78.

73 Maria Montessori to Donna Maraini, September 19, 1911, AMI Archive.

74 Maria Montessori to Donna Maraini, August 1911, AMI Archive.

75 Maria Montessori to Donna Maraini, undated, AMI Archive.

76 Maria Montessori to Donna Maraini, August 25, 1911, AMI Archive (also the following citation).

77 Maria Montessori to Olga Lodi, in "*Caro Olgogigi*," p. 554.

78 Josephine Tozier, "The Montessori Schools in Rome," in *McClure's Magazine* 38, no. 2 (December 1911), p. 133.

79 Kramer, *Maria Montessori*, p. 153.

80 Dorothy Canfield Fisher, *A Montessori Mother* (New York: Henry Holt, 1912), p. 224.

81 Anne E. George, "Dr. Maria Montessori: The Achievement and Personality of an Italian Woman Whose Discovery Is Revolutionizing Education Methods," in *Good Housekeeping* 55, no. 1 (July 1912), p. 25 (also the following citation).

82 Anne E. George, "The First Montessori School in America," in *McClure's Magazine* 39, no. 2 (June 1912), p. 178.

83 Tozier, "The Montessori Schools in Rome," p. 128.

84 S. S. McClure, *My Autobiography* (New York: Frederick A. Stokes, 1914), p. 252.

85 Fisher, *A Montessori Mother*, p. 225.

86 Carolina Montessori (ed.), *Maria Montessori Sails to America: A Private Diary, 1913* (Laren, Holland: Montessori-Pierson Publishing, 2013), p. 28.

87 Maccheroni, *Come conobbi Maria Montessori*, p. 80.

88 Marta Gandiglio, "Sulle tracce di Maria Montessori," thesis, University of Rome, 1997–1998, AMI Archive.

89 Maria Montessori to Donna Maraini, undated, between December 1912 and January 1913, AMI Archive.

90 Maria Montessori to Donna Maraini, telegram, February 1, 1913, in "Maria Montessori e le sue reti di relazioni," p. 139.

91 Kramer, *Maria Montessori*, p. 185.

92 Maccheroni, *Come conobbi Maria Montessori*, p. 187.

93 Letizia Comba (ed.), *Donne educatrici: Maria Montessori e Ada Gobetti* (Turin: Rosenberg & Sellier, 1996), p. 66.

94 Mario Montessori, "Maria Montessori mia madre," in *Sélection du Reader's Digest*, September 1965, p. 70

95 Carolina Montessori (ed.), *Maria Montessori Sails to America*, p. 6.

96 Maria Montessori 100 Years: 1907–2007 Centenary of the Montessori Movement (Chennai, India: Kalakshetra Publications, 2007), p. 181.
97 Maria Montessori to Donna Maraini, August 28, 1912, AMI Archive.
98 Maria Montessori to Donna Maraini, undated, between December 1912 and January 1913, AMI Archive.
99 Kramer, Maria Montessori, p. 178.
100 Ibid., p. 315.
101 Gandiglio, "Sulle tracce di Maria Montessori" (also the following citation).
102 Gutek and Gutek, Bringing Montessori to America, p. 70.
103 Giovanna Alatri, Il mondo al femminile di Maria Montessori, Regine, dame e altre donne (Rome: Fefè, 2015), p. 8.
104 Sheila Radice, The New Children: Talks with Dr. Maria Montessori (London: Hadder and Stoughton, 1920), p. 35.
105 Kramer, Maria Montessori, p. 172.
106 Gutek and Gutek, Bringing Montessori to America, p. 68.
107 Ibid., p. 111.
108 Alatri, Il mondo al femminile, p. 200.
109 Grazia Honegger Fresco, "Roma: il corso Montessori del 1910 e La casa dei Bambini," in Il Quaderno Montessori 51 (1996), pp. 109–136.
110 Gutek and Gutek, Bringing Montessori to America, p. 112.
111 Edith Sharon to Samuel McClure, May 1912, in Gutek and Gutek, Bringing Montessori to America, p. 114.
112 Maria Montessori to Samuel McClure, June 29, 1913, in Gutek and Gutek, Bringing Montessori to America, p. 150.
113 Gutek and Gutek, Bringing Montessori to America, p. 63.
114 Maria Montessori, Letter to the Editors, in Times Educational Supplement, September 1, 1914, AMI Archive.
115 Carolina Montessori (ed.), Maria Montessori Sails to America, p. 28.
116 Kramer, Maria Montessori, p. 174.
117 Ibid., p. 183
118 Alatri, Il mondo al femminile, p. 199 (also the following citation).
119 Carolina Montessori (ed.), Maria Montessori Sails to America, p. 1.
120 Ibid., p. 42.
121 Ibid., p. 32.
122 Ibid., p. 29.
123 Kramer, Maria Montessori, p. 186.

PART FOUR

1 Maria Montessori to Donna Maraini, August 1911, AMI Archive.
2 Rita Kramer, Maria Montessori: A Biography (New York: Da Capo Press, 1988), p. 15.
3 Gerald L. Gutek and Patricia A. Gutek, Bringing Montessori to America (Tuscaloosa: University of Alabama Press, 2016), p. 124 (also the following citation).
4 Kramer, Maria Montessori, p. 190 (also the following citation).
5 Ibid., p. 195.
6 Ibid., p. 196.

7 Gutek and Gutek, *Bringing Montessori to America*, p. 137.
8 Kramer, *Maria Montessori*, pp. 197–200.
9 Gutek and Gutek, *Bringing Montessori to America*, p. 148.
10 Ibid.
11 Maria Montessori to Samuel McClure, telegram, January 7, 1914, in Gutek and Gutek, *Bringing Montessori to America*, p. 158.
12 Kramer, *Maria Montessori*, p. 229.
13 Maria Montessori to Donna Maraini, August 28, 1912, AMI Archive.
14 Maria Montessori to Samuel McClure, April 14, 1914, in Gutek and Gutek, *Bringing Montessori to America*, p. 179.
15 Kramer, *Maria Montessori*, p. 206.
16 Gutek and Gutek, *Bringing Montessori to America*, p. 183.
17 Franz Hammerer, *Maria Montessoris pädagogisches Konzept* (Vienna: Jugend & Volk, 1997), p. 186.
18 Gutek and Gutek, *Bringing Montessori to America*, p. 169.
19 Marta Gandiglio, "Sulle tracce di Maria Montessori," thesis, University of Rome, 1997–1998, AMI Archive.
20 Maria Montessori, Notes on Her Childhood, AMI Archive.
21 Carolina Montessori (ed.), *Maria Montessori Writes to Her Father: Letters from California, 1915* (Laren, Holland: Montessori-Pierson, 2015), p. 4.
22 Ibid., p. 3.
23 Ibid., p. 8.
24 Ibid., p. 12.
25 Gutek and Gutek, *Bringing Montessori to America*, p. 194.
26 Ibid., pp. 197–201 (all citations in the paragraph).
27 Ibid., p. 200.
28 Ibid., p. 201.
29 Carolina Montessori (ed.), *Maria Montessori Writes to Her Father*, p. 13.
30 Ibid., p. 15.
31 Dorothy M. Gaudiose, *Maria "l'Americana": La vita di Mary Pyle* (Cinisello Balsamo: San Paolo, 1995), p. 50.
32 Carolina Montessori (ed.), *Maria Montessori Writes to Her Father*, p. 25.
33 Ibid., p. 32.
34 Ibid., p. 50.
35 Kramer, *Maria Montessori*, p. 219.
36 Ibid.
37 Ibid., p. 220.
38 Carolina Montessori (ed.), *Maria Montessori Writes to Her Father*, p. 71.
39 Maria Montessori to Alessandro Montessori, August 29, 1915, in Carolina Montessori (ed.), *Maria Montessori Writes to Her Father*, p. 87.
40 Ibid., p. 83.
41 Ibid., pp. 83–88 (all citations in the paragraph).
42 Kramer, *Maria Montessori*, p. 222 (all citations in the paragraph).
43 Anna Maria Maccheroni, *Come conobbi Maria Montessori* (Rome: Edizioni Vita dell'infanzia, 1956), p. 27.
44 Eladio Homs, *Maria Montessori "Barcelonina,"* in Marziola Pignatari (ed.), *Maria Montessori cittadina del mondo*, p. 260.

45 Maccheroni, *Come conobbi Maria Montessori*, p. 98.

46 Marcella Vigilante, "Il buon pastore nella didattica montessoria na," thesis, Istituto Superiore Scienze Religiose, 2005–2006, p. 101.

47 Fulvio De Giorgi (ed.), *Maria Montessori: Dio e il bambino e altri scritti inediti* (Brescia: La Scuola, 2013), p. 143.

48 Maccheroni, *Come conobbi Maria Montessori*, p. 113.

49 De Giorgi (ed.), *Maria Montessori: Dio e il bambino*, p. 137.

50 Dani Cañigueral Viñals, *La historia de Montessori i Barcelona*, Treball de Recerca, p. 18, AMI Archive.

51 Maria Montessori to Padre Pietro Tacchi Venturi, September 23, 1917, in "Maria Montessori e le sue reti di relazioni," in *Annali di storia dell'educazione e delle istituzioni scolastiche*, no. 25 (Brescia: Marcelliana, 2018), pp. 37–42 (all citations in the paragraph).

52 Ibid., p. 46.

53 Per la libera personalità del Fanciullo, photocopy, AMI Archive.

54 Raniero Regni and Leonardo Fogassi, *Maria Montessori e le neuroscienze* (Rome: Fefè, 2019), p. 151.

55 Maria Montessori, *La mente del bambino* (Milan: Garzanti, 2017), p. 62.

56 Maria Montessori, *Il segreto dell'infanzia* (Milan: Garzanti, 2017), p. 55.

57 Ibid., p. 72 (also the following citation).

58 Augusto Scocchera, *Maria Montessori: Una storia per il nostro tempo* (Rome: Edizioni Opera Nazionale Montessori, 2005), p. 84.

59 Ibid., p. 64.

60 Kramer, *Maria Montessori*, p. 257.

61 Raniero Regni, *Infanzia e società in Maria Montessori: Il bambino padre dell'uomo* (Rome: Armando, 2007), p. 199.

62 Lucia Fancello, "La Casa dei Bambini di tirocinio a Napoli," in *La Coltura popolare* 10, no. 1 (January 1920), pp. 20–31.

63 Mary R. Cromwell, "Il Metodo Montessori in Francia durante la guerra," in *La Coltura popolare* 9, no. 1 (January 1919), p. 51.

64 Maria Montessori to Augusto Osimo, in Claudio A. Colombo and Marina Beretta Dragoni (eds.), *Maria Montessori e il sodalizio con l'Umanitaria* (Milan: Ed. Humanitarian Collection, 2008), p. 6.

65 Maria Montessori to Augusto Osimo, summer 1917, in Tiziana Pironi, "Da Maria Montessori a Margherita Zoebeli: l'impegno educativo nei confronti dell'infanzia traumatizzata dalla guerra," in *Annali online della Didattica e della Formazione Docente* 8, no. 12 (2016), pp. 115–128.

66 Maria Montessori to Padre Tacchi Venturi, July 12, 1917, in "Maria Montessori e le sue reti di relazioni," p. 47.

67 Suzanne Stewart-Steinberg, *L'effetto Pinocchio* (Rome: Elliot, 2011), p. 394.

68 Maria Montessori to Augusto Osimo, September 20, 1916, in Irene Pozzi, "La Società Umanitaria e la diffusione del Metodo Montessori (1908–1923)," in *Ricerche di Pedagogia e Didattica, Journal of Theories and Research in Education* 10, no. 2 (2015), p. 109.

69 Augusto Osimo, January 1921, Humanitarian Archive, protocol 214, folder 1744/20, unpublished, by kind concession of Carolina Montessori.

70 Paola Giovetti, *Maria Montessori: una biografia* (Rome: Mediterranee, 2009), p. 123.

71 Kramer, *Maria Montessori*, p. 221.

72 Ibid., p. 227.

73 Leonardo De Sanctis (ed.), *Le ricette di Maria Montessori cent'anni dopo* (Rome: Fefè, 2008), p. 63 (also the following citation).

74 Maria Montessori, *La scoperta del bambino* (Milan: Garzanti, 2018), p. 77.

75 Grazia Honegger Fresco, *Maria Montessori, una storia attuale* (Turin: Il leone verde, 2018), p. 212.

76 Maria Montessori to Augusto Osimo, December 20, 1921, Humanitarian Archive, unpublished, by kind concession of Carolina Montessori.

77 "Il materiale Montessori in cataloghi editi a New York, Londra, Bucarest, Berlino, Gonzaga tra gli anni Dieci e Trenta," in *Il Quaderno Montessori* (Castellanza: Associazione Centro Nascita Montessori, 1993), p. 14.

78 Kramer, *Maria Montessori*, p. 267.

79 Sheila Radice, *The New Children: Talks with Dr. Maria Montessori* (London: Hadder and Stoughton, 1920), p. 109.

80 Ibid., p. 104.

81 Ibid., p. 106.

82 Ibid., p. 60.

83 Maria Montessori to Mother Elizabeth, August 14, 1921, in Fulvio De Giorgio (ed.), *Maria Montessori: Il peccato originale* (Brescia: Scholè, 2019), p. 19.

84 Kramer, *Maria Montessori*, p. 351.

85 Radice, *The New Children*, p. 75.

86 Manfred Berger and Clara Grunwald, *Wegbereiterin der Montessori Pädagogik* (Frankfurt: Brandes & Apsel, 2000), p. 60.

87 Kramer, *Maria Montessori*, p. 291.

88 Franz Hammerer, *Maria Montessoris pädagogisches Konzept* (Vienna: Jugend & Volk, 1997), p. 186.

89 Kramer, *Maria Montessori*, p. 282.

90 "Mussolini and Montessori: an Established Principle," in *Times Educational Supplement*, April 4, 1925.

91 De Sanctis (ed.), *Le ricette di Maria Montessori*, p. 65.

92 Augusto Scocchera (ed.), *Introduzione a Mario M. Montessori* (Opera Nazionale Montessori, 1998), p. 154.

93 Kramer, *Maria Montessori*, p. 315.

94 Ibid., p. 314 (also the following citation).

95 Gaudiose, *Maria "l'Americana,"* p. 53.

96 Ibid., p. 54.

97 Ibid., p. 55.

98 Marilena Henny Montessori, "L'altra Maria," in *Le ricette di Maria Montessori, cent'anni dopo* (Rome: Fefè, 2008), p. 66.

99 "Maria Montessori e le sue reti di relazioni," p. 94.

100 Renato Foschi, Erica Moretti, and Paola Trabalzini (ed.), *Il destino di Maria Montessori* (Rome: Fefè, 2019), p. 58.

101 Ibid., p. 164.

102 Grazia Honegger Fresco (ed.), *Montessori: perché no?* (Turin: Il leone verde, 2017), p. 80 (also the following citation).

103 Maria Montessori to Benito Mussolini, May 26, 1928, in Giuliana Marazzi, "Montessori e Mussolini: la collaborazione e la rottura," in *Dimensioni e problemi della ricerca storica*, Università "La Sapienza" di Roma, 1 (2000), pp. 177–196.

104   Police notation, October 10, 1932, State Archive, AMI Archive.

105   Maria Montessori to Emilio Bodrero, May 15, 1931, in "Maria Montessori e le sue reti di relazioni," p. 205 (also the following citation).

106   Central State Archive, Private Secretariat of the Duce, Ordinary Correspondence, 1922–1943, B 288, F. 15230-15279.

107   Radice, The New Children, p. 37.

108   Clara Tornar, "Maria Montessori durante il fascismo," in Cadmo 2 (2005), p. 21.

109   "Il caso Montessori," in La vita italiana, May 1934, p. 615.

110   Mario Montessori, "Maria Montessori mia madre," in Sélection du Reader's Digest, September 1965, p. 74.

PART FIVE

1   Letizia Comba (ed.), Donne educatrici: Maria Montessori e Ada Gobetti (Turin: Rosenberg & Sellier, 1996), p. 25.

2   Jean-François Condette and Antoine Savoye, "Une éducation pour une ère nouvelle: le congrès international d'éducation de Calais (1921)," in Les Études sociales 163 (July 2016), pp. 43–77.

3   "Il metodo in Romania," in Il Quaderno Montessori, Winter 2001–2002, p. 58.

4   Marta Gandiglio, "Sulle tracce di Maria Montessori," thesis, University of Rome, 1997–1998, AMI Archive.

5   Grazia Honegger Fresco, Maria Montessori, una storia attuale (Turin: Il leone verde, 2018), p. 45.

6   Anna Maria Maccheroni, Come conobbi Maria Montessori (Rome: Edizioni Vita dell'infanzia, 1956), p. 187.

7   Paola Giovetti, Maria Montessori: una biografia (Rome: Mediterranee, 2009), p. 132.

8   Gandiglio, "Sulle tracce di Maria Montessori" (also the following citation).

9   Giovetti, Maria Montessori, p. 132, p. 78.

10   Maria Montessori to Donna Maraini, May 15, 1934, AMI Archive.

11   Grazia Honegger Fresco, Radici nel futuro: la vita di Adele Costa Gnocchi (1883–1967) (Molfetta: La meridiana, 2001), p. 65.

12   Sheila Radice, The New Children: Talks with Dr. Maria Montessori (London: Hadder and Stoughton, 1920), p. 52.

13   Ibid., p. 57.

14   N. Padellaro, "Inauguration of the XV International Montessori Course," in Annali dell'istruzione elementare 5, no. 1 (1930), pp. 34–37.

15   Giovetti, Maria Montessori, p. 90.

16   Grazia Honegger Fresco (ed.), Maria Montessori: perché no? (Turin: Il leone verde, 2017), p. 61

17   Gandiglio, "Sulle tracce di Maria Montessori."

18   "La scuola Montessori di Laren," in Il Quaderno Montessori 7, no. 25 (Spring 1990), p. 107, AMI Archive.

19   Gandiglio, "Sulle tracce di Maria Montessori."

20   Augusto Scocchera, Maria Montessori: Una storia per il nostro tempo (Rome: Edizioni Opera Nazionale Montessori, 2005), p. 115.

21   Ibid., p. 118.

22 *Il Quaderno Montessori*, nos. 31–32 (1991).

23 Gandiglio, "Sulle tracce di Maria Montessori."

24 Maria Montessori to Donna Maraini, December 21, 1938, unpublished, by kind concession of Carolina Montessori, AMI Archive.

25 Honegger Fresco, *Radici nel futuro*, p. 58.

26 Camillo Grazzini, "Maria Montessori's Cosmic Vision, Cosmic Plan and Cosmic Education," in *NAMTA Journal* 38, no. 1 (Winter 2013).

27 Fulvio De Giorgi (ed.), *Maria Montessori. Dio e il bambino e altri scritti inediti* (Brescia: la Scuola, 2013), p. 135.

28 Giovetti, *Maria Montessori*, p. 108.

29 Scocchera, *Maria Montessori*, p. 190.

30 Ibid., p. 108.

31 Honegger Fresco, *Maria Montessori, una storia attuale*, p. 160.

32 Scocchera, *Maria Montessori*, p. 103 (also the following citations).

33 Frank A. Stone, *The New World of Educational Thought* (New York: MSS Information Corporation, 1973), p. 174.

34 Rita Kramer, *Maria Montessori: A Biography* (New York: Da Capo Press, 1988), p. 310 (also the following citation).

35 Giovetti, *Maria Montessori*, p. 96.

36 Ibid., p. 81.

37 "Montessori in India," in *On the Watch Tower* 61, no. 1 (November 1939) (Theosophical Publishing House, Adyar, Madras).

38 Giovanna Alatri, *Il mondo al femminile di Maria Montessori, Regine, dame e altre donne* (Rome: Fefè, 2015), p. 241.

39 Maria Montessori to Donna Maraini, February 1940, unpublished, by kind concession of Carolina Montessori, AMI Archive.

40 Giovetti, *Maria Montessori*, p. 109.

41 Ibid., p. 133.

42 Ibid., p. 137.

43 "Montessori in India," in *The Theosophist* 60, no.1 (October 1938–March 1939), AMI Archive.

44 Giovetti, *Maria Montessori*, p. 110.

45 Gandiglio, "Sulle tracce di Maria Montessori."

46 Kramer, *Maria Montessori*, p. 344.

47 Giovetti, *Maria Montessori*, pp. 111–112.

48 Ibid., p. 113.

49 Ibid., p. 114.

50 Kramer, *Maria Montessori*, p. 345.

51 Giovetti, *Maria Montessori*, p. 108.

52 Ibid., p. 133.

53 Marjan Schwegman, *Maria Montessori* (Bologna: il Mulino, 1999), p. 26.

54 Giovetti, *Maria Montessori*, p. 119.

55 Ibid., p. 108.

56 Ibid., p. 123.

57 Ibid., p. 100.

58 Maria Montessori to Donna Maraini, December 31, 1945, unpublished, by kind concession of Carolina Montessori, AMI Archive.

59 Kramer, *Maria Montessori*, pp. 349–351.

60 Maria Montessori to Giuliana Sorge, undated, almost certainly 1947, in Honegger Fresco, *Maria Montessori, una storia attuale*, p. 251.

61 Maria Montessori to Luigia Tincani, July 29, 1949, in De Giorgi (ed.), *Maria Montessori: Dio e il bambino*, p. 362.

62 Ibid., p. 360.

63 Maria Montessori to Joosten, 1946, unpublished, by kind concession of Carolina Montessori, AMI Archive.

64 Maria Montessori to Donna Maraini, August 18, 1946, AMI Archive.

65 Kramer, *Maria Montessori*, p. 352.

66 Maccheroni, *Come conobbi Maria Montessori*, p. 186.

67 Kramer, *Maria Montessori*, p. 353.

68 Phyllis Povell, *Montessori Comes to America: The Leadership of Maria Montessori and Nancy McCormick* (Lanham, MD: University Press of America, 2010), p. 12.

69 De Giorgi (ed.), *Maria Montessori: Dio e il bambino*, p. 111.

70 *Maria Montessori parla ai genitori: Il pensiero montessoriano spiegato alle famiglie* (Turin: Il leone verde, 2018), p. 65 (also the following citation).

71 Ibid., p. 72.

72 Maria Montessori to Donna Maraini, undated, surely July 1947, unpublished, by kind concession of Carolina Montessori, AMI Archive.

73 Kramer, *Maria Montessori*, p. 354.

74 Maria Montessori to Giuliana Sorge, undated, almost certainly 1947, in Honegger Fresco, *Maria Montessori, una storia attuale*, p. 251.

75 Kramer, *Maria Montessori*, p. 362.

76 Augusto Scocchera (ed.), *Introduzione a Mario M. Montessori* (Opera Nazionale Montessori, 1998), p. 157.

77 Honegger Fresco, *Maria Montessori, una storia attuale*, p. 164.

78 Maria Montessori, *Formazione dell'uomo* (Milan: Garzanti, 1949), p. 11.

79 Maria Montessori, *La mente del bambino* (Milan: Garzanti, 2017), p. 25.

80 Raniero Regni and Leonardo Fogassi, *Maria Montessori e le neuroscienze* (Rome: Fefè, 2019), p. 89.

81 Maria Montessori, "Per i minorenni delinquenti," in *La vita*, July 14, 1906, p. 3.

82 Scocchera (ed.), *Introduzione a Mario M. Montessori*, p. 145.

83 Maria Montessori, *Il bambino in famiglia* (Milan: Garzanti, 2000), p. 61.

84 Raniero Regni, *Infanzia e società in Maria Montessori: Il bambino padre dell'uomo* (Rome: Armando, 2007), p. 266.

85 Marziola Pignatari (ed.), *Maria Montessori cittadina del mondo* (Rome: Comitato italiano dell'Omep, 1967), p. 15.

86 Maria Montessori to Clemente Maraini, July 1911, in Giovanna Alatri, *Il mondo al femminile di Maria Montessori* (Rome: Fefè, 2015), p. 17.

87 Gandiglio, "Sulle tracce di Maria Montessori."

88 De Giorgi (ed.), *Maria Montessori: Dio e il bambino*, p. 111.

89 Pignatari (ed.), *Maria Montessori cittadina del mondo*, p. 157.

90   Ibid., p. 201.
91   *AMI Communications*, January–February 1953.
92   Gandiglio, "Sulle tracce di Maria Montessori" (all citations in the paragraph).
93   "In Memory of Mario Montessori," in *AMI Communications*, 1 no. 2, 1982, pp. 5–6.
94   Honegger Fresco, *Maria Montessori, una storia attuale*, p. 181.

AUTHOR'S NOTE

1   Orio Vergani, *Misure nel tempo* (Milan: Baldini & Castaldi, 2003), p. 28.

Bibliography

BOOKS

Addis Saba, Marina. *Anna Kuliscioff: Vita privata e passione politica*. Milan: Mondadori, 1993.

Alatri, Giovanna. *Il mondo al femminile di Maria Montessori: Regine, dame e altre donne*. Rome: Fefè, 2015.

Babini, Valeria P. *La questione dei frenastenici: Alle origini della psicologia scientifica in Italia 1870–1910*. Milan: FrancoAngeli, 1996.

Babini, Valeria, and Luisa Lama. *Una donna nuova*. Milan: FrancoAngeli, 2010.

Badinter, Élisabeth. *L'amore in più: Storia dell'amore materno*. Milan: Longanesi, 1982.

Bailey, Richard. *A. S. Neill*. New York: Bloomsbury Academic, 2014.

Ball, Thomas. *Itard, Séguin and Kephart: Sensory Education: A Learning Interpretation*. Columbus, OH: Merrill, 1971.

Barausse, Alberto. *I maestri all'università: La Scuola pedagogica di Roma 1904–1923*. Perugia, Italy: Morlacchi, 2004.

Barbera, Mario. *L'educazione nuova e il metodo Montessori*. Milan: Ancora, 1946.

Bartolini, Stefania (ed.). *Per le strade del mondo: Laiche e religiose tra Otto e Novecento*. Bologna: il Mulino, 2007.

Battista, Giuseppina. *L'educazione religiosa in Maria Montessori*. Milan: Massimo, 1989.

Baumann, Harold. *1907–2007, hundert Jahre Montessori-Pädagogik*. Bern: Haupt Verlag, 2007.

Bedeschi, Lorenzo. *L'antimodernismo in Italia: Accusatori, polemisti, fanatici*. Milan: San Paolo, 2000.

Berger, Manfred. *Clara Grunwald: Wegbereiterin der Montessori Pädagogik*. Francoforte: Brandes & Apsel, 2000.

Bertin, Giovanni Maria. *Il fanciullo montessoriano e l'educazione infantile*. Rome: Armando, 1975.

———. *Pedagogia italiana del Novecento: Autori e prospettive*. Milan: Mursia, 1989.

Bertini, Giovanni. *Il metodo Montessori*. Florence: Bemporad-Marzocco, 1953.

Bonaventura, Massa. *Maria Pyle: Una creatura meravigliosa alla scuola di Padre Pio*. San Giovanni Rotondo, Italy: Convento Santa Maria delle Grazie, 1970.

Boni Fellini, Paola. *I segreti della fama*. Rome: Centro editoriale dell'Osservatore, 1955.

Borghi, Battista Q. *Montessori dalla A alla Z. Lessico della pedagogia di Maria Montessori.* Trento: Erikson, 2019.

Bortolotti, Lando. *Roma fuori le mura: L'Agro romano da palude a metropoli.* Roma-Bari, Italy: Laterza, 1988.

Bucci, Sante. *Educazione dell'infanzia e pedagogia scientifica: Da Fröbel a Montessor.* Rome: Bulzoni, 1990.

Buseghin, Luciana. *Alice Hallgarten Franchetti: Un modello di donna e di imprenditrice nell'Italia tra '800 e '900.* Selci-Lama, Italy: Pliniana, 2013.

Buseghin, Maria Luciana. *Cara Marietta: Lettere di Alice Hallgarten Franchetti 1901–1911.* Città di Castello, Italy: Tela Umbra, 2002.

Buttafuoco, Annarita. *Le Mariuccine: Storia di un'istituzione laica:l'asilo Mariuccia.* Milan: FrancoAngeli, 1998.

Butturini, Emilio. *La pace giusta: Testimoni e maestri tra '800 e '900.* Verona: Mazziana, 2007.

"Caro Olgogigi": Lettere ad Olga e Luigi Lodi: Dalla Roma bizantina all'Italia fascista, 1881–1933. Milan: FrancoAngeli, 1999.

Castoldi, Massimo. *Insegnare libertà.* Rome: Donzelli, 2018.

Catarsi, Enzo. *La giovane Montessori.* Ferrara, Italy: Corso, 1995.

Cavalletti, Sofia, and Gianna Gobbi. *Educazione religiosa, liturgia e metodo Montessori.* Rome: Paoline, 1961.

Charnitzky, Jürgen. *Fascismo e scuola: La politica scolastica del regime, 1922–1943.* Florence: La Nuova Italia, 1996.

Chattin-McNichols, John. *The Montessori Controversy.* Albany, NY: Delmar, 1991.

Cives, Giacomo. *Maria Montessori pedagogista complessa.* Pisa, Italy: ETS, 2001.

Colomba, Letizia (ed.). *Donne educatrici: Maria Montessori e Ada Gobetti.* Turin: Rosenberg & Sellier, 1996.

Conti, Bruna, and Alba Morino. *Sibilla Aleramo e il suo tempo: Vita raccontata e illustrata.* Milan: Feltrinelli, 1981.

Cornelio, Angelo Maria. *Vita di Antonio Stoppani: Onoranze alla sua memoria.* Turin: UTET, 1898.

Curli, Barbara. *Italiane al lavoro 1914–1920.* Venice: Marsilio, 1998.

D'Amelia, Marina (ed.). *Storia della maternità.* Roma-Bari, Italy: Laterza, 1997.

De Bartolomeis, Francesco. *Maria Montessori e la pedagogia scientifica.* Florence: La Nuova Italia, 1961.

De Giorgio, Fulvio. *Maria Montessori: Il peccato originale.* Brescia: Scholè, 2019.

De Giorgio, Michela. *Le italiane dall'Unità a oggi: Modelli culturali e comportamenti sociali.* Roma-Bari, Italy: Laterza, 1992.

De Sanctis, Carlo. *Giuseppe Ferruccio Montesano.* Bari, Italy: Grafiche Cressati, 1962.

De Sanctis, Leonardo (ed.). *Le ricette di Maria Montessori cent'anni dopo.* Rome: Fefè, 2008.

Di generazione in generazione: Le italiane dall'Unità a oggi. Rome: Viella, 2014.

Dolza, Delfina. *Essere figlie di Lombroso: Due donne intellettuali tra '800 e '900.* Milan: FrancoAngeli, 1990.

Donne e diritti: Dalla Sentenza Mortara del 1906 alla prima avvocata italiana. Bologna: il Mulino, 2004.

Eckert, Ela. *Maria und Mario Montessoris Kosmische Erziehung: Vision und Konkretion.* Berlin: LIT, 2007.

Educazione al femminile: Dalla parità alla differenza. Florence: La Nuova Italia, 1992.

Falchi, Federica. *L'itinerario politico di Regina Terruzzi: Dal mazzinianesimo al fascismo.* Milan: FrancoAngeli; Paris: Julien Crémieu, 1927.

Fare gli italiani. Vol. 1: *La nascita dello Stato nazionale.* Bologna: il Mulino, 1996.

Finazzi Sartor, Rosetta. *Maria Montessori.* Brescia: La scuola, 1961.

Fisher, Dorothy Canfield. *A Montessori Mother.* New York: Henry Holt, 1912.

———. *The Montessori Manual for Teachers and Parents.* Cambridge, MA: Robert Bentley, 1964.

Forti Messina, Annalucia. *Il sapere e la clinica.* Milan: FrancoAngeli, 1998.

Foschi, Renato. *Maria Montessori.* Rome: Ediesse, 2012.

Foschi, Renato, Erica Moretti, and Paola Trabalzini (eds.). *Il destino di Maria Montessori.* Rome: Fefè, 2019.

Fynne, Robert John. *Montessori and Her Inspirers.* London: Longmans, Green, 1924.

Gandiglio, Marta. "Sulle tracce di Maria Montessori: Testimonianze di allievi amici e stimatori, 1930–1999." Thesis, University of Rome, 1997–1998, AMI Archive.

Gaudiose, Dorothy M. *Maria "l'Americana": La vita di Mary Pyle all'ombra di Padre Pio.* Cinisello Balsamo, Italy: San Paolo, 1995.

Genitori e figli nell'età contemporanea: Relazioni in rapida trasformazione. Florence: Istituto degli Innocenti, 2003.

Ghizzoni, Carla. *Educazione e scuola all'indomani della grande guerra: Il contributo de "La Civiltà Cattolica," 1918–1931.* Brescia: La scuola, 1997.

Gidel, Henri. *Marie Curie.* Paris: Flammarion, 2008.

Giovetti, Paola. *Maria Montessori: una biografia.* Rome: Mediterranee, 2009.

Grant, Cecil. *English Education and Dr. Montessori.* London: Wells Gardner, 1913.

Gutek, Gerald L. *The Montessori Method: The Origins of an Educational Innovation.* Lanham, MD: Rowman & Littlefield, 2004.

Gutek, Gerald L., and Patricia A. Gutek. *Bringing Montessori to America.* Tuscaloosa: University of Alabama Press, 2016.

Hammerer, Franz. *Maria Montessoris pädagogisches Konzept.* Vienna: Jugend & Volk, 1997.

Hansen-Schaberg, Inge. *Clara Grunwald: Ein Leben für die Montessori-Pädagogik.* Berlin: Bibliothek für Bildungsgeschichtliche Forschung, 2003.

Heid, M. L. *Uomini che non scompaiono.* Florence: Sansoni, 1944.

Holman, Henry. *Séguin and His Physiological Method of Education.* London: Pitman, 1914.

Honegger Fresco, Grazia. *Maria Montessori, una storia attuale.* Turin: Il leone verde, 2018.

———. *Montessori: perché no? Una pedagogia per la crescita: Che cosa ne è oggi della proposta pedagogica di Maria Montessori in Italia e nel mondo?* Turin: Il leone verde, 2017.

Honegger Fresco, Grazia (ed.). *Radici nel futuro: La vita di Adele Costa Gnocchi (1883–1967).* Molfetta: La meridiana, 2001.

Honegger Fresco, Grazia, and Lia De Pra Cavalleri. *Il materiale Montessori in cataloghi editi a New York, Londra, Bucarest, Berlino, Gonzaga tra gli anni Dieci e Trenta.* Castellanza: Il Quaderno Montessori, Associazione Centro Nascita Montessori, 1993.

Istituto Centrale di Statistica. *Sommario di statistiche storiche dell'Italia, 1861–1965.* Rome: Istat, 1968.

Kirkpatrick, Jerry. *Montessori, Dewey and Capitalism.* Upland, CA: Kirkpatrick Books, 2008.

Klein-Landeck, Michael (ed.). *Fragen an Maria Montessori: Immer noch ihrer Zeit voraus?* Freiburg, Germany: Verlag Herder, 2015.

Kramer, Rita. *Maria Montessori: A Biography.* New York: Da Capo Press, 1988.

La cura dell'anima in Maria Montessori: L'educazione morale, spirituale e religiosa dell'infanzia. Rome: Fefè, 2011.

La scuola italiana dall'Unità ai nostri giorn. Florence: La Nuova Italia, 1992.

L'audacia insolente: La cooperazione femminile 1886–1986. Venice: Marsilio, 1986.

Leenders, Hélène. *Der Fall Montessori: Die Geschichte einer reformpädagogischen Erziehungskonzeption im italienischen Faschismus.* Bad Heilbrunn, Germany: Klinkhardt, 2001.

Leonarduzzi, Alessandro. *Maria Montessori: Il pensiero e l'opera.* Brescia: Paideia, 1967.

Leopoldo e Alice Franchetti e il loro tempo. Città di Castello: Petruzzi, 2002.

Lillard, Angeline Stoll. *Montessori: The Science Behind the Genius.* New York: Oxford University Press, 2005.

L'infanzia svantaggiata e Maria Montessori: Esperienze psicopedagogiche, educative e sociali dal '900 ad oggi. Rome: Fefè, 2013.

Lo Sapio, Giovanna. *Giovanni Bollea: Uomo e scienziato.* Rome: Armando, 2014.

Maccheroni, Anna M. *Come conobbi Maria Montessori.* Rome: Edizioni Vita dell'infanzia, 1956.

Maino, Maria P. *A misura di bambino: Cent'anni di mobili per l'infanzia in Italia 1870–1970.* Roma-Bari, Italy: Laterza, 2003.

Maria Montessori cittadina del mondo. Rome: Comitato italiano dell'Omep, 1967.

Maria Montessori e il sodalizio con l'Umanitaria: Dalla Casa dei bambini di via Solari ai corsi per insegnanti, 1908–2008. Milan: Raccolto, 2008.

Maria Montessori e le sue reti di relazioni. Brescia: Scholè, 2018.

Maria Montessori 100 years: 1907–2007 Centenary of the Montessori Movement. Chennai, India: Kalakshetra Publications, 2007.

Matellicani, Anna. *La "Sapienza" di Maria Montessori: Dagli studi universitari alla docenza 1890–1919.* Rome: Aracne, 2007.

Mazzetti, Roberto. *Il bambino, il giuoco, il giocattolo.* Rome: Armando, 1962.

———. *La donna, la casa e il bambino nella ricerca della Montessori.* Salerno: Beta, 1971.

McClure, Samuel S. *My Autobiography.* New York: Frederick A. Stokes, 1914.

Michelet, André. *Les outils de l'enfance.* Vol. 1: *La pédagogie de l'action.* Neuchâtel, Switzerland: Delachaux et Niestlé, 1972.

Milano e l'Esposizione internazionale del 1906: La rappresentazione della modernità. Mian: FrancoAngeli, 2008.

Montessori, Mario M. *L'educazione come aiuto alla vita: Comprendere Maria Montessori.* Turin: Il leone verde, 2018.

Montessori, Mario M., Jr. *Education for Human Development: Understanding Montessori.* Santa Barbara, CA: Clio Press, 1992.

Montessoriana: Incontri italiani. Pescara, Italy: Libreria dell'Università Editrice, 2010.

Montessori in Contemporary American Culture. Portsmouth, NH: Heinemann, 1992.

Montessori in India: 70 years. Chennai, India: Indian Montessori Foundation, 2007.

Montessori-Pädagogik, aktuelle und internationale Entwicklungen. Münster, Germany: Lit Verlag, 2005.

Müller, Thomas, and Romana Schneider. *Montessori: Teaching Materials, Furniture and Architecture 1913–1935.* San Francisco: Wittenborn Art Books, 2002.

Negro, Silvio. *Roma, non basta una vita.* Vicenza: Neri Pozza, 1997.

———. *Seconda Roma, 1850–1870.* Vicenza: Neri Pozza, 2015.

The New World of Educational Thought. New York: MSS Information Corporation, 1973.

Neyret, Madeleine. *Hélène Lubienska de Lenval, 1895–1972: Pour une pédagogie de la personne.* Paris: Lethielleux, 1994.

Pagella, Mario. *Storia della scuola: Sintesi storica della scuola dalle origini ai giorni nostri, con particolare riguardo alla scuola italiana.* Bologna: Cappelli, 1980.

Papa, Emilio Raffaele. *Storia di due manifesti: Il fascismo e la cultura italiana.* Milan: Feltrinelli, 1958.

Paulucci, Paolo. *Alla corte di Re Umberto: Diario segreto.* Milan: Rusconi, 1986.

Pazzaglini, Marcello. *San Lorenzo, 1881–1981: Storia urbana di un quartiere popolare a Roma.* Rome: Officina, 1984.

Pelicier, Yves, and Guy Thuillier. *Édouard Séguin, "L'instituteur des idiots."* Paris: Economica, 1980. Contains an appendix entitled *"Traitement moral, hygiene et education des idiots de Édouard Séguin, 1846."*

———. *Un pionnier de la psychiatrie de l'enfant: Édouard Séguin, 1812–1880.* Paris: Comité d'Histoire de la Sécurité Sociale, 1996.

Pesci, Furio. *Antropologia e pedagogia a Roma da Giuseppe Sergi a Maria Montessori: Letture per il laboratorio di storia della pedagogia.* Rome: Aracne, 2003.

Pieroni Bortolotti, Franca. *Alle origini del movimento femminile in Italia, 1848–1892.* Turin: Einaudi, 1963.

Povell, Phyllis. *Montessori Comes to America: The Leadership of Maria Montessori and Nancy McCormick.* Lanham, MD: University Press of America, 2010.

Practical Visionaries: Women, Education and Social Progress, 1790–1930. Harlow, UK: Longman, 2000.

Radice, Sheila. *The New Children: Talks with Dr. Maria Montessori.* London: Hodder and Stoughton, 1920.

Ragnatele di rapporti: Patronage e reti di relazione nella storia delle donne. Torino: Rosenberg & Sellier, 1988.

Regni, Raniero. *Infanzia e società in Maria Montessori: Il bambino padre dell'uomo.* Rome: Armando, 2007.

Regni, Raniero, and Leonardo Fogassi. *Maria Montessori e le neuroscienze: Cervello, mente, educazione.* Rome: Fefè, 2019.

Rossi Barilozzi, Stefania. *Adele Costa Gnocchi, 1883–1967: Un'antesignana dell'educazione dalla vita prenatale al bambino di tre anni.* Perugia, Italy: Era Nuova, 2016.

Sanfilippo, Mario. *San Lorenzo 1870–1945: Storia e storie di un quartiere popolare romano.* Rome: Edilazio, 2003.

Sante De Sanctis tra psicologia generale e psicologia applicata. Milan: FrancoAngeli, 2004.

Scaraffia, Lucetta, and Anna M. Isastia. *Donne ottimiste: Femminismo e associazioni borghesi nell'Otto e Novecento.* Bologna: il Mulino, 2002.

Schultz-Benesch, Günter. *Der Streit um Montessori.* Freiburg: Herder Verlag, 1961.

Schwegman, Marjan. *Maria Montessori.* Bologna: il Mulino, 1999.

Scocchera, Augusto. *Maria Montessori: Quasi un ritratto inedito.* Florence: La Nuova Italia, 1990.

———. *Maria Montessori: Una storia per il nostro tempo.* Rome: Opera Nazionale Montessori, 2005.

Scocchera, Augusto (ed.). *Introduzione a Mario M. Montessori.* Rome: Opera Nazionale Montessori, 1998.

Séguin, Édouard. *Idiocy and Its Treatment by the Physiological Method.* New York: Teachers College, Columbia University, 1907.

———. *Rapport et memoires sur l'éducation des enfants normaux et anormaux.* Paris: Alcan, 1895.

Severini, Marco. *Giulia, la prima donna: Sulle protolettrici italiane ed europee.* Venice: Marsilio, 2017.

Soldani, Simonetta (ed.). *L'educazione delle donne: Scuole e modelli di vita femminile nell'Italia dell'Ottocento.* Milan: FrancoAngeli, 1989.

Standing, Edwin M. *Maria Montessori: Her Life and Work.* London: Hollis & Carter, 1957.

Stewart, William A. C. *Progressives and Radicals in English Education, 1750–1970.* London: Palgrave Macmillan, 2014.

Stewart-Steinberg, Suzanne. *L'effetto Pinocchio, Italia 1861–1922: la costruzione di una complessa modernità.* Rome: Elliot, 2011.

Stiller, Diana. *Clara Grunwald und Maria Montessori: Die Entwicklung der Montessori-Pädagogik in Berlin.* Hamburg: Diplomica Verlag, 2008.

Storia della famiglia italiana, 1750–1950. Bologna: il Mulino, 1992.

Storia dell'infanzia. Vol. 2: *Dal Settecento a oggi.* Rome: Laterza, 1996.

Sulea-Firu, Ilie. *Montessori-Erinnerungen.* Zurich: Assoziation Montessori Schweiz, 1991.

Sutherland Neill, Alexander. *All the best, Neill: Letters from Summerhill.* London: Routledge, 2016.

Tomasi, Tina. *Massoneria e scuola.* Florence: Vallecchi, 1980.

Tornar, Clara. *La pedagogia di Maria Montessori tra teoria e azione.* Milan: FrancoAngeli, 2007.

Trabalzini, Paola. *Maria Montessori: Da "Il metodo" a "La scoperta del bambino."* Rome: Aracne, 2003.

Trent, James W. *Inventing the Feeble Mind: A History of Mental Retardation in the United States.* Berkeley: University of California Press, 1995.

Trisciuzzi, Leonardo. *La scoperta dell'infanzia: Con estratti dai diari di Pestalozzi, Tiedemann, Darwin, Taine, Ferri.* Florence: Le Monnier, 1976.

Waltuch, Margot R. *A Montessori Album: Reminiscences of a Montessori Life.* Cleveland Heights, OH: NAMTA, 1986.

Ward, Florence E. *The Montessori Method and the American School.* New York: Macmillan, 1913.

Young-Bruehl, Elizabeth. *Anna Freud: una biografia.* Milan: Bompiani, 1993.

Zago, Giuseppe (ed.). *Sguardi storici sull'educazione dell'infanzia: Studi in onore di Mirella Chiaranda.* Fano, Italy: Aras, 2015.

Zola, Émile. *Il mio viaggio a Roma: 31 ottobre–15 dicembre 1894.* Naples: Intra Moenia, 2013.

ARTICLES

Babini, Valeria P. "Tra scienza e femminismo: Maria M. prima del 'Metodo.'" In *Centro di Studi Montessoriani,* January 2003.

Beck, Robert H. "Kilpatrick's Critique of Montessori's Method and Theory." In *Studies in Philosophy and Education* 1, nos. 4–5 (1961).

Bollea, Giovanni. "Jean Itard, Édouard Séguin, Maria Montessori: medici educatori e nuova immagine del bambino handicappato." In *Vita dell'infanzia* 48, no. 6 (July–August 1999).

Bouman, Jan C. "The Montessori Method: Science or Belief?" In *AMI Communications* 1 (1964).

"Building the Brain's 'Air Traffic Control' System: How Early Experiences Shape the Development of Executive Function." In *Working Paper* 11, Center on the Developing Child at Harvard University, 2011.

Cañigueral Viñals, Dani. "La historia de Montessori i Barcellona." In *Treball de Recerca,* AMI Archive.

Catarsi, Enzo. "Maria Montessori al Congresso femminista di Londra nel 1899." In *Vita dell'infanzia,* February 1984.

Cives, Giacomo. "Maria Montessori tra scienza, spiritualità e laicità." In *Studi sulla formazione*, 2015.

Condette, Jean-François, and Antoine Savoye. "*Une éducation pour une ère nouvelle: le congrès international d'éducation de Calais (1921).*" In *Société d'économie et de sciences sociales* 163 (2016).

Cossentino, Jacqueline. "Big Work: Goodness, Vocation, and Engagement in the Montessori Method." In *Curriculum Inquiry* 26, no. 1 (2006).

Credaro, Luigi. "La scuola pedagogica di Roma (1904–1923)." In *Rivista Pedagogica* 28, no. 5 (October–December 1935).

Cromwell, Mary R. "Il Metodo Montessori in Francia durante la guerra." In *La Coltura popolare* 9, no. 1 (January 1919).

De Giorgi, Fulvio. "Maria Montessori modernista." In *Annali di storia dell'educazione e delle istituzioni scolastiche* 16 (2009).

De Vroede, Maurice. "Francisco Ferrer et la Ligue Internationale pour l'education rationelle de l'enfance." In *Paedagogica Historica* 19 (1979).

"Discorso di Maria Montessori." In *Conferencia, Journal de l'Université des Annales*, January 1937.

Fancello, Lucia. "La 'Casa dei Bambini' di tirocinio a Napoli." In *La Coltura popolare* 10, no. 1 (January 1920).

Fiorani, Matteo, and Giovanni Bollea. "Per una storia della neuropsichiatria infantile in Italia." In *Medicina e Storia* 11 (2011), pp. 21–22.

George, Anne. "Dr. Maria Montessori: The Achievement and Personality of an Italian Woman Whose Discovery Is Revolutionizing Education Methods." In *Good Housekeeping* 55, no. 1 (July 1912).

———. "The First Montessori School in America." In *McClure's Magazine* 39, no. 2 (June 1912).

Grazzini, Camillo. "Maria Montessori's Cosmic Vision, Cosmic Plan and Cosmic Education." In *NAMTA Journal* 38, no. 1 (Winter 2013).

Guarnieri, Patrizia. "Piccoli, poveri e malati: Gli ambulatori per l'infanzia a Roma nell'età liberale." In *Italia Contemporanea* 223 (2001).

Homs, Eladio. "Maria Montessori 'Barcelonina.'" In *Vita dell'infanzia*, May 1952.

Honegger Fresco, Grazia. "Roma: il corso Montessori del 1910 e La casa dei Bambini presso il Convento delle Suore Francescane di via Giusti 12." In *Il Quaderno Montessori* 51 (1996).

———. "La scuola Montessori di Laren." In *Il Quaderno Montessori* 7, no. 25 (Spring 1990).

"How It All Happened: Dr. Montessori Speaks." In *AMI Communications*, 1970, AMI Archive.

"Il movimento Montessori a Napoli." In *Vita dell'infanzia* 3 (March 1967).

"In memoria di Mario Montessori." In *AMI Communications* 1, no. 2 (1982).

"Julius, Evola, Il caso Montessori." In *La vita italiana*, May 1934.

Le Maire, Giuseppina. "Come vivono i poveri di Roma: Il quartiere di San Lorenzo." In *Nuova Antologia* 39 (1904).

Lillard, Angeline, and Nicole Else-Quest. "Evaluating Montessori Education." In *Science* 313, no. 5795 (September 29, 2006).

"Luci e ombre del metodo Montessori di Barbera." In *La Civiltà Cattolica* 81, no. 2 (1930).

Maccheroni, Anna M. "10 novembre 1910." In *Vita dell'infanzia* 10–11 (1953).

———. "Il bambino cerca di vivere." In *Vita dell'infanzia* 5–7 (1952).

Marazzi, Giuliana. "Montessori e Mussolini: la collaborazione e la rottura." In *Dimensioni e problemi della ricerca storica* 1 (2000).

"Maria Montessori et la France: Genèse d'une histoire de Martine Gisloul." In *History of Education and Children's Literature* 9, no. 2 (2014).

"Maria Montessori Writes to Her Friend Giuliana Sorge and Reflects on the Nobel Prize for Peace." In *AMI Journal* 1, no. 2 (2013).

Michael, Knoll. "John Dewey und Maria Montessori: Ein unbekannter Brief." In *Pädagogische Rundschau* 50 (1996).

Montessori, Mario. "Maria Montessori mia madre." In *Selection du Reader's Digest*, September 1965.

"Montessori in India." In *On the Watch Tower* 61, no. 1 (November 1939). Adyar, India: Theosophical Publishing House.

"Mussolini and Montessori: An Established Principle." In *Times Educational Supplement*, April 4, 1925.

Padellaro, Nazareno. "L'inaugurazione del XV corso internazionale Montessor." In *Annali dell'istruzione elementare* 5 (1930).

Palau i Vera, Joan. "Un assaig d'aplicació del mètode Montessori a la Casa de la Maternita." In *Quaderns d'Estudi* 39 (April 1920).

Pesci, Furio. "L'educazione morale e religiosa nell'opera di Maria Montessori." In *History of Education and Children Literature* 6, no. 2 (2011).

Pironi, Tiziana. "Da Maria Montessori a Margherita Zoebeli: l'impegno educativo nei confronti dell'infanzia traumatizzata dalla guerra." In *Annali online della Didattica e della Formazione Docente* 8, no. 12 (2016).

Pozzi, Irene. "La società Umanitaria e la diffusione del metodo Montessori (1908–1923)." In *Ricerche di Pedagogia e Didattica, Journal of Theories and Research in Education* 10, no. 2 (2015).

Recchia, Germana. "Maria Montessori: nei dintorni dell'uomo nuovo." In *Laboratorio Montessori*, February 2013. See also http://www.paedagogica.org/doc/recchia_germana_UNICO_MONTESSORI_def.pdf.

Sáiz, Milagros, and Dolors Sáiz. "La estancia de Maria Montessori en Barcelona: la influencia de su método en la psicopedagogía catalana." In *Revista de Historia de la Psicologia* 26, nos. 2–3 (2005).

Sandri, Patrizia. "L'educazione degli 'ineducabili': i contributi di Jean Itard, Édouard Séguin e Maria Montessori." In *MeTis* 6, no. 2 (2014).

Scocchera, Augusto. "Due reattivi 'teologici' di Maria Montessori." In *Vita dell'infanzia* 41, nos. 5–6 (1992).

Thayer-Bacon, Barbara. "Maria Montessori, John Dewey, and William H. Kilpatrick." In *E&C/ Education and Culture* 28, no. 1 (2012).

"The Theosophist." In *Montessori in India* 60, no. 1 (October 1938–March 1939), AMI Archive.

Thrush, Ursula. "Erdkinder, i figli della Terra." In *Il Quaderno Montessori* 8, nos. 31–32 (1991).

Tornar, Clara. "Maria Montessori durante il fascismo." In *Cadmo* 2 (2005).

Tozier, Josephine. "The Montessori Schools in Rome." In *McClure's Magazine* 38, no. 2 (December 1911).

"Un'identità incompiuta: Maria Montessori nel carteggio di Mère Marie de la Rédemption." In *Orientamenti pedagogici* 64, no. 3 (2017).

Wagnon, Sylvain. "Les théosophes et l'organisation internationale de l'éducation nouvelle, 1911–1921." In *Revista de Estudios Históricos de la Masonería Latinoamericana y Caribeña* 9, no. 1 (2017).

Whitescarver, Keith, and Jacqueline Cossentino. "Montessori and the Mainstream: A Century of Reform on the Margins." In *Teachers College Record* 100, no. 12 (December 1998).

Wilson, Carolie. "Montessori Was a Theosophist." In *History of Education Society Bulletin* 36 (1985).

Zanzi, C. "Le Case dei bambini della Montessor." In *Rivista Pedagogica* 11 (1918).

BOOKS BY MARIA MONTESSORI

Lezioni di antropologia pedagogica. Rome: Sabbadini, 1906.

Il metodo della pedagogia scientifica applicato all'educazione infantile nelle Case dei Bambini. Città di Castello: Casa Editrice S. Lapi, 1909.

Antropologia pedagogica. Milan: Vallardi, 1910.

Dr. Montessori's Own Handbook. London: William Heinemann, 1914.

L'autoeducazione nelle scuole elementari. Rome: Ermanno Loescher, 1916.

I bambini viventi nella Chiesa. Naples: Morano, 1922.

Das Kind in der Familie. Berlin, 1923.

La vita in Cristo. Rome: Ferri, 1931.

Mass Explained to Children. London: Sheed & Ward, 1932.

Psicogeometria. Barcellona: Araluce, 1934.

L'Enfant. Paris: Desclée de Brouwer, 1936.

Education for a New World. Adyar-Madras, India: Kalakshetra Publications, 1946.

To Educate the Human Potential. Adyar-Madras, India: Kalakshetra Publications, 1947.

What You Should Know about Your Child. Colombo, Ceylon: Bennet, 1948.

The Discovery of Child. Adyar-Madras, India: Theosophical Publishing House, 1948.

De l'enfant à l'adolescent. Paris: Desclée de Brouwer, 1948.

Educazione e pace. Milan: Garzanti, 1949.

The Formation of Man. ABC-CLIO, 1949.

The Absorbent Mind. Adyar-Madras, India: Theosophical Publishing House, 1949.

Collected Speeches and Writings: The California Lectures of Maria Montessori, 1915. Santa Barbara, CA: Clio Press, 1997.

Dio e il bambino e altri scritti inediti. Brescia: La scuola, 2013.

Maria Montessori Sails to America: A Private Diary, 1913. Laren, Holland: Montessori-Pierson, 2013.

Maria Montessori Writes to Her Father: Letters from California, 1915. Laren, Holland: Montessori-Pierson, 2015.

Maria Montessori parla ai genitori: Il pensiero montessoriano spiegato alle famiglie. Turin: Il leone verde, 2018.

Il peccato originale. Brescia: Scholè, 2019.

ARTICLES BY MARIA MONTESSORI

"Sul significato dei cristalli del Leyden nell'asma bronchiale." In *Bollettino della Società Lancisana degli Ospedali di Roma* 16, no. 1 (1896).

"Sulle cosiddette allucinazioni antagonistiche." In *Policlinico* 4, fasc. 2 (February 1897), pp. 68–71, and fasc. 3 (March 1897).

"Miserie sociali e nuovi ritrovati della scienza." In *Il risveglio educativo* 15, no. 17 (December 10, 1898.

"Scuole di redenzione." In *Il risveglio educativo* 15, no. 23 (1899).

"La questione femminile e il Congresso di Londra." In L'Italia femminile 1, no. 38 (1899).

"Riassunto delle lezioni di didattica date in Roma nella Scuola Magistrale Ortofrenica." In Laboratorio Litografico Romano (Rome, 1900).

"La via e l'orizzonte del femminismo." In Cyrano de Bergerac 2, no. 7 (1902).

"Norme per una classificazione dei deficienti in rapporto ai metodi speciali di educazione." In Atti del Comitato Ordinatore del II Congresso Pedagogico Italiano, 1899–1900 (Naples: Trani, 1902).

"L'antropologia pedagogica." Milan: Conferenza tenuta agli studenti di filosofia nell'Università di Roma, Vallardi, 1903.

"Sui caratteri antropometrici in relazione alle gerarchie intellettuali dei fanciulli nelle scuole." In Archivio per l'Antropologia e l'Etnologia 33, no. 2 (1904).

"Influenza delle condizioni di famiglia sul livello intellettuale degli scolari." In Ricerche d'Igiene e Antropologia Pedagogiche in rapporto all'Educazione. Bologna: Zamerani e Albertazzi, 1904.

"Caratteri fisici delle giovani donne del Lazio." In Atti della Società Romana di Antropologia 12, no. 1 (1905).

"Proclama alle donne italiane." In La vita, February 26, 1906.

"A proposito dei minorenni corrigendi." In La vita, June 3, 1906.

"Gli odierni riformatori per i minorenni corrigendi." In La vita, June 6, 1906.

"Sulla questione dei minorenni corrigendi." In La vita, June 16, 1906.

"Per i minorenni delinquenti." In La vita, July 14, 1906.

"Ancora sui minorenni delinquenti." In La vita, August 6, 1906.

"Lottiamo contro la criminalità." In La vita, September 8, 1906.

"L'importanza della etnologia regionale nell'antropologia pedagogica." In Ricerche di Psichiatria e Nevrologia, Antropologia e Filosofia dedicate al prof. Enrico Morselli nel XXV anno del suo insegnamento universitario. Milan: Vallardi, 1907.

"La Casa dei Bambini, dell'Istituto Romano dei Beni Stabili." Conferenza tenuta il 7 aprile 1907. Rome: Officina Tipografica Bodoni, 1907.

"Metodo per insegnare la scrittura." In L'educazione dei sordomuti, fasc. 5 (May 1908).

"La morale sessuale nell'educazione." In Atti del I Congresso Nazionale delle donne italiane, Rome, April 24–30, 1908. Rome: Stabilimento Tipografico della Società Editrice Laziale, 1912.

Letter to the Editors. In Times Educational Supplement, September 1, 1914. AMI Archive.

"La croce Bianca." In La cultura popolare 9 (1917).

"Il nuovo metodo di educazione." In Opera Montessori, January–February 1932.

CRISTINA DE STEFANO is a journalist and writer. She lives and works in Paris as a literary scout for many publishing houses around the world. Her books *Belinda e il mostro: Vita segreta di Cristina Campo* (2002) and *Americane avventurose* (2007) have been translated into French, German, Spanish, and Polish. Her biography *Oriana Fallaci: The Journalist, the Agitator, the Legend* was published by Other Press in 2017.

GREGORY CONTI has translated numerous works of fiction, nonfiction, and poetry from Italian including works by Emilio Lussu, Rosetta Loy, Elisa Biagini, and Paolo Rumiz. His translations of Stefano Mancuso's *The Incredible Journey of Plants* and *The Nation of Plants* were published by Other Press in 2020 and 2021. He is a regular contributor to the literary quarterly *Raritan*.